David Bradford was born in Leura in the Blue Mountains of New South Wales and grew up in Seaforth and then Pennant Hills. He graduated in medicine from Sydney University in 1965, and after working for two years at the Repatriation General Hospital, Concord, he joined the army and spent a year on active service as a regimental medical officer (RMO) in South Vietnam. When his wartime service ended in 1968, David moved to England and set out on the long path towards a surgical career, obtaining two surgical degrees, and worked as a registrar in orthopaedics at St George's, a London teaching hospital. After a career change in 1973, he spent the next six years as a general practitioner in Clapton in the East End of London. During that time David began to do some work at the Lydia Department (a clinic for venereal diseases) at St Thomas's Hospital.

From 1975 onwards, David's enduring medical interest has been in the field that is now called sexual health medicine, which deals with all the ills (both physical and psychological) threatening people's health in the sexual arena of their lives, while at the same time promoting the goal of good sexual health for all individuals and communities. Since his return to Australia in 1979, David has worked exclusively in sexual health medicine, first in Melbourne, Victoria, and from 1993 onwards, in Cairns, in North Queensland. He spent some time as Chief Venereologist for Victoria, and as Director of Sexual Health for the Cairns Health Service District. Having experienced the early days of the HIV epidemic in Australia, which presented the greatest professional challenge of his career, David's work has been mainly concerned with sexually transmitted infections (STIs) and HIV/AIDS. Now semi-retired, David is still fully committed to the prevention of sexual ill health in people and communities everywhere.

THE GUNNERS' DOCTOR

Vietnam Letters

DAVID BRADFORD

RANDOM HOUSE AUSTRALIA

Random House Australia Pty Ltd
100 Pacific Highway, North Sydney, NSW 2060
www.randomhouse.com.au

Sydney   New York   Toronto
London   Auckland   Johannesburg

First published by Random House Australia 2007

National Library of Australia
Cataloguing-in-Publication Entry

Bradford, David, 1941–.
The gunners' doctor: Vietnam letters.

ISBN 978 1 74166 470 6.

1. Bradford, David, 1941– – Correspondence. 2. Vietnam War,
1961–1975 – Personal narratives, Australian. 3. Physicians – Vietnam –
Correspondence. 4. Vietnam War, 1961–1975 – Medical care. I. Title.

959.7043394

Cover photographs: *Top* – Gunner Galea (with the Vietnamese hat) and
Gunner Lemm on Operation Ainslie; *Bottom* – troopers from 3 Cavalry Regiment
on top of an armoured personnel carrier on Operation Kenmore, by the South
China Sea.
Cover design by Darian Causby/www.highway51.com.au
Typeset in Futura Book and Bookman by Midland Typesetters, Australia
Printed and bound by Griffin Press, South Australia

10 9 8 7 6 5 4 3 2 1

CONTENTS

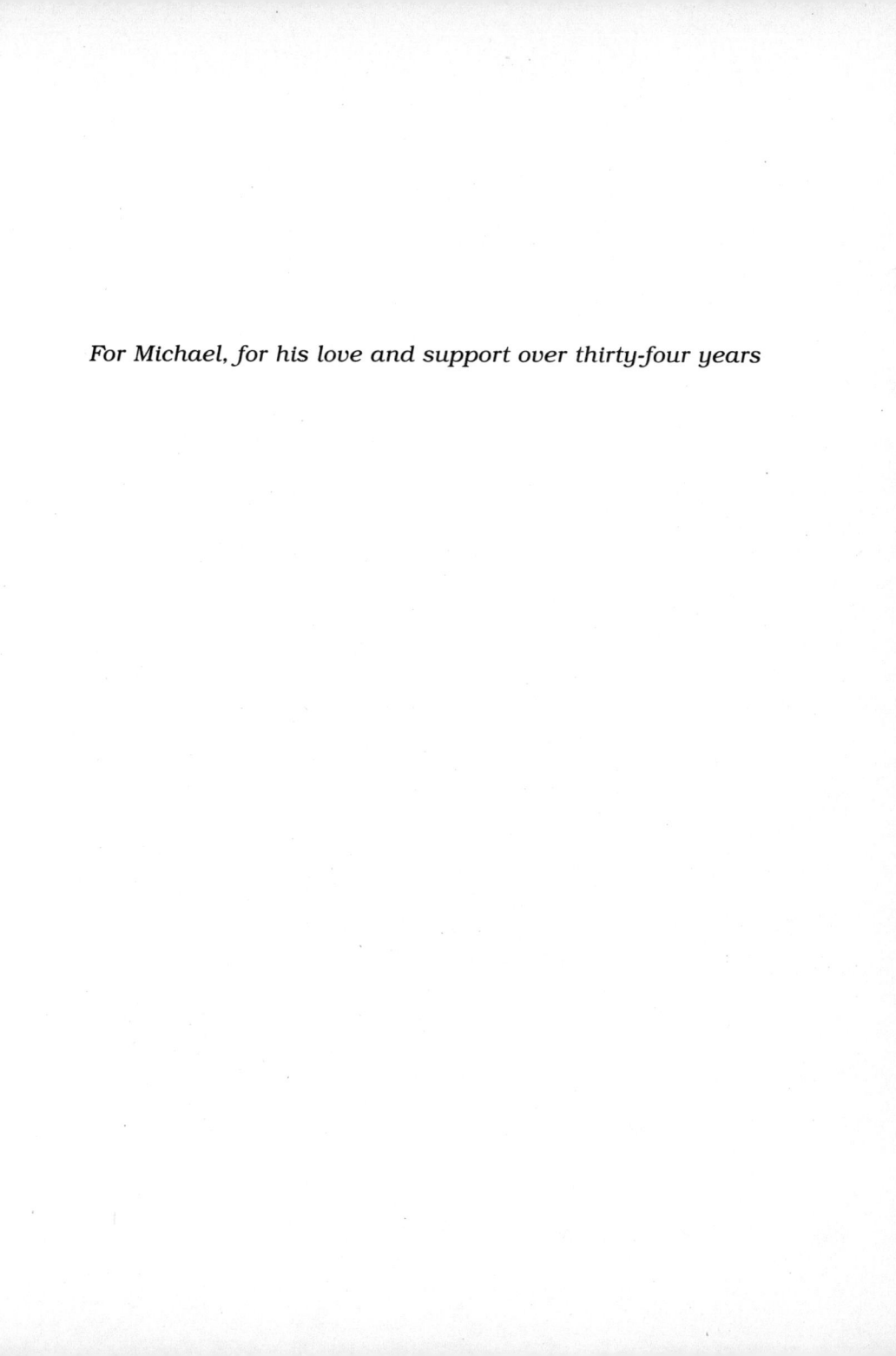

For Michael, for his love and support over thirty-four years

Acknowledgements

I acknowledge and thank all the officers and soldiers who served with me in Vietnam and who feature in these letters, but especially Bob Allen, Alex Berry, Peter Williams, Jeff Banks, John Dickinson, Jack Blomley, Digger James and Tony Williams.

My colour slide collection and Bob Allen's became inextricably mixed over the year in Vietnam. Some of the pictures reproduced in this book were probably taken by him although I would be unable to say which ones. I acknowledge their use with thanks.

PREFACE

The Vietnam War left an indelible mark on Australia, but it ended more than thirty years ago and the soldiers who fought there are no longer young. It happened in another world at another time. The divisiveness, discord and heartache resulting from Australia's participation are almost forgotten today except by those who served, those who protested, and their immediate families. And even their memories are fading.

I served in Vietnam for a year as a young doctor in the Australian Army. The Vietnam War was an important event in my life although memories of people, places and events have become blurred. I rapidly lost touch with men with whom I served and only once, in the eighties, attended a veterans' reunion. During my time in Vietnam from May 1967 to May 1968 I wrote almost daily letters home to my family. I was unaware that my mother had preserved all these letters. My father died in 2003 and eventually, in mid 2005, when my mother was well into her eighties, she moved to nursing hostel accommodation. While packing up, she unearthed my old letters stored away in a shoebox in the back of a cupboard. She told me I should have them. The collection is virtually complete except for the odd lost page and a few letters absent because they appear to have been eaten by a voracious mouse. Why he chose the particular letters he did will remain a mystery.

In November 2004, I made a trip back to Vietnam with my life partner, Michael. Over three weeks, we did a tour of the country, visiting Hanoi, Ho Chi Minh City, Hue, and Hoi An. Just stepping back onto Vietnamese soil after thirty-seven years was an emotional experience, but the highlight was one day spent revisiting Nui Dat where the Australian Task Force base had been located during the war, and Vung Tau where the Australian Field

Hospital (or 8 Field Ambulance as it had been called for much of my time in the country) struggled to maintain a toe-hold in the sandhills. So much had changed. There was little to indicate Australians had ever been there – the ruined gates of the old task force, the crumbling asphalt of Luscombe airstrip and the lone white cross in the rubber plantation at the site of the Long Tan battle of August 1966 are all that remain. Not one trace of the former Field Hospital remains at Vung Tau's Back Beach where modern hotels and resorts now cover the sandhills.

But it was a far more moving, heartrending and sometimes painful experience to read my own letters written thirty-nine years before. My faded memories sharpened and refocused. The letters revealed a different world, different values, and a different me. They provide a snapshot of my daily experience as an army doctor during a time of war, giving some indication of the effect the war and Army life had on me over the course of that twelve months. The letters paint a picture of some of the people I worked and lived with, especially those officers and soldiers who became important to me at that stage of my life. They cover the period of the 1968 Tet Offensive when the real seeds of defeat for the Americans and their allies in Vietnam were sown. They also tell something of life in Australia in the late sixties for a middle class family whose son and brother was in Vietnam.

The chapters that follow are only possible because the letters have been preserved. My own memory, unreliable and fuzzy now about these events, could never have allowed me to write an account with such immediacy. At the time I also kept a diary, which I still possess, but it was brief and scrappy. It has enabled me to put a date on one or two of the undated letters and place some fragments of letters more or less accurately. The letters are presented as they were written, however, for the reader's sake, they have been tidied up a little, and I have purposely omitted some material. Letters home from a family member situated in some far-flung corner of the globe, particularly when they are very frequent letters, inevitably contain details and repetitions that would bore the most attentive reader. I have cut such items but have done my best to retain anything that readers might find interesting and important. At the end of some letters, I have also explained information contained in that letter which might other-wise prove difficult for the reader to follow. Some of these notes also serve to round out cultural or emotional contexts.

The letters are predominantly about the Australian and New Zealand soldiers who constituted my medical practice – the officers and gunners of 4 Field Regiment, Royal Australian Artillery (RAA), which included a New Zealand battery; and the officers and troopers of a squadron of the 3 Cavalry Regiment, who also served in Vietnam between 1967 and 1968. The letters are also about officers and soldiers from the Royal Australian Army Medical Corps (RAAMC), to which I, as an army doctor, belonged. They pay tribute to my fellow soldiers and for that reason, if for no other, I believe they are worth publishing.

I have presented the letters chronologically so that the reader can follow and share my year in Vietnam. Each chapter contains the letters written over a calendar month. At the end of each chapter I have added a short reflective account, giving my impressions of events as I remember them now in the light of the letters and sharing my current thoughts and feelings on those events.

In November 1967, as an army doctor in Vietnam, I celebrated my twenty-sixth birthday. In November 2006, semi-retired, I celebrated my sixty-fifth birthday. I hardly recognise the person portrayed in the letters and although inevitably I feel some sympathy for him, I don't like some of his attitudes. In bringing things to mind I had long forgotten, the letters now revive strong feelings about the same experiences. At times my feelings now are at odds with what I had written home to my family then.

In any case, my letters were never entirely an accurate picture. There were many things I could not tell my family about my year in Vietnam. Of course, like most soldiers, I wanted to shield them from the dangers and risks that were inherent in being a combatant in a war zone. But there were more deeply personal things I could not share. Some of my deepest emotions and needs, I believed then, were unacceptable and reprehensible. I had been raised as a devout Evangelical Christian, and still adhered to a Christian faith and, in the main, a Christian perspective and morality. But by the time I went to Vietnam I had, albeit uneasily, accepted that I was gay. I could not tell my family how much my soldier patients meant to me, although some inkling of my true feelings does shine through in some of the letters. I could not share with them my doubts and fears about God, faith, the war, communism, when I knew they were at home supporting me with prayers, daily thoughts, letters, tapes and parcels. I couldn't let the side down and I did not want to deliberately hurt them. And I could never be totally and fully myself in my letters, because I did not know myself totally and fully.

It is easy to be wise after the event, and an older writer can be as self-deluded as a younger one. There are times, if I do say so myself, when the youthful writer of these letters shows perception and wisdom beyond his years and where his words ring true. No doubt there will be times in my reflections on the letters when readers will feel they would prefer to hear what the young Army doctor had to say rather than read the musings of his older counterpart. We all bring our own experiences, memories and perspectives to our reading of this material. I hope my youthful but guarded comments and my more mature thoughts, derived from a re-reading of the letters, offer inspiration and insight into some aspects of human nature, and the experiences of men at war.

INTRODUCTION

Signing up for war service

As will become apparent in the course of these letters, my war service was unremarkable. I enlisted *voluntarily*. That was perhaps remarkable. I had no previous experience of any kind of military service, nor any family military history – although my father did spend ten days, just before his marriage in 1941, at Sydney showground awaiting the army's pleasure, only to be permanently discharged from the forces because he was a pharmacist. Presumably they had all the pharmacists they needed on active service.

In 1967, I enlisted in the Citizen Military Forces as a full-time duty (CMF-FTD) medical officer (MO). This meant that, provided I completed twelve months service in Vietnam, I could then relinquish army service whenever I wished. Because I was a doctor, I became an officer, at the rank of captain, in the Royal Australian Army Medical Corps (RAAMC) in February 1967 and underwent basic training for six weeks at Healesville School of Army Health in Victoria. At the end of that course, although expecting I would be joining 8 Field Ambulance in Vung Tau 'to obtain expertise in military surgery', as I had been more or less promised on enlistment, I was instead assigned to 'the gunners' as their regimental medical officer (RMO). Accordingly, in early April 1967 I 'marched in' to the headquarters of 4 Field Regiment at Wacol in Queensland.

Members of the regiment were almost all away on their last exercise in Australia prior to embarking for South Vietnam (SVN), so I was given a vehicle and driver and told to join them at Tin Can Bay near Gympie. When

1

I arrived and met the commanding officer (CO) he took me to the dug-out and sandbagged tent which served as regimental aid post (RAP) for the regiment on exercise and which became my temporary home for the next two weeks. As the CO and I approached the RAP, my future medical sergeant, Bob Allen, looked out and, as he told me later, exclaimed to one of his fellow medics, 'Good God, will you just look at this? What on God's earth have they sent us now?' The whole regiment knew a doctor was coming and my arrival was eagerly awaited as they had not had a permanent doctor for years. But my youthful and unmilitary appearance as I walked towards him made Bob Allen wonder what exactly he had been saddled with. I was tall, thin, gangly and uncoordinated. I can sympathise with his original impression as it was not an auspicious beginning.

After Tin Can Bay, I did two weeks of a Battle Efficiency Course at Greenbank, not far from Wacol, which I'm glad to say had to be aborted because orders came through for the date of my departure with the regiment for Vietnam. I was sent off for a week's pre-embarkation leave with my family in Sydney, then flew back to rejoin the regiment. I left Australia with members of the headquarter battery of the regiment on Monday 1 May 1967 by air and arrived in the Australian Task Force base at Nui Dat the next afternoon, having spent Monday night in Darwin. The first letter home to the family is dated 2 May 1967.

The RMO's duties

It will become fairly clear during a reading of the letters what my duties were as the regimental medical officer (RMO) for 4 Field Regiment. In summary, I performed hygiene inspections, ran sick parades, gave vaccinations, provided emergency care, visited the three active gun batteries regularly whether they were in the task force or out on a temporary fire support base on operation, visited the Cavalry Squadron (for whom I was also medical officer), stood in for the senior medical officer at the Forward Detachment of 8 Field Ambulance if he happened to be away, and provided advice to the CO of 4 Field Regiment on the health of his officers and gunners and the hygiene of the regiment. As well, because 'winning hearts and minds' was a prominent part of US General Westmoreland's strategy in South Vietnam I, like all other medical personnel, took part in many clinics for villagers under the army's Civil Aid Program. The letters refer frequently to these so-called Medcap (medical civil aid program) clinics.

I also took part in several military operations in South Vietnam including Paddington, Ainslie, Kenmore, Santa Fe, Duntroon and Coburg, during all of which I manned a regimental aid post at the relevant fire support base (FSB). I had five days rest and recreation (R&R) leave in Taipei in November 1967 and a further three weeks medical detachment at the Free World Forces Headquarters in Saigon straight after R&R. For the rest of the time I remained at Nui Dat until my return to Australia on 8 May 1968. I personally saw no enemy action, was never fired upon, mortared, rocketed, bombed or physically attacked in any way. I felt really afraid only twice during my whole time in Vietnam – once flying by helicopter at dusk from Saigon back to Nui Dat in dreadful weather, the whole way at tree-top level, because the pilot feared rocket fire from the ground if the chopper were any higher; and again one afternoon while we packed up supplies and hurried to leave a small village where, with a medic and a handful of gunners, I had been carrying out a medical clinic for the villagers. We had heard a brief burst of gunshot fire in the distance, the crowds had suddenly evaporated and the village had fallen ominously silent. What it was all about was never revealed but the accompanying soldiers were quite sure a group of Vietcong must have returned suddenly and unexpectedly to the village – hence our hasty evacuation. A tiny medical detachment was in no position to engage any enemy, let alone a group of highly trained and dedicated Vietcong fighters on their home ground.

I occasionally assisted in the resuscitation of battle casualties and these events are documented in the letters. On these occasions I would call by radio for the casualties to be evacuated. 'Dust-off' (i.e. medical evacuation) helicopters would quickly appear on the scene and fly the wounded to hospital. These were the most exciting parts of my work in South Vietnam but such situations happened rarely. In no sense could I claim to have been a war hero. As I have said, mine was an unremarkable war.

Most wars, for most soldiers, contain many more hours of inaction than hours of fighting. The Vietnam War was no different from others in this respect. War is a weary business but even more it is a boring business. So when not performing official duties, I read books (medical and recreational), wrote letters home (prolifically) and talked to the soldiers. 'Yarning' is a time-honoured occupation in the Australian Army and fills much of the inactive time of the military, especially when on 'active service'. I was no exception for I found talking to the soldiers – my patients, even when they were well and not requiring my professional services, as was mostly the case – an interesting and profitable experience. So rewarding in fact that these 'yarns' helped change my previous patterns of thinking, broadened my outlook and influenced the course of my life.

This army existence would normally be thought unexciting for a young doctor at the commencement of his professional career, but I found it sufficiently fulfilling not to seriously want to be doing anything else. There are a number of reasons, I recognise now, why this was so.

My background

I had a sheltered upbringing. I was the eldest of three children, two boys and a girl, and was brought up in what an outsider would describe as a 'very religious' home. My parents were Evangelical Christians and the family attended a Baptist church. No one in the family drank alcohol, smoked, swore or danced, and on Sundays we did nothing secular – my father's car ran out of petrol on several Sundays over my childhood years because he had forgotten to fill it up the day before, and 'filling up' on a Sunday was unthinkable. Driving on a Sunday was only acceptable because it was necessary to get to church. It was the rarest event for any member of the family to 'go to the pictures' and by the time I left for Vietnam in 1967, I had seen *The Coronation of Queen Elizabeth II*, *Richard III*, *Julius Caesar* and *The Sound of Music*. The family did not acquire a television set until after I left for Vietnam. 'The devil in the lounge room', as Christian people at that time liked to describe it, was highly suspect.

We three children had made a Christian commitment at an early age. As teenagers we had been baptised by full immersion in the baptistery at our local church and believed sincerely and fervently that the most important thing in life was to do God's will (i.e. to find out what it was for us personally and then to do it obediently).

Lest it be thought this upbringing was a cheerless one, it has to be said that in fact my childhood was carefree, and full of fun and laughter. My adolescence was similar, but was a little clouded by the teasing and bullying I underwent at high school because of my Christian profession, my unworldliness, my gangly, awkward appearance and my total lack of interest and capacity in any team sport whatsoever. My parents were people who practised what they preached and, realising that their children's upbringing was 'different' and lacked some of the 'worldly' pleasures other children enjoyed, they went out of their way to 'make up' by ensuring our family home life was happy. They truly shared in our joys and sorrows, triumphs and minor tragedies.

At the end of 1964, at age twenty-three, I graduated in medicine from Sydney University and the Royal North Shore Hospital. My university experience had not been particularly fulfilling. I had been beset throughout my university course with the strong feeling that I was unsuited to medicine. When I first met sick patients in teaching hospital and it began to dawn on me that human existence was considerably more complicated than I had hitherto believed, I found the experience painful and confronting. I discussed my doubts about medicine with my parents and for the first time I knew I caused them some sadness. My dad had dearly wanted to be a doctor himself but was prevented by the Depression years and had settled for a career as a pharmacist instead. Besides, both my parents had a deep interest in Christian missions overseas and both believed that the highest calling for any young Christian man was to become a medical missionary. Try as I would I could detect no desire within myself either to be a doctor or a medical missionary. Yet 'once having put my hand to the plough', there could be no turning back, as Father reminded me. Time enough for a change in career after I qualified and worked as a doctor for some time, if I still felt the same unsuitability for medicine then.

There was another big problem which I could never bring myself to discuss with my father or mother, nor anyone else for that matter, and which I tried hard and very unsuccessfully not to think about myself. I knew I was homosexual. Young women had never stirred the remotest physical or emotional interest in me. I had never taken a girl out, kissed a girl with any passion, or fantasised about women. On the other hand, young men had always stirred strong desires and emotions. I remembered vividly the day I returned to high school for my fourth year when I was just fourteen years old. I looked around the classroom and suddenly saw my school mates, or some of them, in a new light – they had transformed over the holidays and become desirable, highly sexually attractive and danger-ously interesting human beings.

At first, I thought it was a phase I was going through. It was not, and I was to struggle in silence against this 'sinful' attraction over the ensuing years. I managed to resist any sexual contact with another male, but my mind was full of thoughts and desires I found difficult to control. At university in psychiatry lectures, I had heard about 'sublimation' and decided the only way for a real Christian to deal with homosexual feelings and yearnings was to 'sublimate' them somehow into other channels of productive work or study. By the time I graduated, though, I could no longer believe that my homosexual orientation was just a 'phase' or that there was any prospect of being 'cured'.

Coming to terms with being homosexual is rarely easy for any young person, even in the 21st century, but in the mid 1960s for someone who was a committed Evangelical Christian it was little short of appalling. I realised that somehow I would have to live with it. Being a believing Christian as I then was, there could be no prospect whatsoever of succumbing to homosexual temptation. It equally seemed unfair to any potential female partner, and unthinkable to me, to try and settle down in marriage, when I knew only too well my homosexual disposition. In 1965 therefore, rather sadly, I looked forward to a life of celibacy and sexual restraint. All of this I endured alone and never discussed with another individual.

In the annual lottery for a hospital intern placing, I scored a position at the Repatriation General Hospital (RGH), Concord, in Sydney as a junior resident medical officer (JRMO). RGH Concord had recently acquired the status of teaching hospital and the first intake of six JRMOs, including me, arrived in January 1965. After an initial adjustment period and experiencing the usual anxiety and stress any new doctor faces when he finds himself responsible for the medical care of sick patients, I found that my student fears had been groundless. I decided, after my first year, that being a doctor wasn't so bad after all, and that my patients, the old diggers of World Wars I and II, were interesting and amazing people.

In the last few months of my second year at the hospital 'the powers that be' decided that this new batch of JRMOs was being denied any 'casualty' experience, as RGH Concord lacked a casualty department at that stage. We were accordingly rostered, in turn, to spend a few months at the Army Hospital (2 Camp Hospital – 2CH, as it was then called) at Ingleburn south of Sydney.

From the moment of my arrival at 2CH, in late 1966, I felt I had met my destiny. For a heady two or three month period, I was surrounded by patients who were all male, largely young, to my mind stunningly good looking, yet medically or surgically 'needy' in some way. And I was one of their doctors – I personally looked after two full wards. I had not only been given permission; I had been literally forced into 'doctoring' the clientele of my dreams! I worked tirelessly from dawn till dark; I actually resented time 'off-duty' and volunteered for extra duties; I ministered to this new flock of patients like some latter day Florence Nightingale, as if they were extreme 'VIPs' instead of ordinary average young Australian males who had been caught up in the army machine for a variety of different reasons. This was sublimation on a very grand scale.

For the record, I must reassure readers that due to medical and military professionalism, and my 'unworldly' upbringing, my reputation remained unsullied during my whole time in the army and I managed with little effort to avoid all sexual or emotional entanglements with any of my fellow officers or soldiers. The patients at 2CH and the men of 4 Field Regiment were never in any moral danger despite having a gay medical officer, albeit a highly closeted and 'non-practising' one.

National Service, on a selective basis using a birthday ballot, was introduced in 1964, and in late 1966 Prime Minister Harold Holt increased Australia's commitment to the war in Vietnam. 2CH received the less serious medevacs from Vietnam almost weekly. The more serious ones requiring specialist surgical care went to RGH Concord. RAAMC officers at 2CH spoke of the army's need for fit young doctors to volunteer for work in South Vietnam and the superb surgical experience such privileged medical volunteers might obtain working in the Australian Field Ambulance in Vung Tau. For an impressionable, idealistic, sublimated homosexual doctor who found looking after young soldiers a rewarding, fulfilling and exciting experience, the attraction of frontline military service in a time of war seemed a godsend. Perhaps I could become a medical missionary overseas after all, with a slightly different clientele.

I remember clearly the day in November 1966 when I decided to enlist and go to Vietnam. For this I need no letter to jog my memory. It was a Wednesday evening and officially my day's work was finished at Ingleburn. However, a large medevac – mostly of non-serious medical patients – was expected to arrive at 7 pm via the Richmond RAAF airbase direct from Vietnam and I had volunteered to stay behind and assist in the assessment of the new arrivals. A busload eventually appeared at 8 pm and a group of walking but tired, smelly, largely unwell soldiers staggered off the bus. They were given cups of tea and directed to chairs in the waiting room so that in turn they could be examined by the three MOs on duty before being assigned a bed for the night. After he had examined and assessed them, the MO decreed whether they were fit to proceed home the next day, or whether their medical condition required that they stay as inpatients in the hospital.

I worked through my group of assigned patients who were a motley lot. There were PUOs (pyrexias, or fevers, of unknown origin) who had to stay until their fever settled or a definitive diagnosis could be made. Others who had chronic ear infections could go home next day with future ear, nose and throat (ENT) referrals arranged. Soldiers with chronic pustular acne and other intractable skin rashes, and soldiers with hearing damage, occasioned by exposure to artillery gunfire, could be discharged home in the morning with appropriate referrals. The non-specific urethritis cases (then one of the commonest forms of sexually transmitted infection [STI]), where the luckless individuals had urethral discharges unresponsive in Vietnam to serial antibiotic therapy, were a problem. The doctor had to be sure they were non-infectious to wives or girlfriends, so these patients had to stay at the hospital for more treatment and testing before they could be allowed home. Finally there were the 'psych' cases, soldiers who had developed stress-related symptoms which rendered them incapable for service in a war zone because of their unpredictability, their labile emotions, their lack of control, or in a few cases their frank psychoses – these all needed to stay until the visiting psychiatrist could assess them.

My last patient was an appealing, thin young man of laconic disposition, whose brittle cynicism failed to disguise some deep-seated mental anguish. His skin was an unhealthy bronze and the whites of his eyes were bright orange. He had been seriously unwell with fever, pains in the joints, vomiting, abdominal pain and lack of appetite for ten days and the doctors at Vung Tau had decided his days in the war zone were over. He had only become jaundiced during the flight home. His liver was enlarged and tender on palpation. He obviously had acute infectious hepatitis. As in most cases of acute hepatitis, he had started to feel a little better as soon as the jaundice appeared. After I examined him, he asked me the score and I said, 'Sorry soldier, it's a week at least here in the hospital until your jaundice starts to fade before we can be sure you're no longer infectious and we can let you go home – but you *will* get better and you *will* be right as rain in a few weeks.' 'So, home's out of the question, doc, for a week or so you reckon?' 'They're the rules I'm afraid – sorry.' The young soldier smiled grimly and said: 'Well at least I'm out of that fucking horrible place I suppose – even hospital's better than that shit!'

We talked for a further fifteen minutes, while he told me his experiences as an infantryman. He had been fired on, had shot and killed several Vietcong, had been mortared, had had an R&R in Manila (where he caught gonorrhoea *and* syphilis), and had served eleven months in Vietnam. He was a battle-seasoned, regular army warrior at age twenty-three. While I talked with him, my mind became clear – I decided I had to go to Vietnam. There were people there like this war-weary but winsome soldier who needed me.

While on annual holidays in December 1966 I wrote to the Army and volunteered my services. I was given an appointment at Eastern Command Army Headquarters in Victoria Barracks, Sydney, for a gentlemanly talk with an RAAMC desk-bound colonel and within a few weeks I was in uniform.

Bound for Vietnam, I was filled with enthusiasm, fervour, personal doubts, fears and longings. It was a potent mix.

I have changed with time as we all do. After successfully obtaining a surgical degree in England and working for a time as a surgical and orthopaedic registrar, I found that surgery was not for me. My true interests lay elsewhere – all that VD (venereal disease, now more appropriately called sexually transmitted infection) experience and those many VD lectures in South Vietnam couldn't be ignored. I eventually became a sexual health physician and have spent the past twenty-five years of my life working in that field. My Vietnam War experience directly led to my chosen specialty, but it took me many years before I realised what I was best suited for and what I really wanted to do.

I am no longer 'a bigoted Baptist', if I ever was one. I claim no particular religious affiliation and I can no longer believe the certainties and verities of Evangelical Christianity which were once so real and clear to me. For this I cannot blame the army or my Vietnam War service. I now wince a little when I read some of my definite and firmly expressed views in the letters. That long year in Nui Dat undoubtedly opened my mind and gave me a new perspective on life and its problems and difficulties.

Some things haven't changed. My sympathy for the dilemmas all young men face, be they soldiers or civilians, remains the same. My respect for the soldiers I served with in Vietnam is profound. My gratitude to them for what they unwittingly taught me is inexpressible. I am eternally grateful to all those who wrote and supported me, especially members of the Pennant Hills Baptist Church, and the members of my wider and immediate family during that year of war service. Each person in my family was something of an inspiration to me during my time in Vietnam, especially my mum and dad. But it is entirely due to my mother that this book is possible at all and I thank her sincerely for preserving my letters and for agreeing to their publication.

1

MAY 1967

Letters

HQ Battery
4 Fd Regt
AFPO 4,
GPO Sydney
Tuesday 2/5/67

Dear family,

Here is my first letter from SVN! We arrived this arvo at about two o'clock at Vung Tau, and after waiting there about an hour were flown into Nui Dat by Caribou aeroplane. The flight from Brisbane to Darwin was very pleasant – all mod cons; air hostesses etc, but the flight from Darwin to Vung Tau was altogether different. We were all packed into a Hercules and there we stayed for eight hours – very little to see and very little space to move about in, so we were all relieved to get here I can tell you. The gunner sitting next to me, John Dickinson by name, read a book by the French novelist Emile Zola – *Germinal*, all the way, which seemed to me very intellectual for a mere gunner.

The YMCA had a hot cup of tea at Vung Tau airport which was very acceptable. A great crowd of American soldiers were there too, and a funnier looking lot you've never seen. They all seem to have weak eyes – at least 50 per cent were wearing glasses.

The conditions at Nui Dat aren't too bad – the (officers') mess is quite comfy and I have a tent to myself. At the moment the present RMO of the regiment is living with me, but he leaves for Australia on Sunday. He is a nice chap and has been giving me warning of all I can expect in the next twelve months. It is almost the monsoon season here, so we can look forward to six months of heavy rain in the near future. It is hot and sticky tonight but not unbearable. It is a relief to be here in many ways.

Down the road, 8 Field Ambulance has an outpost in our Task Force Headquarters with about ten beds. The MO there, I met at Healesville, so it is nice there is someone I know reasonably well near at hand.

We have electric light in the tent and a proper bed with sheets. So it is real comfort.

I do hope you are all well and bearing up and that you've got over Saturday night.[1] It seems so long ago now, that I've just about got over it, but I do miss you all a lot. Do take great care of yourselves, won't you?

Will write again soon,

Much love,

David

---

[1] On the previous Saturday night, my family plus a contingent from the Pennant Hills Baptist Church farewelled me at Sydney Airport. It was a large group and an emotional send-off.

Nui Dat
Thursday 4/5/67

Dear family,

Well, I am gradually settling in to life up here in SVN. It is still all a bit strange and unreal, but I should be more at home next week when the previous RAP (regimental aid post) staff leave for Australia – at the moment we are all in each other's way and not knowing who does what. I had a *fascinating* day today doing a hygiene inspection, which consists of looking wisely into deep pit latrines, and poking vaguely around the various kitchens in the regiment. I have to submit a monthly report about it all.

I am just about used to having guns going off in the middle of the night and having helicopters, jets and things, whizzing by in the air all day – it is a bit noisy on the whole.

All the task force are camped amongst rubber trees, which are curious light greenish-leaved trees. The weather hasn't been too bad the last two days – pretty sticky but not much rain, except last night when it just suddenly started pouring and stopped after half an hour as suddenly as it started. I met the padre yesterday evening when the present doc took me over to 6 Battalion to meet the doctor there. He is a bit of a failure I think. But he was very pleasant anyway – asked me gloomily if I knew anything about VD.

It is nearly lights out now so I had better finish. On Sunday I will have a tent to myself and will settle in properly.

There is a chapel just across the road. I will investigate on Sunday.

Hope you're all well.

Very much love,

David

Nui Dat

Saturday 6/5/67

Mother dear and all the rest,

I am sitting in my tent sweltering at the moment writing this at my little desk. It is about 8.30 pm (10.30 pm your time). We have electric light in the tents but tonight we have all the flaps down because it is a maximum security night (MSN) in the task force and no lights must show. These MSNs happen every so often when there are special events, like Ho Chi Minh's birthday or the anniversary of Dien Bien Phu battle – when the VC defeated the French – as it is tonight.

It is awfully hot and sticky. I suppose my two previous letters haven't given much idea of what it is like up here, but it's so hard to describe. But for the noise of the artillery, the roar of the trucks and the clatter of the helicopters it is more like the camping ground at Gerroa Beach[1] than anything else – the same red dusty earth – the tents huddled together and the typical Gerroa showers and toilets. In fact I keep thinking I'm at Gerroa. I'm afraid I can't get into thinking there's a war on at all – it's all very strange.

My RAP is a big aluminium shed which will eventually have partitions, but at the moment is an open barn-like room. We have pretty good stocks adequate for our purposes. The doctor at the Forward Detachment just up the road gets casualties in by helicopter if anyone out on operation is wounded and he can use the helicopter to fly anyone who needs it down to Vung Tau.

It is certainly going to take a lot of getting used to and I suppose I am beginning to get a bit of reaction now from all the goodbyes – and Australia seems such a long way away. The chapel has a PD (Protestant Denomination) service at ten o'clock Sunday, so I will try it out tomorrow.

Hope the pharmacy is doing well and that Pip[2] isn't having too much trouble with my old car, the Mighty Austin Lancer.[3]

Very much love,
David

---

[1]   Gerroa Beach is on the New South Wales south coast. Every year from 1957 through to 1964 I spent Christmas–New Year there, living in a tent, as a member of an interdenominational Christian beach mission team seeking to evangelise the campers in the camping ground.

[2]   My younger brother, Phillip.

[3]   I was very fond of my 1962 Austin Lancer, despite the fact that it broke down frequently. We generally referred to it as 'Mighty Austin Lancer' or 'MAL'. While I was in Vietnam, various family members used it; especially Pip.

Nui Dat
Monday 8/5/67

Dearest Mum,

Just a little note before I go to bed, under my mosquito net, wishing you a very happy mother's day (hope it gets there in time). Have a very good day won't you?

I went to church yesterday morning and was greeted as a celebrity because I can play the organ. They have a little tiny pedal thing with about three octaves, but it's something.

There were about ten there, several of them good Baptists, so even though on the whole there aren't many Christians here I can always meet with some on Sunday mornings. The C of E[1] padre took the service and it was good.

I have been busy today and had my first big wash (as it's Monday) – clothes I mean.

Will write again tomorrow,

All my love,

David

[1]   Church of England/Anglican.

Nui Dat

Tuesday 9/5/67

Dear Mum and Dad,

Well it is 5.30 pm and I have just had my daily shower, out of a shower bucket hanging from a rope – but it was hot water today, so I feel nice and clean. I thought I would start this letter to you before tea and I'll finish it afterwards. This is the best time of day to have a shower, as you are all hot and covered with sweat and not able to sit comfortably in the mess, and the shower sort of cools you down so that at least you look a bit presentable at tea time, which in the artillery still tries to retain something of its 'officers and gentlemen' old colonial gentility.

I have had two letters now from Mum and last night received the photos[1] – they are pretty good aren't they? I will try and buy a frame at our PX store (sort of canteen thing) and put one of the family on my desk.

I won a major victory today (or at least my hygiene sergeant and I did). We wrote off tonight's mince meat, so I guess we will all starve. It really upset the catering officer though and he maintained that mince meat which has been in the deep freeze two years (!), as most of our meat has, always has a dark black rim around it and smells like nothing on earth, 'because of the preservative'. My hygiene sergeant, Fred Wittmer, condemned it out of hand – he is a high-handed young man in many ways – and I meekly backed him up by saying that I certainly wouldn't eat it myself, so I couldn't in fairness let the men eat it. The caterer and his inspector (who was just over for the day) looked at me pityingly and said it was obvious I hadn't been here long

– but anyway the task force hygiene inspector who I happen to have met on the Battle Efficiency Course in Greenbank was called in and we won the day. He was nearly ill and charged off with a specimen to the brigadier to tell him what he was about to get for tea tonight. At any rate truth and honour and hygiene have been upheld and the enemy has retreated with its tail between its legs. The gunners may be the crack regiment of the army but their ideas of hygiene are appalling.

Enough of that though. How are you all at Penno?[2] And is the shop progressing, or 'pretty deadly' at present?[3] I hope everything is OK. I may have found you a new customer – the soldier who runs the post office (AFPO4) lives in Castle Hill and commented on the address in one of my letters – so if I'm kind to him, he might send his mother along to the 'new chemist'. He says there are a lot of 'Hills District' soldiers up here in the task force (all potential customers).

I did a big wash yesterday – all my singlets and socks and 'things'. Our greens are done by a local Viet laundry in Baria just down the road about two miles [a bit over three kilometres]. They smell strongly of fish soap when they come back but I guess you get used to it.

I nearly had some excitement – the doc at the Forward Detachment was away and I had to do his calls. The helicopter which is always there by day had to go on a 'dust-off' (i.e. to pick up some casualties) who had been blown up in a minefield, but they must have been too bad for us to deal with as they went straight to Vung Tau we heard later.

8.30 pm – Well I've had tea and two cans of soft drink in the mess and have now excused myself 'to write some letters'. Actually there are very few officers left in our mess (headquarter battery) most of the time. The other three batteries have their own officers' messes and as they are all about half a mile or more away in different directions, their officers stay there, and all that are left here are the 2IC (second in command), the adjutant, myself and three lieutenants. The adjutant, Brian Mitchell, is a nice chap – in fact he was the other officer who came up with me on the flight last Monday and at Brisbane Airport he very kindly took me under his wing and introduced me to all his relatives who had come to see him off. His wife even kissed me goodbye. And told me 'to look after Brian', so it was all very touching – I'm glad I had already said my goodbyes in Sydney though. The 2IC is easy enough to get on with, but not as nice a person as the CO (commanding officer), who isn't due here until 28th May. The lieutenants are quiet and nice chaps so we are all quite a happy family.

And so I had better close off now as I haven't really any more news. Tony Williams (the doctor I knew at Concord) has just returned from out in the scrub on operation with his battalion (7 RAR) to the task force, but they are situated on the other side of the area (about one and a half miles [2.4 kilometres] away). I will pop over and see him tomorrow if I get a chance but at present at night we have to stay in our own area as we are approaching Ho Chi Minh's birthday which is always a time when the VC become more active, so they say. Not that there's much danger of course here, unless they drop a few mortar bombs on the task force, but this is pretty unlikely with all our radar patrols, air surveys and artillery fire missions.

I think of you all most of the day.

All my love,

David

[1]   These were photos of the family taken during my week's pre-embarkation leave in Sydney.

[2]   Pennant Hills.

[3]   Only 12 months before I left for Vietnam, my father opened a pharmacy business in Castle Hill, and was still building up his clientele.

Nui Dat

Wednesday 10/5/67

Dear Dad,

I wasn't going to write any letters tonight, as I was going to bed early, but the big American guns (155 mm compared to our 105 mm ones) are pounding away and firing right over our heads so it seems especially loud. I guess one of the patrols from an infantry battalion has come across something some distance away and is calling down fire on it. You can hear the whistle of the shells as they go overhead – you get used to the noise though and I can usually sleep through it now.

Today I did my first 'Medcap' (medical civil aid program) clinic – well, it was the army dentist and I, accompanied by an interpreter, and a couple of warrant officers (WOs) from the Civil Aid Unit.

'Winning hearts and minds' is their motto. They are known as 'the man from WHAM' and there is a rather rude little ditty based on the Superman rhyme about the man from WHAM 'being faster than a VC bullet and more powerful than a water buffalo'. We descended in our Land Rovers on the nearest township of Hoa Long (pronounced 'Wha' as in a baby's cry – Long). The army has built a sort of aluminium shed with a dentist's office, where he pulls teeth all afternoon to the wail of screaming kids, and a doctor's office. The villagers file in one by one and the interpreter vaguely tells me what is wrong e.g. 'He is sick in head', or 'His body too warm', or (if you will excuse the language), 'He very sick in arse'. In fact my main trouble is understanding the interpreter. They are a poor sick lot of people on the whole and TB is rife amongst them. The Medcap program is really only political, most army doctors feel, as the amount you can achieve on an occasional arvo is pretty small. There is no real follow up, and if you want to send anyone to hospital, say for surgery, or chest X-ray or treatment of TB, well, they may or may not get there. Still, it was interesting to actually meet the people. They certainly seem friendly enough, although dirty in the extreme – some bowed very politely in true old Chinese style when they left with their little packet of pills. The kids were nice – just like kids anywhere (bright little faces and full of mischief). They come up to you and say as clearly as anything: 'How are you?' and grin. They pick up some terrible Aussie swear words I believe, but I didn't hear any this afternoon. The smells were pretty bad and my RAP sergeant was looking rather green – as he already had an upset stomach anyway – by the end of the afternoon, after he'd had to cover several babies and kids with calamine lotion. But we survived OK.

How is your brilliant mechanic coming on with my old car? Any closer to a solution or has he lost those 'high hopes' he was holding out for it? I can't believe valves are the only trouble with that poor old engine!

Now I must get to bed as the guns have settled down for a while. 'End of mission' as they say when a target has been hit enough. They will fire periodically throughout the night (this is routine – called 'H&Is' – 'harass and interdict', which is designed generally to worry the VC) but no one here notices anymore.

Much love, Dad, and to all the family,
David

Nui Dat
Friday 12/5/67

Dear Mum,

How are you? It is three nights since I wrote to you. You really lose track of time here as one day is much the same as another. Nothing very eventful has happened – the usual war news – one patrol or another has sighted a mortar pit, or a tin shed, or a tunnel system and our artillery have decimated it and our ears as well. It's the queerest[1] war! Or perhaps all wars are queer like this?

The usual sick parade in the morning; an occasional visit up the road to see Jack Blomley at the Forward Detachment to look at a slide (under the microscope) together, or something, and so it goes on. I might be 1,000,000 miles from a war, and yet sometimes it seems very near – like this afternoon when the man from WHAM (Civil Aid Corps) brought in two Vietnamese ladies (plus hangers-on) for me to see. One was in the advanced stages of something or other (pulmonary TB I would think) and the other had something wrong with her tummy – goodness knows what. It is so difficult not being able to speak the language. I will really have to try and learn a bit while I am here. Apparently they come from a family from which a sixteen year old daughter was accidentally shot by one of our soldiers not long ago, so the Civil Aid people try to look after them a bit and fuss over them. I shipped the TB one off to a civilian hospital in Vung Tau where there's an Australian surgical team and gave the other some tummy pills.

I got hauled over the coals by the second in command later on for allowing locals into the RAP, but I took no notice as I'm boss of the RAP if nothing else, and anyway the 2IC suffers from the SM (small man) syndrome in my opinion. I'll be glad when our commanding officer (CO) arrives at the end of the month as I get on well with him.

When you see poor sick people like those this afternoon you realise what an awful business war is and wonder what hope there is for little kids growing up in such a place – nothing but war and poverty and disease.

Have I told you about Jack Blomley, the doc up the road? He is a 'character' – an old GP (about forty-five-ish I suppose) and rough as nails, but for all that he's a good sensible type and we get on pretty well. He is fat and always in a perfect lather of perspiration – I've never seen anything like it – you could fill a bucket if you wrung out his shirt. And he smokes an awful old pipe – but he is certainly comforting to have close at hand. He was called out in the middle of the night the other day, to the American artillery camp, because one of their shells had gone off too soon and injured a couple of gunners. Anyway he drove straight down and was bailed up at the gate by the guard who thought he was a VC. He said he had American guns trained on him from every side but Jack was nothing daunted – he pulled out his pistol and told them he'd —— well shoot them all dead if they didn't let him in. Didn't they know a —— Aussie doctor when they saw one? So it has its funny side, the war up here!

Much love to you all,
David

[1] Back in the sixties, 'queer' did not have the connotation 'gay'. It was a commonly used word meaning 'weird'. How the language changes!

Nui Dat
Monday 15/5/67

Dear old Mum,
I have just finished work – a day of splashing around a lot of beautiful red paint all over our new shelves in the RAP ('red' because that's all the Q store could give us; and besides I like it). This was interspersed by various people coming in with all manner of little ills; upset stomachs, cut fingers. We now have the RAP looking much better – my sergeant (Bob Allen) is very handy with hammer and nail and has managed to knock up some pretty good shelves and partitions out of ammunition boxes so I can now examine patients in a sort of partitioned-off office without everyone else in the building watching.

Yesterday I went to chapel after sick parade and played the organ – there were a good number there yesterday (about thirty I suppose) and Padre Wellings took the service. I don't really think he and Dad would see eye to eye on theology or practical Christianity, but he seems a nice enough man. Apparently the army chapel is planning to help the Civil Aid work in the area, especially in Hoa Long where I did that Medcap last week. The Civil Aid people are planning a youth club at Hoa Long and they want any servicemen who have experience in Church youth clubs at home to help out now and again. Quite a few of the boys at the service came afterwards and said they'd be willing to help. Also they're asking for chaps who have connections at home to write and ask them to send over little things to give out to some of the village kids like soap, combs, toothbrushes, toothpaste, coloured pencils etc. So maybe Pip's Endeavourers[1] could be interested? They particularly want hygienic things and I don't wonder – if ever there's a neglected goddess in Sth Vietnam, it's the goddess of Hygiene. Also they're getting some youth fellowships to send over medical stuff to help with the Medcap work like Elastoplast, crepe bandages, cotton wool, lint, eye shades etc; so it's all rather a good thing for the army blokes. Some of the boys at the chapel were really enthusiastic about it, as I guess they feel then they're doing something more than just fighting a war. A lot of 'those higher up' look on the work of the Civil Aid Unit as a lot of misdirected over-enthusiasm and say we're here to fight a war and not play nursemaid; but as the Civil Aid people say (and rightly I think) 'if the Allies are ever to win in South Vietnam, it won't be on the battlefield the war will be won'.

I'm just back from tea as I broke off to have a shower, and then someone came in from one of the batteries with a big cut in his head that had to be sutured. No, not a battle injury. They were having a game of football and he fell and hit his head on some ammo boxes. So I sewed him up and sent him up to the hospital for the night. Then in the middle of tea, out of the blue, a great storm blew up and sheets of rain fell for about an hour and stopped as suddenly as it started. It's a crazy country but I guess it's working up for the monsoon season.

Yesterday morning I was awoken by a most curious sound – a loud voice booming over loudspeakers in Vietnamese. At first I thought the VC had overrun us during the night and were calling on us to surrender! After half an hour of this I found it was a plane going around booming out American propaganda to the surrounding villages and also warning them that an insecticide plane was coming shortly. And come it did – a great big plane zoomed overhead just missing the tree tops and spraying the most foul-smelling insecticide everywhere – it circled back three or four times; so it wasn't my lot to have a restful Sunday morning sleep-in.

Today you must have spent in town with the bridesmaids (the terrible foursome).[2] I hope you didn't all come to blows and that something nice was decided on. Did you manage not to get run over, Mum? I guess Kay Patterson in true girl-guide fashion had to pull you back from certain death on several occasions and probably had to stop Merrie falling down several flights of stairs or escalators.

I have just got your fourth letter. The mail arrives at six o'clock and is eagerly snatched up – it certainly is a great feeling to see those letters waiting for you.

You are quite right about the army boys. I am sure a lot of them feel pretty lonely and uncertain. I am getting to know quite a few of them as they drop into the RAP from time to time. We have some interesting characters in the regiment. The steward in the officers' mess is a BEng and quite content to serve beer for his two years national service. We have a very good artist too in one of the headquarter battery gunners.

We are a happy little group in the RAP. Sergeant Allen is a very good worker – he has good ideas for improving the RAP and will do anything you ask him to and will tactfully tell you if he thinks you've made a wrong decision. 'Chuck', really Alex, Berry (the 'Gunner') is as good as ever – he fusses over all the blokes in his battery (106) and you can always be sure he will carry out to the letter anything you tell him to do. The other medic (for 101 Battery) is a happy little soul called 'Shorty' – his real name is Corporal Dutton – he's been here nine months and is due to go home in another six weeks. He is supposed to have a girlfriend in Vung Tau, which is a constant source of amusement to us all as he is really a harmless type; but he has a twinkle in his eye, so I wouldn't be surprised if the rumour were true.

In the mess, the only officer I get on with really well is a 'nasho' (national serviceman) – a 'one pipper' (second lieutenant). He is a school teacher in real life called Peter Harnwell. He is a roly-poly sort of figure with a sense of humour to match and is fun to talk to; but we don't see much of him at present as he is liaison officer to the Yank battery and lives down there, about a mile [1.6 kilometres] away, most of the time. Whenever he comes here he regales us with tales of their dreadful eating habits and how awful iced tea is. The adjutant is a nice bloke too, but very reserved.

I am going to 'Vungers' as everyone calls it (i.e. Vung Tau) tomorrow to look over these four 'glamorous' Aussie nursing sisters, so you had better pray hard for me tomorrow in case I fall in love with one.[3]

Very much love to you all. I am very well and bearing up under the strain,

Look after yourselves,

David

PS. Saturday's *Herald* would be appreciated if you could manage it – we get papers here about three weeks old and they're just a haphazard selection of Sydney, Melbourne and Brisbane papers. An occasional paperback would go well too. Pip knows my tastes.

[1] Endeavourers were young people who attended meetings on a Sunday of an organisation called 'Christian Endeavour' (CE). Endeavourers were encouraged to take an active part in the meetings – chair the meeting, pray out loud, give a short talk on a biblical theme, lead a discussion, choose a hymn and conduct the singing of it, etc. They also were encouraged to take on projects and good works. An older responsible person was appointed by the church as Endeavour Leader to oversee proceedings. Pip was CE Leader at Pennant Hills Baptist for a year or two.

[2] My sister Merrie was busy organising her wedding to Ian Gilchrist which was to be held in November 1967 in the Pennant Hills Baptist Church. She had chosen three bridesmaids and during May the wedding dress and the bridesmaids' outfits had to be decided upon – hence the trip to town. Merrie's bridesmaids were a cousin, a nursing friend, and an old family friend, Kay Patterson (later to become a Liberal Senator for Victoria and one time Minister for Health).

[3] This sort of statement was an example of how sometimes, in the letters, I said things which were untrue and were merely designed to reassure my family at home. The subject of girlfriends was an uncomfortable one for me.

Nui Dat
Wednesday 17/5/67

Dear old Mum and all the family,

Just a short note tonight as I am very tired and intend to go to bed a bit earlier than usual if I can. I have just received your letter, Mum, with the newspaper cuttings enclosed. The clipping about R&R leave in Australia caused much interest in the mess tonight and some 'tut-tutting'. It was news to all of us here and most officers think it is a bad thing and I can see their point – there are going to be a lot of soldiers going AWOL and not turning up when their five days leave are finished to go back to Vietnam. And if it's only to a limited few, it's going to cause quite a lot of discontent. Anyway, it might be a way of getting home for the wedding, but I wouldn't raise your hopes too high.

You needn't worry about minefields – the four sappers, who were blown up, were laying mines outside the perimeter and one accidentally trod on one of them – it was very sad though as a couple of them received severe head and spinal wounds. Anyway, I can assure you I won't be laying any minefields. The paper you read was wrong anyway – the nearest doctor is Jack Blomley in the Forward Detachment – they were flown straight to Vung Tau. And in any case I was doing his calls that morning and if they had been landed here I would have been looking after them.

We had another unfortunate accident last week when an artillery shell fired by one of our batteries 'dropped short' somehow and landed in 7 Battalion's area on the other side of the task force. A couple of diggers were injured and one had to have his leg amputated. When I was down at Vung Tau yesterday I saw the operation through the theatre window. It caused a lot of heartache in the regiment and a great deal of enquiry. Apparently no one was to blame though – they just hadn't allowed for the rubber trees being so tall over that side of the task force area, or something like that.

I met the four sisters from Australia yesterday at 8 Field Ambulance in Vung Tau – they are a great asset and are pulling the place into shape and getting the wards running smoothly. The CO down there is good, but the 2IC (second in command) is a great useless character who does a lot of fine talking and does nothing himself. One of the doctors told me he is the genuine 'con-man'. There seem to be quite a few officers in the army of that sort – all talk and full of their own importance. Fortunately they aren't all like that.

I did my second Medcap at Hoa Long this arvo and I feel a wreck after it. For two and a half hours straight they poured into the little clinic room and today was probably the stickiest day I've experienced here so you can imagine the atmosphere. For all their dirt and disease they are a graceful people though (just like the old Chinese) and the women are certainly quite attractive. I had an Australian sergeant for interpreter today and he was pretty good (better than last week's effort) but it is an uphill battle. I guess I will get a little more accustomed to their diseases, but half the time I don't know what's wrong or whether they're really sick. Some come just to have the 'Bac-si'[1] examine them. When they're obviously sick it could be one of a million things (from worms to chronic malaria). Who knows? A few pills to take away make them happy it seems. At four o'clock we had to leave and they were still clamouring around the door – the kids are everywhere and they trip you up – once you have seen one member of a family, all the others decide they're sick too and you have to give them some pill or other. I tell you I head for the showers pretty quickly when I get back to camp.

I enjoy sick parades in the mornings with the gunners – they are a good lot on the whole and you can't help liking the rascals. Our regiment hasn't had any cases of VD yet (which I think I told you is our greatest problem up here) but when they start getting a day or two R&C (rest and convalescence) leave in Vung Tau I'm afraid the trouble will start, despite all our warnings.

Much love,
David

[1]   Vietnamese for 'doctor'.

Nui Dat
Friday 19/5/67

Mother mine,
Greetings once again from SVN. I hope you are all doing the right thing and celebrating Ho Chi Minh's birthday with suitable festivities? The regiment celebrated last night with a special 'fire plan' (that means a plan for firing the guns in a certain sequence at a certain time) called 'Fire Plan Birthday Uncle Ho' or something like that and dropped 800 shells all around the place – a restful night was had by all as you can imagine.

I have just received your 'table napkin' letter.[1] I'm so sorry to hear about the possibility of a new chemist opening in Castle Hill.

I suppose Dad is pretty upset, but he shouldn't worry too much – I'm sure your business is firmly enough established now. I'll suggest to Bombardier Banks, our post office clerk – the one from Castle Hill – that his 'missus' would get extra special serviceman's wife treatment at Bradford's Pharmacy.

Tell Ian[2] that it would be no good sending my batman[3] over to help him prepare for the wedding as he is non-existent at present. The last doctor here had a batman/driver, but I miss out at the moment although they keep assuring me I'll get one. Meanwhile I sweep my tent, make my bed and clean my shoes myself. Tony Williams (the doctor for 7 RAR) says I'm mad and should tell the senior medical officer at Vung Tau that I am not being treated right, but you know me – a typical Bradford martyr! At the moment I usually have plenty of time to do the chores, and if I get rushed I'll object then.

Today I had to go to Baria (about 3 miles [5 kilometres] away) to the civilian hospital. Apparently one week ago one of our army vehicles ran over a civilian lady and chopped off four fingers of her right hand and broke her leg. I had to go down to get a medical certificate from the doctor looking after her, saying how much damage had been done and also whether an artificial hand of some sort was feasible. I took a Vietnamese interpreter with me but the resident doctor spoke a bit of English and we managed very well. The hospital surprised me – it was fairly neat, although terribly primitive, but the awful results of the war were more apparent there than anywhere else I've been so far. It certainly makes you realise that praying 'Give peace in our time, O Lord' is no light prayer to pray, when you see women and children who have been wounded by VC mortar bombs and mines. If ever a country needed peace to patch up its wounds and to get started towards civilisation, it's poor South Vietnam. As we left the ward the interpreter (a boy about twenty-one with a nice bright face) turned to me and said, 'If this war not over soon, I don't know what will happen!' And yet until the VC are pushed out or controlled somehow there will be no peace here. It's a sad old world isn't it?

I still have my big trouble here. My interpreter took about five minutes of solid talking to convince him I was a doctor, 'But you so young to be a doctor.' Even here, they won't believe me. Maybe I'll age a bit in the next eleven months and one and a half weeks.

I suppose you're sure to have a fire going at home tonight – what an awful thought! The temperature here's in the range 80–95 degrees F day and night most of the year and the humidity at present (the beginning of the Wet) is 99–100 per cent. It certainly has been a lot sultrier the last few days.

Much love Mother dear, and to all the family,
David

[1] My mother, very unusually for her, must have scribbled me a short letter on a paper table napkin. At the time she was working quite long hours in the pharmacy assisting my father, so letter-writing had to be squeezed into her busy schedule, whenever it could be.

[2] My sister Merrie's fiancé.

[3] Army officers of the rank of captain and above often have a private soldier assigned to them as a sort of personal valet and driver. He was called a batman.

Nui Dat
Sunday 21/5/67

Dear Dad,

I have just finished writing my awful hygiene report which has to be in tomorrow morning – this is a monthly chore which I am going to hate – I just don't seem to have the right sort of brain for making suggestions on hygiene improvement. At any rate I have really been tough on the kitchen in our battery as I've had about fifteen cases of diarrhoea in the last twenty-four hours and I'm sure it's the kitchens – they haven't been finished off, they're inadequately fly-screened and the cooks aren't hygienically minded.

Thank you for your letter and your account of the helpful sermon you gave recently.[1] We had a good service this morning – Communion because it's Trinity Sunday and Padre Wellings was pretty good. I think he's good at heart but has fallen off the track a little bit somewhere along the line. Anyway he had some good thoughts this morning and it was helpful. I squeezed away on the old organ. It's a nice break from the daily routine which doesn't change much on a Sunday at present. I believe later when the regiment has settled in and has done more of the work that needs to be done in fortifying our position we'll have Sunday as a 'stand down' day. I am getting busier too what with the beastly hygiene and going down regularly to Vung Tau (by road) with patients whom I want a specialist opinion on, and to visit my gunners who are in hospital.

Thank you for all your prayers for me – I am very conscious of them and thank the church people too, won't you?

Much love, Dad,

David

¹   My dad was a great one for sermons, but if asked to preach at church he took the responsibility very much to heart and liked to test out his thoughts on the family at home beforehand. He often wrote and told me what he was planning to say in a forthcoming sermon. I had great respect for my father and for the genuineness of his Christian commitment. At this stage of my life I was beginning to realise that I could never hope to live up to his high ideals, which was a source of some guilt for me. Dad's sermon letters merely reinforced this feeling.

Nui Dat
Sunday 21/5/67

Dear old Mum,

Just a short one tonight I'm afraid. First to answer your questions:

1. Yes, I am well and don't seem to be much affected by the heat. I thought I was getting diarrhoea this morning but it was only psychological after dishing out so much sulphathalazole to the fifteen cases of the 'runs' yesterday.

2. Yes, I get stacks enough to eat and I still eat like a horse except when we get one of those awful American salads – they have olives and gherkins and asparagus and their ham is terrible. But on the whole the food is good and after my visit to the kitchen yesterday it should be safe to eat too.

3. We lack fresh milk (we have tinned instead) and good tea, but apart from that the food is OK. I'm sick of tinned soft drink but you've got to drink something.

You do sound tired in your last two letters. I hope you're not trying to work too hard. Please look after yourself (you can't be trusted, I know) – forget the ironing and get a washerwoman or something – you can pay for it out of my bank money.

Pip had me in fits of laughter in his last letter – I will write to him and Merrie again soon. Where does he get his twisted sense of humour?

Could you send me a cake of Gamophen (soap) once a fortnight? It would be much appreciated as we only have army issue soap. There is some Gamophen in my RAP but I want to hang on to it for bad skin cases.

Thanks for all the letters – they're great! And do take good care of yourself and of old Dad too, won't you?

Your dutiful son,
David

Nui Dat
Tuesday 23/5/67

A SUPER SERIAL LETTER FOR EVERYONE
Dear Mum and family,

1. Mum

My word but you are getting vague, old thing – your letter is dated Thursday, Friday and Saturday, with 'Friday' and 'Saturday' then crossed out. I must certainly be just like you though as I rang the adjutant this afternoon about something and said 'Hello David, it's Brian here. No – Hello Brian it's etc.' and then got all confused. It's pretty bad when you don't know your own name. I think I had an excuse though – I had just been ringing the Field Ambulance at Vung Tau to ask about one of my patients, and it's not like ringing trunk calls to Melbourne from Sydney or anything simple like that. First you get onto our switchboard (called Enterprise Switch), then to the Task Force switchboard (Ebony); then a radio-telephone link to Vung Tau switchboard (a civil switchboard), then to the Australian Army switchboard at Vung Tau (Emu), then to the 8 Field Ambulance switchboard (Vampire) and so to the required phone. Five switchboards in all and they all keep breaking in and saying 'Are you getting through, sir?' It's a long drawn out struggle just to find out how a patient's getting on, or to ask advice from a specialist.

But seriously, Mum, I don't want you collapsing from overwork while I'm away. Don't worry about writing proper letters if you haven't time. Just jot down any old thing as you go through the day and send that – I don't mind as long as the letters come. Just 'Hello, love from Mum' will do . . . I'm looking forward to the biscuits by the way. They should be good – who cares if they're melted?

Anyway, do please look after yourself – no overworking!

Much love, Mum.

2. Dad

Dear Dad,

I hope the shop is good this week and not giving you any trouble? I've had my own troubles in the last two days since my last letter. The 2IC didn't like my hygiene report because I ran down headquarter battery so much, and he wanted me to change it. He said it was a bad reflection on my hygiene staff, but what he really meant was it was a bad reflection on his administration. Anyway I didn't change it so he's a bit upset with me. He reckons I ought to go round making sure things are done and if they're not done he says I should put people responsible on charges. Imagine me, charging people! I maintain I am purely an adviser on health matters and it's up to him to see that my recommendations are carried out. In actual fact the hygiene staff work well, but are just vastly overworked and short in numbers; but the administration doesn't like taking soldiers off other jobs and putting them on hygiene. I had to get the task force health officer over today and the 2IC broke down a bit and gave us an extra hygiene man, but then pretended it was his own idea. The regimental MO's job is not always a bed of roses. I'm afraid with my being so inexperienced in army ways, he's got it all over me, but I'm learning fast.

I'm getting a batman tomorrow, who will also be our ambulance driver – he'll be attached to me all the time and have no other job so he'll be useful for all sorts of jobs in the RAP, as well as cleaning my boots – it will make life a lot easier.

Much love anyway, Dad.

3. Merrie

Dear Porky girl,[1]

How are you? Still 'love sick' as Pip says in one of his letters?

Well, I suppose (true nurse) you want to know how the RAP is going? Our shelves are almost complete now and painted a lovely red – we have set our stores out in a logical tidy order and have laid out an emergency table which is already covered with red dust. It contains such things as my endotracheal tubes, laryngoscope, and drugs like adrenaline, Solu-Cortef and giving sets (for IV fluids). We have plenty of normal saline and albumen in our kerosene fridge and we even have a sucker and oxygen manual resuscitator mask, so we're not too badly off. I've already done a few 'major' surgical operations such as removing warts, cysts, draining abscesses and suturing and NO infections post-op as yet, so we're reasonably sterile, even though we have no sterile drapes, no masks and *no gloves*. It just shows you what you can get away with, doesn't it?

I've just indented (that means 'ordered') an infra-red lamp for our many bruises and strains, and a proctoscope for our many cases of piles, both of which we may or may not be supplied with, depending on the whim of the medical and dental stores at Vung Tau. I'm mainly treating skins and ears at present – there are some really terrific rashes up here if you like rashes. We seem to have an outbreak of diarrhoea under control now, with all my brilliant public health measures swinging into action at the first signs of the 'trots', but I had to send one case to hospital.

I received my first copy of *The Australian Baptist* today much to the astonishment of most of the mess.

My love to you and all the sisters and nurses at Hornsby Hospital. Hope the nursery is going well.

Much love.

4. Pip[2]

Dear Pipsqueak,

Thank you for the lovely thank-you letter you sent me last week. I'm glad you liked your birthday gift which as you can imagine made a large hole in my 'money-bins'.

Well, are you still alive after the Boys' Brigade[3] canoe trip? I'm sure something must have gone wrong or it wouldn't have been a proper BB outing – the canoes probably sank after the first 100 yards or so? I am looking forward to hearing the full details.

Today a great event occurred! A special work party of gunners was detailed to sandbag my tent. This is a mighty job which entails piling sand bags two layers thick up to the base of the roof proper of the tent. This is supposed to protect the tent occupant from mortar attacks, should these ever occur. It also has the effect of shutting out any fresh air that may have conceivably got in otherwise and leaves the tent rather like the black hole of Calcutta; but they reckon the doc ought to be protected, if not very comfortable.

I am sorry about the vulgar terms in my letters, but Vietnam is a bit of a vulgar country in more ways than one. I'm glad (my former) car is going again. Maybe Mr Hughes has made a success of it at last.

Can you forward over 'Christian Youth and Dating' ASAP as I think I will need to consult it? I am giving a valuable and intensely gripping, fascinating and altogether not-to-be-missed lecture on 'hygiene' (which is a euphemism for VD) in a couple of days. I bet you are sorry to be missing it.

Anyway 'all the best for the festive season', Uncle Phil – until my next epistle, bon soir.

5. Ian[4]

Dear Ian,

Just a short note to say how sorry I am about your old chartered accountancy exams. It must be a big disappointment for you and Merrie, but I'm sure you'll not let it get you down – and there's always next time. I expect your sister has left[5] by now too so your family will be a bit lonely. Thank you very much for the 'flash' photos.[6] I look at them a lot.

Kind regards,
David

[1] 'Porky' or 'Porko' were my father's nicknames for Merrie, my sister. She was more thin than chubby, in fact – most of my father's nicknames had little logic to them. She had trained in nursing at the Royal North Shore Hospital, and her time there overlapped with mine as a medical student. Merrie then did her obstetrics training at Hornsby District Hospital, completing that just prior to her marriage.

[2] My brother Philip was almost invariably called 'Pip' or 'Pippy', the latter

name causing him intense annoyance. He was in his final year of a
Bachelor of Arts degree at the University of New South Wales in 1967,
majoring in psychology.

3 A Christian youth group modelled on military lines (boys only; there was
also a Girls' Brigade) of which Pip was a leader.

4 Ian Gilchrist, my sister's fiancé, was studying chartered accountancy. He
was the only son of a well-known Sydney Evangelical family.

5 Ian's sister, Robyn, went to work in Papua New Guinea as a missionary
in 1967. She remained there for about five years.

6 The flashlight photos were taken by Ian at Sydney Airport on the night I
left to return to the regiment in Brisbane.

Nui Dat
Wednesday 24/5/67

Dear Mum,

Just a little note on Empire Night to say hello – or don't they have
'cracker' night on 24th May anymore? If it is cracker night I suppose
the usual smoke pall is hanging over Sydney and the fire brigade is
as overworked as usual. It does seem funny being so far away from
you all – it is raining here tonight and for once the temperature is
down to about 75 degrees F, so it is quite pleasant sitting here in my
ultra sandbagged tent. The biscuits arrived tonight and are very good
– the chocolate ones have melted a bit, so it's probably not worth
sending chocolate biscuits anymore. The others are good and fresh
so we'll have a feast tomorrow afternoon in the RAP. My medical
journal arrived tonight too and a letter from the 'little creatures',[1] so
I am getting a constant stream of mail – one or two letters every day
which is just nice.

I went to Hoa Long again this afternoon and spent the usual
somewhat frustrating time struggling with the language. It makes me
very sad to see so many little kids, so obviously sick, and I just don't
know what's the matter with them most of the time. I wish I had been
a better student and read a bit more widely in my student days. A few
patients whom I've sent to Vung Tau for X-rays and operations have
been fixed up; most had TB whom I suspected of it and have started
treatment so I suppose that's some good gained.

There is an Australian Surgical Team from Prince Henry Hospital NSW working at the main civilian hospital in Vung Tau and the Civil Aid people are going to take me down to meet them sometime soon. I may even know some of them and they might be able to give me some clues.

I have now been here three weeks and a day and am getting to be quite an old hand – I am now eligible to wear one ribbon and to get a war service home, so how about that? It takes another six months to get the second ribbon.

Do keep praying for me won't you? As I see what little chance these people have ever had it keeps reminding me of that verse 'unto whomsoever much is given, much shall be required'.

Anyway, very much love, Mum – tomorrow is pay day so I will buy a camera next week and send you some slides.

Your dopey son,

David

---

[1] This refers to my three Lloyd cousins who lived in the Blue Mountains: Peter, Robbie and Ian, sons of my mother's younger brother, Bill. The eldest boy, Peter, was about twelve years my junior. My family always referred to them as 'the little creatures', a strange term which their maternal grandmother had once used to describe them. They were 'special' cousins as they often came to stay with us for holidays and my sister, brother and I felt considerable affection for them.

Nui Dat
Saturday morning 27/5/67

Dear Mum,

Just a short note this morning in order to catch the post. I couldn't write last night as I was busy fixing up a big surprise for you all – I am sending home a parcel (not dirty washing) which will probably take four or five weeks I suppose, but it will be good when it gets there. I won't tell you what it is, but leave it as a big surprise.[1] Anyway I packed it up all safely this morning with Sergeant Allen's help and posted it. This morning has been pretty quiet (very small sick parade) so I've had time to churn out this letter and to pack up the parcel.

Must go now – will write a proper letter tonight.

Much love and look out for a parcel in the mail.

Love from

David

<hr>

[1] The contents of the parcel are finally revealed in my letter of 25/6/67 if readers can't contain their curiosity.

Nui Dat

Saturday evening 27/5/67

Dear family,

I'm afraid my letter writing has been rather poor this week as I have actually been quite busy and last night and this morning I was busy fixing up the little present I'm sending you all in the mail. As you see, I'm like Dad, bursting to tell you what it is, but I will be strong. You just have to wait and see.

Well, they say, be sure your sins will find you out. Tonight for the first time for ages and seeing it was Saturday night I went to the movies. To go to the movies you have to go out of your own area i.e. cross the road and walk about 100 yards to the task force officers' mess – where all the 'big wigs' hang out – there's majors and colonels everywhere. I forgot to tell our switchboard where I was going (I'm usually pretty good about things like that) and of course tonight was the very night they wanted me. A sergeant got bitten by wasps and all his face was swollen up like a great balloon. And no one could find me – of course they did in about fifteen minutes so all was well and the poor bloke got his Phenergan injection, but that's what happens when I go to the movies.

It's nice to know the nurses at Hornsby think Merrie is a 'happy nut'. I overheard my RAP sergeant say I was 'very religious, but a good bloke' the other day and one of the officers in the mess said it was a nice change to have 'a teetotaller who didn't preach at you'. I'm glad to say we do get on very well in the RAP. Sergeant Allen is a very worldly-wise young man and can swear in quite an amazing fashion when provoked; but he really has a heart of gold and I would be lost without him. He is quite soft underneath and pours out all his troubles to me now and again – I'm finding that the RMO is really more like a father confessor here – they, the gunners, drift in any old time of day and tell you all sorts of hair-raising things, but they're mostly really all kids at heart – I just listen wisely and can never think of anything to say, but I guess a good listener is what most of them need anyway.

Pip's canoe trip sounds like a real saga – I hope he's recovered by now?

I don't know any more about the hygiene kits for Hoa Long yet – may know more tomorrow.

Much love to you all – look after yourself, Mum.

David

Nui Dat
Monday 29/5/67

My dear Mum,

It is early Monday morning (7.10 am) and I got up a bit earlier to write this letter while I listen to the news. It was a busy night last night – two boys from a reinforcement unit out on patrol were shot and were brought to the Forward Detachment.

The rainy season has well and truly started with quite heavy rain yesterday afternoon and last night. The big American guns have been firing almost constantly since yesterday arvo, as they've heard of a big VC battalion down near the coast. The guns get on your nerves a bit after a while, but I slept through them pretty well last night. Today I have eighty-five medicals (medical examinations) to do on 101 Battery, which is going home in two weeks, so I'll be extra busy today.

Thank you for the papers, the biscuits and all your letters. I'd better go off to breakfast now and get ready for sick parade.

Lots of love dear old thing and look after yourself, won't you?

Your son

David

PS Went to chapel yesterday morning – no further news of the Civil Aid work, but I'll let you know as soon as I can.

Nui Dat
Monday 29/5/67

For Merrie
To: The Pork Publishing Company, Castle Hill Rd
Dear Sir, madam, mistress, 'it',
Just a note matey, on behalf of us digs 'ere in Sth Vietnam to thank youse folks a ——— of a lot for the first volume in your new service to the Gunners 'ere at the Regt. Most of us feel that *Playboy* would have been a better choice frankly, but ya can't look a gift 'orse in the mouth can ya, and I reckon Wodehouse will hafta do for the time bein'.

That's enough of that! The books are very much appreciated and I will hand on to other Wodehouse fans[1] when I've finished.

You would have been interested last night when the two soldiers were shot by machine gun out on patrol. Jack rang me to give him a hand, so I had to dash up to the Forward Detachment, arriving in time to help get them into 'the chopper'. All they'd had time to do for the two boys was stick shell dressings (which are a large pre-packed army dressing with tapes attached) over their wounds – chest wounds in one case and loin and spinal wounds in the other – and put drips up before the chopper arrived. Old Jack was in his usual lather of perspiration, sucking on his foul old pipe and swearing like a trooper at anyone who happened to get in his way – he even swears at the brigadier over the phone on occasions – but he really is a good doctor even if a little unpolished. There's no mucking about with him – he rings for a chopper at a glance and sticks drips up and that's it. One boy was very bad – had a big chest wound and needed the oxygen mask, while the other probably had a spinal injury. They were the first actual battle casualties I've seen, and it's a sobering sight. The staff were all dashing around like old veteran hospital sisters, although this was their first sight of battle casualties of any severity too. At any rate they (the casualties) would have been at Vung Tau within twenty minutes of their arriving up the road, so I hope they'll both be OK. They're both still alive today we heard, but one only just. The medics up at the Field Ambulance were terrific – they're a motley lot but all hoe in when it's necessary.

Tonight is another maximum security night, but all's quiet so far.
Will write again soon,
Your dopey brother,
Dave

[1] 'P. G. Wodehouse knew a lot of his readers had time on their hands. They were in institutions of one kind or another – boarding schools, hospitals, prisons – and he did his best to keep them happy' (Peter Craven, *The Australian*, 21–22 October 2006). Add in 'the army on service overseas' and that included me back in 1967.

Nui Dat
Monday 29/5/67

Dear Philip-Pirrip,
Well how are the aching limbs and shiny nose? Recovered from the Boys' Brigade canoe trip? I trust it hasn't cramped your form for amorous activities at the Evangelical Union[1] house party! But how could it with you being such a tall, dark, handsome 'over-twenty-one-year old'.

You really must get a subscription to *The Baptist*, Uncle Phil. It's a laugh a minute. The leading article this week was on 'Baptists and others', and made the remarkable statement that Baptists 'because of our distinctive view of baptism' must always be a 'race apart'. It made me so mad I've written a letter to the editor, but I haven't been game to post it yet. They will take it the wrong way if I do send it, I suppose, and label me an 'ecumenical'. John Moroney, the Anglican vicar I met in Melbourne when I was at Healesville, says in his most recent letter that if many more Baptist young people follow my example the Baptists will have to be compensated for 'their redundant under-water snorkels and other equipment'.

Sergeant Allen bought me a Yashica camera in 'Vungers' today – I gave him the money to do just that – for only US$45. It looks terrific, so I'll send some slides home when I get some taken.

Hope the UNSW EU house party is a great success,
Your old bro,
Dave

1   University of NSW Evangelical Union. EU was a Christian student group
     which offered prayer and bible study groups as well as social activities
     to university students.

Nui Dat

29/5/67

Dear Mum,

People back home DO seem to have trouble with my address but at
least with *your* letters there's no chance of them going astray – you put
everything in quite correctly plus your appended 'Psalm 91'[1] written
on most envelopes. But don't worry, I like that.

The good old commanding officer (CO) – Lieutenant Colonel Reg
Gardner – arrived today, which is a matter for great rejoicing in the
regiment as the 2IC is regarded as a 'pill' by all and sundry, whereas
the CO is respected and well liked. The CO has the happy knack of
setting people at ease, even the gunners, so I like him.

I've had an exhausting day doing medicals on all the battery which
is going home in two weeks time. If they have any infectious diseases,
particularly 'you-know-what', they're not allowed to leave SVN; however I didn't have to fail anyone today. Word got around that you don't
go home if you have any infection, so they all behaved themselves in
the last month. It's amazing what a deterrent going home is. I felt a bit
flaked out though after looking down 170 ears, feeling 85 tummies,
and inspecting other more intimate parts of the anatomy all day – it's
a bit soul destroying.

I'm glad Mrs Brown[2] approves of our involvement in Vietnam. I'm
sure I don't know what to think – at least I know it's right for me to be
here, so that's really all that matters. I like and appreciate the soldiers
more every day and I understand a little better, I think, the bond
that binds ex-servicemen together. There is a tremendous sense of
comradeship between the gunners, which is the best thing about
the Australian soldier and I do feel proud to be a member – at least
I don't feel a newcomer anymore and it is nice to feel genuinely liked
and respected by the men. I only hope I'm more than just 'a good doc'
and am able to help them a bit more than just professionally, but
'spiritually' too.

The sunsets here are lovely and I can see them[3] because they're good strong yellows and blues and not 'pastelly' reds and pinks like ours. The mountains around the task force area are bluish, but more greenish-blue than our Blue Mountains – I think you would like them.

Apart from the sickness, the war and poverty, I think South Vietnam could be quite a beautiful land. There was more rain today so the mud is beginning to get really sticky – it just won't come off boots and so it comes into all the buildings.

I too sometimes wake up with a heavy heart and think how far off Sydney is and how far away you all are, but I think it's mainly the thought of shaving in cold water and having to face another day of our delightful toilet facilities that worries me most. But I feel assured of being in the place where I ought to be, and I'm not really lonely or homesick. I just have this feeling of how awful it would be to have 'wasted' the time I have up here, so please pray that I won't.

Thanks a lot for the Gamophen – it's like gold here. I'm telling all the 'bad skins' to get their folks to send it up to them, so I ought to get a commission from the manufacturers.

Much love to you all, from

'The quack from Nui Dat'

PS I'm enclosing one of our *restricted* evening information sheets issued nightly to all officers to show you a typical army document. Don't let the Press get it – you'd better cut it up into little bits and eat it after you've looked at it.

---

[1]   My mother would just write 'Psalm 91' on the outside of the envelope, certain I would know what it meant. Verses 5 and 7 were especially relevant – King James version: 'Thou shalt not be afraid for the terror by night; nor for the arrow that flieth by day; A thousand shall fall at thy side, and ten thousand at thy right hand; but it shall not come nigh thee.'

[2]   Our next door neighbour at Pennant Hills.

[3]   I am totally red-green colour blind but can see yellows and blues very well in compensation.

Nui Dat
Wednesday 31/5/67

Dear Dad,

Today has been an interesting day; being Wednesday, it was my Medcap day at Hoa Long and I actually diagnosed my first case of leprosy (at least I'm pretty sure it was). I sent him to Baria civilian hospital and the Vietnamese doctor there thought it probably was too. The man had a funny infected scaly-looking rash on one of his palms which he said had been there one month. The Vietnamese interpreter said he thought it was leprosy and sure enough he had anaesthetic patches on his forearms and his ulnar nerves were as thick as whip-cord behind the elbows when I examined him properly. I probably would have missed it but for the interpreter – I'm still hopeless with diagnosis over here.

Tomorrow should be a good day. Sergeant Allen (my RAP sergeant) has to go to Vung Tau, so the Civil Aid blokes have promised to come down too and introduce me to the Australian Surgical Team working in Le-Loi hospital at 'Vungers'. As I refer any 'sickies' found at Hoa Long to them I'll be pleased to get to know them and see how they work and what facilities they have. I'll probably spend all day with them if I can arrange it. I'll have to go to 8 Field Ambulance in Vung Tau too and see some of my patients there, so it will be a nice break from usual routine. We doctors in 'the Nui Dat Medical Association' are a bit upset with 8 Field Ambulance at the moment – we regard them as an idle lot who don't understand the situation up here (at Nui Dat) at all and they certainly don't have much common sense. Their greatest diagnostic success lately was one case whom Jack Blomley sent down for something or other and he ended up in the VD ward (although it would have been a physical impossibility for him to have acquired VD). The other night, too, when those two boys were so badly shot up and we flew them down to Vung Tau in a chopper, the Field Ambulance failed to tell us over the phone beforehand that the Australian surgeon had the night off in the town and so they had to be transferred to the American army hospital; whereas if we'd known, we could have sent them straight to the Yanks without mucking around and waste of precious time. (Don't for goodness sake publish that around.) The trouble is the 2IC down there is only interested in being a big time army officer and not interested in medicine.

After I finished my Medcap this afternoon the four Civil Aid fellows from Hoa Long invited Sergeant Allen and myself around to where they live and it really is an eye-opener. The four of them share a little room about 24 ft by 7 ft [7.3 metres by 2 metres] in the 'married quarters' of the local Popular Forces (South Vietnamese equivalent of our Citizen Military Forces) compound. The four Australian guys are attached to Hoa Long as their particular area of Civil Aid. You really have to take your hat off to them. They live with absolute squalor all around them – the soldiers (Vietnamese) have all their kids (dirty and unkempt), dogs and hens, garbage, refuse etc. all around them in this wired-in compound. After 5 pm it isn't safe to go out, so the Aussies are cooped up in their little room from dark to daylight – have to do all their cooking on little hexamine stoves. They've fixed themselves up a decent shower and toilet, but before that they had to shower under a pump in the middle of the compound in full view of all inter-ested Vietnamese. They're such nice blokes too – just ordinary rough old soldiers but genuinely interested in doing something helpful for the people. They say they get closer to the people that way and are trusted more than if they just arrive every day from the task force area armed to the teeth. They're pretty game though as the compound could be attacked any night by the VC and they have no radio or any means of letting the task force know. The Vietnamese Popular Forces are pretty hopeless soldiers too – on the last operation they went on, a couple of blokes wore thongs and several had to come back because they'd left their food behind.

I took some photos with my new US$45 Yashica Electro 35 camera, which is a beauty. It's a really classy camera.

I will ask the Civil Aid blokes about useful Medcap equipment to have sent up as Padre Wellings seems to be turning out 'a bruised reed'[1] on this issue. He never knows any more from one Sunday to the next. I'll write as soon as I get more definite information.

As you can see from the stains on the paper I'm spraying insect repellent furiously but it does no good at all. The insects continue to crawl through my hair and down my neck. It's most uncomfortable sitting under a light at night.

Has Mum solved the problem of the venetian blinds yet at the front of the church?[2] I'll be most interested to hear her solution for the Wedding Day!

I wouldn't worry too much about the changes at Castle Hill. I have great faith in your shop weathering any storms. I told our postman Bombardier Banks to send his 'missus' in to your shop but he was non-committal. I think she must be firmly wedded to your main opposition. It doesn't stop him telling me about his 'crook knee' every time he sees me though.

Did Pip tell you I wrote a letter to *The Australian Baptist*? After two days wondering whether I should send it, I finally sent it this morning, so if in a few weeks no good Baptists speak to you, you'll know it's your trouble-making son again. Actually I think it was a good letter – I just said that the 'race apart' attitude of Baptists made Baptist young people suspicious of other Christian young people's inter-denominational activities, which was a shame.

Hooroo Dad,

David

PS Keep looking for that big present in the post.

[1] 'A bruised reed' is used to describe someone who is weak or unreliable. The biblical reference is from Isaiah 42.3 – King James version: 'A bruised reed shall he not break, and the smoking flax shall he not quench.' My father was very fond of this verse, as it supposedly referred to God's patience with unreliable humans. He often said so-and-so was a bruised reed.

[2] Most Baptist churches are fairly spartan and austere in decoration but the Pennant Hills Baptist Church was more austere than most and the three long windows at the front of the church were shaded by venetian blinds. These were not particularly beloved by my sister or mother and how to deal with them for the wedding becomes a regular semi-serious theme in the letters.

Reflections

Arriving in Nui Dat was a severe shock. Any romantic notions I might have had about being an army doctor in time of war were severely tested over my first few days there. I was trying my best to come to terms with the enormity of what I had done in volunteering for the army and for service in Vietnam. The environment was alien, uninviting, rough and unsafe. I was expected to provide care and support to others when I felt little support and total inexperience myself. I knew I had no one to blame but myself that I was in this predicament. Yet, I somehow felt I was stuck with something I should have been forewarned about and better equipped to deal with. Of course I could not allow members of my family back home to get an inkling of these my true feelings, hence the letters are low key and rather non-committal. They also show that I was exceptionally naïve and wet behind the ears.

The task force area was spartan, divided up into smaller unit areas by barbed wire fences. The mess halls, admin services (orderly rooms) and RAPs at Nui Dat were aluminium buildings with glassless louvred windows, the command posts were dug-out bunkers and the living quarters were tents – the latter sandbagged to about shoulder-height all around. It was an all-male camp so toilet facilities were rudimentary. 'Piss phones' (i.e. urinals) made from ammunition casing were scattered all over the place, often with little or no screening; shower blocks were concrete ground slabs with suspended shower buckets above; and toilets were 'thunder boxes' over holes in the ground (deep pit latrines). Screening for all these facilities was very variable – shower areas often had no screening at all or screens only to about waist height. Sitting on one of the thunder boxes when all the guns were firing (particularly the big 155 mm American guns) was quite an experience. The shock wave transmitted through the earth forced a wave of warm foul air from way below you, nearly lifting you off your seat. It gave a whole new meaning to the expression 'the bowels of the earth'! The weather was hot and very humid most of the time and air circulation was poor under the rubber trees. No wonder that, when in camp, most soldiers and many officers worked without shirts on.

Things were not wholly bad, though. I was fortunate enough to have been given a medical sergeant, Bob Allen, whose years of army training entirely made up for my inexperience. My hygiene sergeant, Fred Wittmer, was knowledgeable and confident about hygiene matters. The other members of my medical team, Chuck Berry and Shorty Dutton, were friendly and capable. I had the wit to recognise my good fortune and to acknowledge my limitations. I was quite willing to learn from my more junior colleagues even though formally I was their boss.

I was fortunate too with the fellow officers with whom I lived in close quarters in the headquarter battery. They were all friendly, approachable and easy-going with perhaps the notable exception of the 2IC, Major Gerry Salom. The poor major comes in for considerable criticism in the letters and looking back I believe this criticism is unjustified. No 2IC worth his salt in time of war could allow himself to be friendly and easy-going at all times with his junior officers. In retrospect, I think the good major probably went out of his way to make allowances for and manage an RMO who was obviously inexperienced in the ways of the army and the ways of the world. Of course he was stuck with me as I was stuck with him and he probably recognised that, for all my youthful arrogance, I had the makings of a reasonable doctor. If he had wished, he could have made life considerably more difficult for me. All in all, I got off lightly with him and my feelings for him in retrospect are considerably warmer than they were in 1967–68.

Brian Mitchell, our adjutant, was my idea of what a professional Australian army officer ought to be. He was handsome, intelligent, rational, always fair-minded and just in his dealings; egalitarian and even-handed with the ORs, friendly with his fellow officers but always with a hint of reserve; totally and utterly dependable. He was a credit to the Royal Military College, Duntroon. I would like to have known him better and I remember him with great respect and affection.

About the commanding officer (CO), Lieutenant Colonel Reg Gardner, I will have more to say later in the book when I join him on R&R. Suffice to say now that he was a gentleman artillery officer of the old school, with a surprisingly witty and risqué sense of humour and genuine human warmth and kindness. Padre Wellings, a Presbyterian Church minister gets a few serves in the letters, but he was a pleasant man and I am sure did his duty as best he could. My father, if they had ever met, definitely would have endorsed my unkind reference to him as 'a bruised reed'. He smoked cigarettes and drank alcohol; looking back now I think he was probably one of those men who have to grapple with a lifetime of depression. He looked depressed and his Sunday homilies were a bit depressive in outlook. His time in Vietnam cannot have been easy for him. I definitely could and *should* have been nicer to him.

Captain Tony Williams was a colourful character. He is another person I regret losing contact with over the years. I hero-worshipped him at Concord Hospital as he was a registrar when I was only a brand new junior resident. He was first and foremost a very good, competent and caring doctor. He was also unusually kind to junior residents and wouldn't hesitate to step in and help if you were in trouble – if you couldn't manage a procedure (putting up a drip, doing a lumbar puncture, inserting a chest drain etc.) you would hope and pray Tony was the registrar on call to come to your aid. He had a certain rather naughty allure about him as well; always indefinable, but you couldn't help feeling his innocent smile and open face belied the real Tony. He had an interest in army medicine and had been in the Citizen Military Force (CMF) for some years, yet it was a surprise when he announced he was going to Vietnam. His decision certainly influenced my own decision. He had a much more exciting and braver war than I did and put his life at risk on several notable occasions. Once he was winched in from a hovering helicopter at night to attend to wounded soldiers when enemy fire made it impossible for a 'dust-off' helicopter to land. He told me later he asked the pilot how he knew he was landing him in the right place and not in the middle of the enemy force and the pilot replied that he was 'pretty sure it's the right spot, mate'. After Vietnam, Tony had a distinguished career as a psychiatrist in the New South Wales Health Department and has only recently retired.

Despite constant reiteration of my hatred of hygiene inspections throughout the letters I knew very well that lack of attention to hygiene in a fixed military camp like Nui Dat could be catastrophic. No military force can fight effectively if large numbers of soldiers have gastroenteritis. When browsing in a major bookstore once, through an official history book of the RAAMC, which covered the period from the beginning of World War II to the end of the Vietnam campaign, I found the only official reference to my army service: a quote from one of my hygiene reports on headquarter battery in 1967. Ironic that hygiene is my one and only true claim to military fame.

It has to be remembered that, for all my two years at a teaching hospital after graduation, I was a very young inexperienced doctor; I had no false ideas about my medical knowledge – I knew there were big deficiencies in my training. My experience with major trauma was negligible because 2CH in Ingleburn was little more than a cottage hospital and sending me and others there had been merely paying lip service to our need for exposure to emergency medicine. During my time at Ingleburn the worst acute trauma I saw was a young soldier who came off his motorbike practically outside the hospital and suffered several major lacerations and an open compound fracture of his ankle. This was hardly enough experience to prepare one to deal with battle casualties in a war zone. So I was glad that my first Vietnam experience of major trauma was with Jack Blomley and I was relieved to find I acquitted myself passably well. It was shocking to see young men seriously wounded by mine explosions and later by bullet wounds, but in the sixties, severely damaged young people were commonplace in urban and regional hospitals around Australia. Carnage on the roads was a daily event and doctors were inured to the sights of major injury. There were no seat belts; no speed limits on open roads; road traffic laws were less enforced; drink driving was considered a misdemeanour and a badge of honour rather than a serious crime and cars were far less roadworthy – witness my Austin Lancer! Young men drove hotted-up old cars – friends squashed into back (and sometimes front) seats three or four abreast, often with girlfriends on their knees. Frequently they came to grief. Of course, road trauma still happens today, but it is much less common now.

At Healesville School of Army Health they had tried to instil some knowledge of tropical medicine into us fledgling army medicos. Leprosy wasn't mentioned though and in any case the lectures were so boring and impractical on those hot sunny afternoons that they in no way prepared me for Medcaps in Hoa Long. I learnt to do the best I could under the circumstances, which were far from ideal. Sometimes the medicine was exciting (as when I actually diagnosed a case of leprosy – admittedly with the interpreter's help). The people intrigued me – at first they were a shock to the system with their alien smells, scabby skin rashes and incomprehensible complaints and demands. But I am sorry for the image I conveyed of them and of their beautiful country in the early letters home. They were desperately poor certainly, often dirty, but nevertheless a gracious, long-suffering, resourceful and resilient people. The local midwife and her young ever-smiling assistant, clad always in a black pyjama-suit (she even *looked* like a VC), were excellent to work with and they kept up a stream of witty and flirtatious banter with us all afternoon, only some of which we could understand. They would occasionally go off into gales of merry laughter usually for inexplicable reasons but no doubt brought on by something we ignorant 'round-eyes' had said or done which tickled their fancy. It's almost certain that, after dark, they doctored local VC members just as expertly as they had assisted us with the villagers' needs during the afternoon. I think we always just assumed that they did. The black pyjama-suit probably *was* the young assistant's military uniform which she had the cheek to wear to the Medcap clinics and she was most likely a part-time Vietcong Army medic in real life. I can't help chuckling to myself now when I think how much soap and how many Band-aids from the good people of Pennant Hills probably found their way into the Vietcong supply chain.

It may seem odd that I devoted my free time on Sundays to playing the organ in the task force chapel. However, this was no hardship for me as I greatly enjoyed it. I had been one of the organists at Pennant Hills Baptist Church for a year or more before I joined the army and it was one of the things I genuinely missed after I left home. Perhaps more than the actual Sunday services, playing the organ brought me a great deal of solace in Vietnam.

I was very aware that at home during May 1967, apart from dealing with a son and brother in Vietnam, members of my family were preoccupied with two matters: the progress of my father's fledgling pharmacy business and my sister's approaching wedding. Every letter from home made some mention of these two concerns and on one level it was a great comfort to be kept up-to-date and to know the family still saw me as having an interest and a part in these important family affairs. But, from the distance of forty years, I have to admit that for me there was a degree of unreality in what was going on back home with the family. My own day-to-day concerns were very real and seemed so all-consuming, demanding and so full of uncertainty that I didn't have enough mental energy left over to deal with the family's big issues as well.

Although nothing much happened on the war front and few serious demands were made of me, May was a difficult month for me emotionally. I hadn't yet found my feet.

2

JUNE 1967

Letters

Nui Dat
1/6/67

My dear Mother,
Two letters from you today! This must be brief, so I'll try to summarise:
What I did today:

After sick parade (long and of course involved because I wanted to get away early), I drove down to Vung Tau with Sergeant Allen. He dropped me at the Le-Loi hospital where the Australian Surgical Team is working. A new team just arrived from Royal Prince Alfred Hospital in Sydney with two surgeons, an anaesthetist, a registrar, who was in my year at one stage before he did a BSc(Med), and is terribly 'brainy', four theatre sisters, a path. assistant and one other doctor (a physician – MRACP – who's been here 3 months already). They were all quite pleased to see another Sydney-sider and it was a valuable day's visit I think as the physician, Peter Miles, let me sit in on his outpatient clinic (which is very like my Medcap) and showed me a few things I was missing, so I feel a bit more confident now.

It is nice to know I can refer people down to them and that the patients will be in reliable hands. The surgeons are mad keen to do some surgery, naturally, and drilled me on looking out for hare lips and cleft palates in kids (as one is a plastic surgeon). They have

49

two quite nice operating theatres, although the wards aren't the best. I felt a little envious of them in their nice cool white shorts and long socks and their air-conditioned room at the Grand Hotel – they even have showers – while I was sweating and probably smelling horrible in my dirty old army greens. Still, I think I have the best of both worlds – I can do Civil Aid work and as well I have the army, which I do enjoy. It is rather good fun being a soldier sometimes. I had lunch with the surgical team at a big American officers' club in Vung Tau ('the Pacific') – quite a nice meal but very American-style, for 65c (US). We were surrounded by Yankee officers on every hand – they sure are a funny looking lot.

The registrar (Doug Baird) had 'crook ears' and had to go to the US Hospital to consult an ear, nose and throat (ENT) surgeon, so he took me over to meet him. This US doctor, Dr Maurice Alvaro, isn't quite through his ENT diploma course as he has one year to go, but got drafted into the army for two years much to his great disgust. He does all the ENT work over here, but typical army fashion, he has no gear for doing his ENT operations, so he gets no practical surgical experience at all. Armies are the same the world over.

I wish I were an artist, or a terrific writer, to describe Vung Tau adequately for you. It's incredibly like Manly and the Corso, except with funny little shops made out of packing cases (in some instances) open onto the street, with occasional bigger French looking houses, hospitals, or office type buildings scattered here and there. The roads are filled with every imaginable form of conveyance – great army trucks, tanks, little Lambrettas, bicycles, mechanical rickshaws, jeeps, American cars all driving madly, helter-skelter through the narrow streets. And then the pavements packed with people of every description – soldiers (Yankees, Aussies, Koreans, Sth Vietnamese with their flashy looking badges), some on business, some drunk, or nearly so, some just shopping or taking photos, some with attractive Vietnamese girls on their arms; little kids everywhere – some smoking, but all pestering soldiers for sweets or cigarettes or money, in various stages of clothing or lack of same; and then ordinary Vietnamese people wandering around vaguely – they never seem to do any work – the main business in 'Vungers' seems to be making money out of soldiers. There are bars everywhere – some very seedy-looking; some garish; some dingy – all dangerous for the young soldier. That's Vung Tau! They say it's the R&R (rest and recreation) centre for the Allies and for the VC. A sort of unwritten agreement exists that there will be no incidents of any sort in Vung Tau. It is a horrible place in many ways, yet could be quite beautiful if cleaned up. But no one could claim it was dull or lacked interest – there must be no other town quite like it in the world. It makes me sad, though, for two reasons: firstly, that people (particularly the girls) can become as degraded as the bar girls of VT so obviously are. I know Eastern culture is different from ours, but I bet 100 years ago, before the Westerners came (mainly the French of course), the local moral standards would NOT have been like they are today. And second, because our soldiers haven't a chance! I am infinitely sympathetic with their problems – cooped up here at Nui Dat for three or four months and never getting out and then allowed one or two days in VT for R&C. What hope does a typical young, only nominal Christian Australian have of remaining true to his wife, fiancée, or sweetheart at home? It is just one of those horrible problems of war and I don't know the answer except perhaps 'Give peace in our time, O Lord!'

(The above paragraph is obviously not a suitable extract for the good church people back home or for the Press, so keep it under your hat).

Much love, Mother dear, and to all the other drongos at home,
David

Nui Dat
Sunday 4/6/67

Dear good woman,
How are you? And how are all your bairns? This particular one is well and happy if a little hot and sticky! You might be interested to know that for the past weekend and until tomorrow morning at 0830 hours your elder son is the senior medical officer in the Nui Dat area – the brigadier's (i.e. he in charge of the task force) chief medical adviser. Jack Blomley, who normally runs the Forward Detachment, suffered such agony with his prickly heat on Saturday that the colonel of 8 Fd Amb decided he ought to come down to the

air-conditioned ward at Vung Tau – it is really awful, the prickly heat; once it gets a go on up here, there's nothing you can do to stop it – and so I had to leave my post and relieve him as they must have a doctor here all the time. Any casualties in the task force area are brought straight in to the emergency ward here and are then 'dusted off' via helicopter to Vung Tau if they need instant surgery. During the day a helicopter sits on the pad just outside the hospital, but goes away at night and can be summoned if necessary by radio. It's been pretty quiet here so far, except for sick parade this morning, as I had to do my own plus all the ones that normally come here for sick parade. It went so long I had to miss chapel – there are only two doctors in the task force area this weekend – Tony Williams from 7 RAR and me. Jack is in Vung Tau and the other battalion doctor is out on patrol.

Tomorrow morning the major (2IC of 8 Fd Amb) is coming up to relieve me and I will go back to the regiment, much to the disgust of the medical staff here as the major is not over-popular. It's quite a funny set-up – it's such a small unit that the doctor is the only officer and all the rest (about fifteen or so) are NCOs or diggers – everyone eats together, showers together and generally lives together in a very democratic way, and Jack is so free and easy that it's about the most easy-going unit in the whole task force area from the soldiers' point of view – a bit different from our posh artillery regiment. No gunner would ever dare prattle away abusing all and sundry to a captain at 4 Fd Regt (except perhaps to me) like they do here. I've heard more soldiers' grievances today than I've ever heard before. They're quite a rough and tough mob the medics here, but pretty good at heart. I must really have a soft spot for soldiers, I think. Sorry this must be awfully boring reading for you, but there isn't anything much of excitement to tell you today.

Headquarter battery of 4 Fd Regt played the US artillery battery on Saturday afternoon at basketball and got severely trounced (the Yanks had a few Negroes in the team and they sure are big and good jumpers). Anyway I took some slides with my new camera which I hope will turn out OK.

There's nothing very serious in the ward to look after here – only a couple of minor injuries (sore knee, half cut-off toe, half cut-off finger, moderate arm burns and two fevers that could be anything – we're just watching the latter to see if anything develops).

I'm sitting in Jack Blomley's tent (which is a shocking mess – makes mine look a palace and you can imagine mine isn't anything to write home about) writing, or rather scrawling, this terribly written epistle, sweating profusely as I write. I haven't any skin troubles at all yet (here's hoping) and in fact the acne seems to have cleared up on my back – perhaps I am at last growing up.

I was sorry to miss chapel this morning as it is my one and only chance for coming aside from the daily routine, but it couldn't be helped, I'm afraid. Although I live in a totally non-Christian and pretty earthy atmosphere all the time, I'm glad to say I have been very conscious of all the prayers of you people back home. It does make me sad to see the ignorance of Christian things amongst the soldiers – I'm sure we church-goers fool ourselves into thinking there is a certain Christian influence in the community – as far as I can see Australian young people are just as pagan as any Vietnamese and we are just not even scraping the surface with Christian witness.

Very much love,
David

Nui Dat
Monday 5/6/67

Dear old Mum,
I have written a lot of letters tonight, so thought I had better end up by writing a few lines to my good old mum. I am back in the regiment after my weekend of glory as SMO for the Nui Dat area – back in time to pour more oil on troubled waters between the 'PITN' (pain in the neck) 2IC and my easily upset hygiene sergeant. I'm glad to be back to my normal routine though.

I got Dad's scarcely legible letter tonight, my third copy of *The Australian Baptist,* and a letter from young cousin Ian[1] which had me in fits of laughter. Also my second paperback from Merrie arrived, so thank you all very much.

It is bedtime now anyway, so I'll write up my little diary and climb under my mozzie net.

I hope your surprise parcel doesn't take too long to arrive (sometimes it's up to six weeks by surface mail), but it will get there in good time, so don't get too anxious.

All my love, Mother dear,

David

PS Psalm 103.13 – like as a father pitieth his children, so the Lord pitieth them that fear Him.

¹   Ian Lloyd, one of the 'little creatures'.

Nui Dat

Tuesday 6/6/67

Dear Dad,

I'm afraid it'll only be a short letter tonight but I figure short frequent letters are probably better than long well spaced out ones. Thank you for your last cheery letter – I enjoy your little sermons in your letters as they are really the only ones I get at present. Padre Wellings' little chats aren't really sermons in the true sense of the word. I even went and read up the story of Daniel in the lion's den after reading your letter and on thinking about it, Daniel's position in Babylon¹ wasn't so different to my position here in the regiment – both pretty pagan environments! I might even try and 'work in' Daniel and the lion's den at the end of my VD lecture to the new troops (108 Battery) who arrive on Thursday – I'm not sure what other answer (than a Christian one) there is to the problem. Medicine's only answer is 'If you can't be good, be careful' – Mr Morality certainly isn't regarded too highly up here.

Tell Mum not to worry about it being 'dangerous'. I'm sure it's pretty safe where I am. The sandbags around the tents are only because the brigadier of the task force thinks everyone ought to be sandbagged (to remind us we are supposed to be at war). The 'sappers', who keep blowing themselves up with their own mines, have been very unlucky. It must be a hazardous job. The two boys we resuscitated the other night, after they were shot on patrol, are still alive and improving.

Thank you for making extracts from my letters for the church people – I'm sorry there aren't more exciting stories or statistics, as I really lead a quiet sort of life.

One of our batteries goes out on Operation Broken Hill to support the 7th Infantry Battalion (7 RAR) who are on patrol, tomorrow for about ten days. Tony Williams the 7 RAR doctor is going out with them so I don't have to go. At the moment I hardly ever move from Nui Dat.

Time for bed, Dad,

Much love to all,

David

PS I am enjoying reading Lord Emsworth and Monty.

---

[1] Daniel was a captive Jew in the city of Babylon under Darius, King of the Medes and Persians. Despite his race, Daniel was respected and he prospered under this pagan king, so much so that the local princes became jealous of his success. They plotted against him and got the king to agree to pass a law forbidding anyone to pray to, or petition, any person or god other than Darius for thirty days. As was his custom, Daniel continued to pray three times daily to the God of Israel. He was arrested and, reluctantly, Darius had him thrown into a den of lions. The next morning, Daniel was miraculously unharmed as God had 'shut the lions' mouths' and 'no manner of hurt was found upon him, because he believed in his god'.

Nui Dat

Thursday 8/6/67

Dear Mum,

I haven't any exciting news to tell you but I thought I would write.

I have just come back from the movies;[1] we have our own outdoor movie theatre in headquarter battery now – made by one of the gunners in his spare time – it has a canvas roof so it doesn't matter if it rains, but no walls so you don't roast so much as you do in one of the messes. Sergeant Allen (my RAP sergeant) is the certified projectionist – just one of his many talents; and I went along tonight at his invitation because there was a good spy film on. I think Sergeant Allen rather likes showing me off to the other gunners – he thinks I'm such a funny curiosity!

Sergeant Allen was most amused because I wouldn't let him stick a lovely nude (one of those 'heavy stuff' photos) up in the RAP. I told him I didn't care whether every other place in the task force had nudes on the wall (as they have – believe me). *Playboy*, which is banned in Australia, makes up for it in sales to Aussie troops over here and everywhere from CO's tent to the Q store has a battery of 'heavy stuff' on every inch of wall space. I said we weren't going to lower the tone of our RAP. He thought it was the funniest thing he had ever heard, but agreed only to paste up the girl's face on the wall, which he did, chortling away to himself and saying: 'You kill me sir, you really do' and going off into gales of laughter again. I don't know – I try to be serious but no one ever takes any notice – the more serious I am, the more they laugh. At least I suppose I'm fulfilling one of my functions and maintaining unit morale.

Another funny thing – every night (except maximum security nights), movies are on at about four or five different places (e.g. our HQ battery, the Task Force officers' mess, one of the gun battery messes), but no one knows until five o'clock in the evening what movies are on where. The CO has now decreed that it's one of the duties of the RMO to find out the various programs for the night and put it up on the noticeboard so that the officers can take their pick. The irony of it all is that I become 'the movie man'. Fortunately, I now have a batman and I've told him that one of his special jobs is waiting on the amenities officer at five o'clock every night for the film list.

The batman arrived up from Holsworthy and they grudgingly allocated him to me. He will make life a bit easier. He's not the brightest, I'm afraid, but if I spell everything out for him I guess he'll do a pretty good job.

106 Battery is out on operation at present – camped in a graveyard! I will probably be going out to pay them a 'morale-boosting' visit, with my cheery smiling face tomorrow in an APC (armoured personnel carrier) if my old friend the 2IC agrees. We had a casualty brought back from there this morning (with much drama) by helicopter. We were expecting some shot up victim, but behold – an unconcerned gunner walked sedately down from the chopper with a bit of cotton wool stuck on his chin. He was cleaning his machine gun and a spring flew out and cut his chin – admittedly it was quite a nasty cut and I had to stitch it up but it was nowhere near the big drama that our wireless report led us to believe (fortunately).

I did my Medcap again yesterday – I'm getting a bit better at it, but it sure makes for an exhausting afternoon. It's getting to be quite a popular trip though, with the soldiers. Yesterday, apart from Sergeant Allen and myself, we took my batman (as 'shot-gun' – i.e. an extra passenger who carries a weapon anytime you go outside the task force area in case you're ever attacked), two of the 'rough and toughies' from the Forward Detachment to help Sergeant Allen daub Castellani's paint and benzyl benzoate cream on kids with rashes, and one of our gunners who wanted to see 'what the people are like'. Every week I have more and more of the gunners asking if they can come too. The American Civil Aid team were there yesterday and took photos – so if you see me in *Time* magazine you'll know how I got there.

About those hygiene supplies – in addition to the list I've given you before, we never seem to have enough little bottles to put small amounts of mixture in for them to take away. Only very small ones are allowed as we never like to give too much stuff away in case the VC end up with it.

Much love,
David

---

[1] After seeing *Julius Caesar* I was hooked! No doubt it was the youthful Marlon Brando, his eyes 'red as fire with weeping' which first won me over to the movies. Family attitudes were changing, too, at a rather more sedate pace than my own, but Vietnam provided an opportunity for me to indulge my taste for the silver screen several nights a week. I felt relatively little guilt.

Nui Dat
Friday 9/6/67

Chao ong, Phil,
It's pronounced 'chow ong', meaning good day, good morning or goodbye when addressing a male of reasonable importance as befits an almost BA. If you're addressing a kid you say 'Chao em', and if it's a married woman you say 'Chao ba' – a confusing language, but your brilliant brother Dave is picking it up rapidly.

Well, your brother is a real 'warrie' now (pronounced 'WAR-EE' for those uninformed in army slang). Today I, in my usual good form as upholder of unit morale, took my life in my hands and joined the convoy out to 106 Battery's position to see how my medic 'Chuck' Berry was getting on. Chuck's battery is now camped in a graveyard about five miles north of here near a charming village called Binh Gia (pronounced bin jar). Already one of the gunners in digging himself a weapon pit removed a few old bones, but it doesn't seem to be upsetting the gunners at all. While I was there visiting today the locals staged a Buddhist funeral in one section of the graveyard – probably only a fake so they could get a good look at the gun position, or so they tell me. Anyway it was interesting to watch – the coffin with a little pagoda on top (very ornate) and all the mourners were jam packed on the back of a five-ton truck. On top of the pagoda was a swastika (apparently a Buddhist symbol) and as they all came along someone on the back was banging a dull sounding drum while someone else would give a sporadic bash on a tin can thing. All around the coffin were gay coloured flags. In the midst of all this performance the gun battery got the command over the 'net'[1] to fire and the boom of our guns added to the funeral ceremonies. Most of the mourners gave a little jump and then went calmly on as though nothing had happened, although the guns were only 100 yards or so away, so used are the people to the sights and sounds of war.

They all seem pretty healthy (the gunners that is), and Chuck was patching them up in his usual reliable manner. I could only stay about fifteen minutes this time as I came in a road convoy and it had to get back, but I 'showed the flag'. It was really quite fun in the convoy. I travelled in a Land Rover in the front seat (as befits my exalted position as RMO), however the seat didn't have any back to it except for two projecting prong type things which didn't add to the comfort of the trip. The two Land Rovers were preceded by APCs and followed by them too. APCs are sort of tank-like conveyances in miniature, so we were pretty safe – it would be a game VC who attacked an APC company. We all had our weapons, with magazines attached, which seemed pretty silly to my medical mind, but there you are – it's the army. As Padre Wellings says, the VC seem not to want to pick a fight in this province anymore, and apparently it's generally believed that the VC dislike tangling with Aussie diggers if they can avoid it.[2]

I hope you like my letter to *The Australian Baptist*, if it's ever printed, which I doubt. I should have left it to you with your magnificent turn of phrase and excellent grammar.

And now for 'people in the pics', in short:

Me: my old cheery usual dumb self, bringing joy and gladness to the hearts of the soldiers in the Nui Dat area – (enough said).

Sergeant Allen: very euphoric (a new medical term for your vocabulary) this week. I think being appointed HQ Battery Movie Projectionist has gone to his head. Still threatening to put up some 'heavy stuff' in the RAP and telling everyone what a joke the RMO is (quite kindly of course). He had cause to 'charge' Gunner Lenz (who is our mess waiter) for being asleep on guard duty one night last week, when Sergeant Allen was duty NCO.

Corporal 'Shorty' Dutton (the 101 Battery medic): going home on Sunday to Australia and being replaced by Private Williams who arrived today with most of 108 Battery which is replacing 101. He, the latter, is a bit of a 'know all' and earns the nickname 'ENOS' i.e. 'e knows everything'!

'Gunner' Chuck Berry: see above.

The 2IC: his usual pompous self.

The CO: settling in and wants to have a long talk to me in the next few days, probably about the problems of a certain disease in the unit, as that is all anyone who wants to have a long talk to an RMO up here, ever wants to talk about. I, of course, don't mention the disease in my letter for fear of bringing a blush to the cheek of 'the young person'.

I think that is all the news for the moment

The parcel you are all eagerly awaiting is not a Vietnamese lady, nor a Vietnamese 'poor boy'. Just learn a little patience. Don't forget Mum's grandma used to say (as Mum was wont repeatedly to tell us throughout our childhoods) 'patience is a virtue' or was it 'pride bears pain'? I forget.[3]

Yours in Baptist 'koinonia' (another word for your vocabulary – means 'fellowship'),

Dave

PS I had a letter on *scented* note paper tonight from that army sister at Singleton whose heart I appear to have broken. What do you think of that?

1   Not the internet, of course, but rather the radio network connecting the 106 Battery command post with the regimental HQ command post. The order to fire came from the battery command post to each gun via a tannoy system.

2   A popular myth, which the Tet Offensive soon discounted.

3   I never met my mother's grandmother, as she died fairly young. She was reported to be a 'lovely lady' who made the grave mistake of marrying a German who deserted her before the outbreak of World War I and returned to the Fatherland. She was my Grandmother Lloyd's mother and was noted for her wise sayings.

Nui Dat
Friday 9/6/67

Dear Mum and everyone else,

I hope you can sort out which is Mum's letter and which is Pip's, but I think it more economical to join them all in one envelope. It's probably too heavy,[1] but Bombardier Banks is one of my good friends – I've cured his knee and now I'm curing one of his rashes so he looks after my mail very well.

Looks like our RAP is going to be pretty busy soon with all these army 'big wigs' descending on us. There is a rumour around that Brigadier Gurner, the RAAMC – i.e. Medical Corps – chief, is up in SVN this weekend and could drop in on all or any of the RAPs anytime. He is to become major general next month. So I had better try to get my batman to acquire some more respectable jungle greens for me. Mine are still getting lost in the laundry all the time. I find it hard to believe that Aunty Jean's acquaintance[2] will drop in on me, a humble captain, though. Major generals just don't do that sort of thing.

It certainly seems a topsy-turvy world at the moment. Today out at Binh Gia we had to stop for about half an hour – typical army convoy – for some reason or other and all these little Vietnamese kids came up to talk to us; they all want cigarettes not just to sell to their elders but to smoke themselves. Of course they get lots of them from the soldiers but it is very sad to see little kids of eight or nine puffing away at cigarettes like hardened soldiers. What hope have the poor kids got? No medical care to speak of, only the merest smattering of an education or none at all, broken families – fathers fighting for the VC or the SVN Army – in short no hope in this world and, but for the grace of God, none in the next world either.

And our own troops – so much materially better off, but not much better spiritually. So many such likeable boys; such good material in lots of ways; I guess the best of our Australian youth, yet little if any moral standards. I feel very helpless sometimes to do anything useful. But I must stop sermonising.

The mystery parcel is box-shaped – quite small. That's all I'll tell you. I hope it gets there in one piece.

Very much love, Mother dear, and to one and all,

Chao ba and all that,

David

PS I refuse to give any more information about the mystery parcel till it arrives so 'Xin-Loi' – sorry about that.

---

[1] I.e. too heavy for the standard letter rate which was then five cents. I can't recall what the weight limit was for the standard letter rate. Bombardier Banks would have known!

[2] Aunty Jean (Love) was not a biological aunt. She was my mother's best friend and a sort of guru to the family. She had been crippled by poliomyelitis as a child and had a strong personality. Her sister, Ida Love, was one-time matron of Crown Street Women's Hospital. The family had 'good connections' and it wasn't surprising that Aunty Jean was acquainted with a major-general in the British army.

Nui Dat
Saturday 10/6/67

To my old sister 'Wosephine',[1]

It is Saturday night and I am sitting in my tent swatting creepy crawlies, and listening to the 'Voice of America' and the emergency meeting of the UN Security Council about the Middle East.[2] So if this letter seems a little disjointed you will understand why. I feel a bit 'down'. The Middle East doesn't sound good at all – a very uncertain world we live in. I just can't get off my mind how many there are who know so little of Christian things or the Christian way, even amongst my own gunners, let alone all the poor people in Hoa Long, South Vietnam generally, not to mention all the other troubled nations of the world.

I have had a quiet day today doing such vital things as patching up ingrown toenails and cutting out sebaceous cysts. It's really a miracle that my minor ops don't get horribly infected – if you could see our sterilizer – it's only a tiny metal thing that we have to heat up on a petrol burner which does little other than make clouds of yellow flames that cover the outside of the sterilizer with inches of soot. We have no access to sterile drapes at all, but still the ops seem to do OK – just your brother's terrific skill.

About those venetian blinds in the church – I have a suggestion – how about a good 'pull down' – i.e. right down for ever. Rather than a 'pull up' as Mum suggests!

I have had four letters from 'the little creatures' since I arrived here so they must be interested in the war effort.

Anyway I feel much brighter now so I will close, read a few lines of the latest Wodehouse book and shuffle off to bed feeling thoroughly cheered.

Love to you two lovebirds,

Davey

---

[1] 'Wosephine' was a shortened version of 'Wosephine Wozzery Gozzard', another of my father's famous nicknames. Where he dreamed it up is anyone's guess. A Google search does not assist!

[2] The Six-Day War between Egypt, Syria, Jordan and Israel, 5–10 June 1967.

Nui Dat
Saturday 10/6/67

Dear old thing,

I have just written to Merrie and feel cheered up, as I was a little down in the dumps tonight. I don't know why, but a letter from an old friend started me off I think. Anyway I am 'me old self' again now so will just write you one page before tottering off to my well-earned siesta.

How are you all at home anyway? Has Pip managed to get his mind off all those EU girls and settled down to some solid study, or is he gazing out the window dreaming of 'sweet nothings'? And how about Dad? Has he decided to run for Secretary of that bastion of the faith, Pennant Hills Baptist Church? I am dying to know. And are you keeping well, old warlike mother of mine? Reading John Buchan, that dreadful old imperialist again, I hear – you are certainly the cause of all the war-like tendencies in the family, I'm sure.

I hope your corns are behaving? I often have to pare down corns here – it's a common complaint, as are all foot conditions.

Anyway, I feel much better after writing to you both. I have forgotten the world and its problems and am off to bed.

All my love,
David

Nui Dat
Monday 12/6/67

Dear Dad,
I will start this letter tonight and finish tomorrow morning as it is late. I was persuaded to go to the movies tonight with some of the officers and was rather glad as it was a funny film[1] and we all had a good laugh. After the film we all sat around talking and one of the captains who works in 'Arty-Tac', i.e. the tactical headquarters of the whole artillery set-up in the task force area, later took me to show me over Arty-Tac. It was quite interesting seeing the nerve centre of the artillery section. In this same building TAC (Task Force Area Command) is situated and the running of the whole task force is done here and the brigadier lives there all the time.

I have just got back to my tent and decided to start this letter for you. I have been thinking about my situation up here a lot, with regard to being a doctor and a Christian and living in an essentially non-medical (as opposed to hospital medicine), non-Christian environment all the time. It needs a lot of wisdom, which I often feel I lack, and it is good to be able to share this with you. I read by chance today a bit of the Prayer Book which Pip gave me before I left Australia. The section for next Sunday (fourth after Trinity) and the Collect seemed very applicable – it talks about: *'that we may so pass through things temporal, that we finally lose not things eternal'*. The authors of those ancient prayers certainly understood practical Christian living and how to pray for grace and strength.

Tuesday morning:

You ask about the Civil Aid (CA) people – this is just another army unit, smaller than most, but just the same as say an artillery regiment or an infantry battalion. It's composed of soldiers posted to the unit, exactly the same as in any other posting, although there are a higher proportion of warrant officers and NCOs who have had a fair bit of experience, than privates. As from last weekend they have a lieutenant colonel for CO (as we have) and next week an army doctor from Australia is coming up as the full-time Civil Affairs doctor attached to the CA Unit. They also have a couple of seconded Vietnamese army soldiers who can speak English, as interpreters – these are the usual interpreters I use every week, although a couple of the CA Australian army soldiers themselves are quite good at Vietnamese. The interpreters haven't had any medical training – Sergeant Anh, the Vietnamese interpreter who helped diagnose my case of leprosy the other day, only picked it because he'd seen it before in the country. I hope you can follow a bit easier now – my letters must be difficult to understand as there is so much army jargon.

I met the 2IC of the CA Unit on Sunday and he's arranging for me to do another Medcap at a village called Binh Gia (pronounced Bin Jar) which is supposed to be one of the nicest villages in the area. It's a predominantly Catholic village and apparently the Christian influence has made a big difference. The place is reported to be nice and clean – it will be interesting to see. We are supposed to be going there this afternoon.

I received the second instalment of soap and insect repellent today, which I am sure will be much superior to the army issue, so thanks a lot, Dad.

Anyway I must close now if I'm ever to get this posted in time to 'catch the mail'.

Much love to all,
David

[1]   I think it was called *The Egg and I* – about twenty years old then, starring Claudette Colbert and Fred MacMurray.

Nui Dat
Tuesday 13/6/67

Dear old Mother-mine,

How are you? And how's the shop going, and the church?

I'm afraid I haven't got much in the way of news to tell you . . .

(Interrupted by a long-winded lieutenant, Bob Birse, who dropped in on his way to bed to talk for two hours).

So now it's Wednesday lunchtime and I'll finish the letter in time to catch the mail.

It's very hot today – hasn't rained for two days but the ground is still dampish and I guess it is only a brief spell of dry weather. You ask about getting washing dry – well it only rains for fairly short periods usually at about the same time every day (but very heavy while it lasts of course). In between times it can be sunny and hot and clothes will dry pretty well. I usually hang things I want to dry quickly in my tent and they don't take long. It's amazing how quickly the undergrowth grows up once the rain starts – what was just dry old dusty ground two weeks ago is now knee deep in greenery. It's quite an amazing place in many ways.

I'm off to Hoa Long this afternoon for my Medcap. It will be hot and smelly down there today I'll bet. I haven't done a Medcap anywhere else yet – the arrangement to go to Binh Gia fell through on Monday but I guess the CA people will be onto me to do it pretty soon.

106 Battery is back from its operation now and so sick parade was long this morning what with one thing and another. The brigadier (Gurner) is up on a visit and today is with Jack at the Forward Detachment. He could pop down here anytime I suppose so I'll have to be on my best behaviour.

Sorry this is such a rushed letter but I will write a better one soon.

Much love,

David

Nui Dat
Wednesday 14/6/67

Dear Mum,
A short letter tonight I'm afraid.

Porky got the long newsy one because you say she has been missing out a bit. Today has been long and busy – a long sick parade, and the Medcap at Hoa Long this afternoon, so I'm tired. Just listening to people's problems is enough to make you very tired (as you know from the shop, I guess). I had to drain an abscess on a teenage boy at Hoa Long too – quite satisfying to relieve his pain.

What did Gran mean about 'the horrible way we are born'? Tell her from me it's not like her to sound like Queen Victoria. I can just imagine, as Dad suggested in his last letter, that Gran Lloyd would enjoy sitting at Vung Tau watching all the people going by. I think she would enjoy the army too, knowing Gran.[1] I think Grandma Bradford would have liked the army but in a different way.[2] I think I must have inherited a lot from her – I am sure she would have appreciated the problems some of the poor boys face up here.

How is the shop boy, David,[3] going? I can understand how he worries Dad – my batman worries me. After he's done his work, cleaning my shoes, tidying my tent, making the bed, he comes over to the RAP and moons around. Then when you get him to do something like sweep it out, he does it OK but finishes very quickly and starts 'mooning' again. It's very disconcerting. Sergeant Allen is trying to get him employed about the place. He's as untidy and un-prepossessing as your David too.

More news tomorrow,
Much love and good night, Mum,
David

PS Going to Vung Tau tomorrow to 8 Field Ambulance to clear up a few things. The brigadier didn't turn up today, by the way.

[1]   Grandma Lloyd was a chair-bound invalid because of chronic rheumatoid arthritis. She loved watching people and would have enjoyed being a spectator of the Vung Tau scene. But she had a marked distaste for the more physical aspects of life. Her reference to 'the awful way in which

we are born' was entirely characteristic. I was teasing her in the message I asked my mother to pass on to her.

2   Grandma Bradford, on the other hand, loved life, boys and young men. She had little time for girls. She had six boys of her own and no daughters which may have been either the cause or the effect of her liking for the male sex. Hence the reference to her understanding of what soldiers went through. Indeed three of her sons served in World War II and one, my uncle Owen, suffered a chronic debilitating skin condition for the rest of his life after return to Australia from PNG. Although she died when I was only seven, I always felt a great kinship with her.

3   David, the shop boy, delivered prescription drugs which had been dispensed by my father during the day. He would arrive after school and do the deliveries on his bike to nursing homes and to housebound patients. He was good-hearted and enthusiastic but somewhat scatter-brained in those days. He worked faithfully for Dad for a number of years.

Nui Dat
Friday 16/6/67

Dear old thing,
Four letters tonight – great!

So Uncle Stace[1] has declared himself an Israeli/Middle East expert has he? That is not surprising. The officers here all cheered madly when they heard about Israel's victory in the Six-Day War. No one in the army has any respect for Arabs as soldiers, but Israeli soldiers are held in high esteem – apparently King David's influence lives on even today. I liked the little quote in the 'Granny's Column' of the *Sydney Morning Herald* you sent me 'And David slew Goliath!' – I showed it to the CO in the mess tonight and he enjoyed the joke too.

Yesterday Brigadier Gurner with an air vice marshall (RAAF-Medical) and Colonel Myer (the CO of 8 Field Ambulance) dropped in at the RAP for five minutes. He didn't enthuse about our ammunition box shelves and partitions and, looking on it with civilised eyes, I suppose it doesn't look too wonderful, but it serves the purpose. He told me my CO had told him earlier in the day that he was 'very satisfied' with his medical officer, so that was nice to know. He also cleared up a little problem or two I had about some army medical matters, so it was a helpful visit. I had a nice long chat today too with my CO. We get along well, so I feel very much part of the regiment and not an outsider, even to the extent of agreeing to donate a pewter mug to the mess for the exclusive use of the unit RMO – it will have the RMO's names engraved on it and their years of incumbency (if that's the right word) – and I will be the first. What a shame to waste a pewter mug on soft drink for a year, they all reckon. I'll have to buy it when I go on R&R. (Australia? Hong Kong? Who knows?) I certainly hope my R&R can be in Australia for Merrie's wedding's sake, but in another way I reckon it will be awfully hard to go home for five days and then come back for another six months – I'd hate to go through all those good-byes again. Still, for your sake and Merrie's, I hope I can get home, as I really would hate to miss the wedding of the century – venetian blinds and all.

. . . just interrupted by Chuck Berry with a patient with a pain in the chest. Probably just heartburn, as he ate two full platefuls of American ration cherries for dessert tonight, and if you could only taste our American ration cherries, you would understand why heartburn is the most likely diagnosis. I gave him an injection of pethidine to keep him quiet for the night and it'll probably be gone by the morning. He forgot his pain long enough to comment favourably on Merrie's photo on my desk – he mistook her for a girl he went to school with somewhere in Brisbane so I guess that's flattery for old Porky girl.

Merrie certainly hasn't changed has she? Sending off a money order AND the money in an envelope together! Did the post office girl ever get paid for the money order though? Will she ever get any better? The only answer is for 4th November to hurry up and come along so that she has a full-time guide dog, ambulance man, armed guard, watch dog, stretcher bearer all rolled into one Ian. He may not be able to pass accountancy exams but he'll need to be pretty versatile to look after my dear sister.

I smiled at your remembrances of Empire nights past. You forgot one long-lived family memory – Dad in knickerbockers at Chatswood Primary School reciting 'Empire Day is the day on which we remember Queen Victoria's birthday'.

Round up of Nui Dat news

CO: (see earlier)

2IC: mellowing a little and bending just a fraction (fortunately) – I think he has decided he must put up with a worthless RMO for a year.

Sergeant Allen: a bit subdued this week – stomach cramps (our food again).

Sergeant Ken Murphy: (a new addition to my rogue's gallery) Sergeant Allen's best friend; fat, jolly, the father of two bouncing baby boys whose photos he flourishes. He is the other partner for Sergeant Allen's TAB on Saturday afternoons and he haunts the RAP.

Chuck: (see earlier)

Private Williams (108 Battery medic): busy organising efficiently, like 'the efficient Baxter' in Wodehouse, an FFI 'free from infection' inspection for me tomorrow morning for his battery. I have to go around the whole battery with the battery commander looking at feet, crutches and axillae. How humiliating for all concerned, except Private Williams who will get ghoulish delight out of the exercise.

Jack Blomley: back on the job – prickly heat is as bad as ever though. The brigadier said I had to ensure he got no pricklier!

And that's all I have room for tonight, so I will close wishing you my best love,

Your faithful son,

David

---

[1] Uncle Stace was my mother's brother, the eldest in the family. He kept up with current affairs and was knowledgeable about many things, especially those of a scientific nature. He was not anti-religion but he did believe religious belief was irrational. It was inevitable that he and my mother sometimes clashed.

Nui Dat

Saturday 17/6/67

Dear Dad,

I think I will be a dermatologist of note after this tour – it's quite amazing the funny skin rashes I see. Prickly heat, which must be quite dreadful for the poor sufferer, is the worst affliction, and I'm stumped to know what to do for it. Calamine is no good; coal tar preparations, like Pragmatar, are hopeless in this climate, as are zinc pastes. Whitfield's ointment and alcohol, ruthless as it sounds, seems to do the best for it, but it's cruel treatment.

Today has had its moments – I had to rush through sick parade which fortunately was small for the regiment itself, but as usual a few Kiwis from the NZ battery came late and a few Cavalry Regiment boys straggled in after them, so I only just made it to 108 Battery in time to do my FFI ('free from infection') inspection – I was wringing wet with sweat by the time I'd popped in and out of all the tents looking at skin rashes, and I then got word that I had to join the big inspection party for the deputy commander of the task force.[1] He is a full colonel – the 2IC of the whole task force, second to the brigadier who's running the war here, so he's big stuff – talk about rough though! He has as much poise and dignity as a lumbering old ox and of course he put my back up immediately. He was inspecting our regiment accompanied by our own 2IC, our quartermaster, the task force hygiene officer, our battery commanders and little old me. He growled at me: "Ow often do you do a 'ygiene inspection of this regiment, doc?' I said brightly that I did it once a month, at which he assumed a look of incredulity and shouted 'Once a month? – You gotta do it once a week, doc, and keep these ——s on their toes'. After that he forgot me and we all trundled around with our 2IC and the battery commanders (BCs) fawning and cringing. Only once did we cross swords again, when he announced that it was silly to wear boots during the day in this climate when the men were just working around the battery task force positions and said 'just thongs' were better and I piped up in a meek voice 'what about hookworm, sir?' That stumped him! To cap it all he decided to inspect our RAP unexpectedly. Saturday is NOT a good day for Sergeant Allen to get the place tidied up as he is always sneaking off to listen to Radio Australia and all the races. He is so good during the week, I usually turn a blind eye to his Saturday activities – there are certain things so deeply ingrained in the army that I don't think you can do much about them and Saturday race day seems to be one of them. Anyway the RAP was in a mess, not bad, but certainly not looking its best, so the colonel gave a dull grunt and swept out again. So, not the most successful day for the regiment but it was quite fun and appealed to my somewhat kinked sense of humour. I must say army 'big wigs' don't overawe me at all and only make me more stubborn. I just put on that vague dumb look I am so famous for. I had to give Sergeant Allen and my batman a blast after it (mild, of course) for form's sake and they forgot the races long enough to tidy the place up a bit.

No more room, Dad. Has my parcel arrived yet? I hope it will soon. Much love,
David

¹ His name was Colonel White.

The Surgery
Nui Dat
Sunday 18/6/67

Dear Uncle Phil,
*Tharunka*¹ arrived, thank you – most disappointing, I found – no good reading material at all and most certainly nothing to bring a blush to the cheek of 'the young person'.

This morning at chapel we had an Anglican padre lately arrived at Nui Dat from Western Australia, but quite good. Charlie Wellings is at present on R&R in Hong Kong buying 'goodies'. Of course, if I had been a really good Baptist, I should have left when I found an Anglican conducting the service, as we can't mix the denominations, you know – 'East is east, and west is west and never the twain shall meet' as Rudyard Kipling so wisely remarked . . . Sorry, I do seem to be raving on tonight. This is because I really have no exciting news since last night and as Robbie Lloyd said in his last letter – 'I'll just have to stall you till the bottom of the page'.

Anyway, here is a Nui Dat news round-up for you:

My batman: He is more like David from Dad's shop every day. He *does* keep my shoes clean and picks up my greens from the laundry, so that helps. He also fulfils that other valuable function of finding out what films are on at what spots at night, so I can inform the officers ('to keep up their morale'). They reckon they're working me in as 'amenities officer' in my spare time.

Sergeant Allen: 'the white angel of Hoa Long', as the gunners call him now. This nickname makes him go 'right off', as he would say. He has very fair hair, you see, and the gunners are always teasing him about our Medcap trips and asking him whether we have many shots fired at us in Hoa Long, and is it very dangerous? His upset stomach is better anyway.

The 2IC: not bad this week

The CO: also has an upset stomach but is recovering under my superb treatment.

Gunner Lenz: our mess steward – still acting as though working in the Charlton Hilton – also is doing twenty-eight days without pay for being caught asleep on guard duty.

Gunner Dickinson: our headquarter battery artist (and the soldier next to me reading Emile Zola on the plane from Darwin to Vung Tau) has presented me with a big canvas painting of a face for the RAP – it's supposed to be Ernest Hemingway in his last hour – it's rather good but a little depressing for an RAP. We are at present deciding where to hang it. He (our artist) has an ear infection, also responding to the Bac-si's (Vietnamese for 'doctor') fabulous treatment. I would like mum to meet Gunner Dickinson – he is a very nice chap, not at all 'arty'. He comes from London.

Bombardier Banks: the AFPO4 postmaster general, is counting the days until he goes home. He works out that he should arrive back in Castle Hill on Christmas Eve, so he said he'd pop in to the pharmacy and hand deliver a card from me. He is quite a character – has a mild touch of prickly heat, again responding to high standard treatment.

Me: my usual charming gracious friendly, buddy-buddy self. Need I say more?

The RAP: We now have two beds (excellent for taking short naps on) but really for short term 'sickies' if necessary. Sergeant Murphy (Sergeant Allen's bosom pal) has almost completed a sign for us – 4 Field Regiment RAP – to hang outside so at last everyone will know what we are. At present we just have a printed notice 'ARRAYPEA' above the door which isn't Strine but Maori, meaning 'house of torture' which a Kiwi put up there before our arrival. It is a bit ambiguous if you're looking for the RAP, though.

Oh well – off to bed. Hooroo till next time,

Dave

---

[1]   University of NSW student newspaper.

Nui Dat
Tuesday 20/6/67

Dear Mum,

I'm afraid I missed writing to you last night but I was very tired after a trip to Vung Tau yesterday and was going to bed early and then got delayed with people dropping in to my tent before I went to bed and so I didn't get around to dropping you a line as I had intended – still, I'll make it a specially long one tonight.

Yesterday was quite a busy day – I decided only on Monday morning to go to 'Vungers' as the ambulance was going down with a patient for 8 Field Ambulance so I thought I might as well go too as there were a few things I wanted to find out about. They really are muddlers down there. This particular patient was being admitted for a routine circumcision, a very common operation up here due to the climate, and we had an appointment for him, but they decided they were too full and couldn't take him yesterday. It wouldn't have been so bad only they'd done the same thing to the same patient only the week before. Talk about a hopeless lot! They lose our pathology tests and muck up our appointments. I'm very glad I wasn't attached to that unit – I'm much happier being the gunners' RMO – at least medically speaking I'm my own boss here. Vung Tau was as messy and smelly as usual – the Vietnamese are really a hopeless-looking race of people – it just looks as though twenty years of war have been too much for them and that they don't care about anything anymore. There was a stabbing in one of the Vung Tau bars a couple of nights ago – an airman was killed. I don't know if he was Australian but VT (township) is now out of bounds for anyone from Nui Dat except on special business. The Field Ambulance and all the Australian Army units in VT are on the sandhills behind the town. VT is still an R&C centre though, where soldiers go for five days holiday once a year – that's separate from their R&R leave which is always outside the country. Usually the soldiers stay in the R&C centre building and lounge around there – it's only when they go to town that they get into trouble.

The Baptist came tonight, with my letter published in it, but with no comment. They cut part of it, though. I guess I shouldn't have sent it as it was a hopeless proposition – you can't change the old 'die-hards', but it does seem rather poor they can edit the letter without a by-your-leave. So if anyone objects to the letter you can tell them that the best part was left out.

I was so sorry to hear you have an upset stomach. I do hope you are better again now. My tummy has been a bit upset since the visit to Vung Tau (just the smells, I think), so perhaps yours is just in sympathy.

I thought of another thing the Christian Endeavourers might like to collect for the Hoa Long kids – tennis balls (old ones) would make them pretty happy, I think; if it's not too late, that is a new suggestion for them.

I am back on hygiene inspection for my second monthly report. It's a gruesome business. I find I spend most of my time talking to the gunners here and there in the various batteries instead of getting on with the job of poking my nose into latrines, while my hygiene sergeant gets impatient.

The rain has been slow in getting a go on – in fact it's predicted that this wet season is going to be the driest for many years. This is bad for the poor people with their rice harvest, but good for us in that we are better protected in the dry than the wet, with helicopters and aircraft.

Much love to you, old thing anyway,
David

Nui Dat
Wednesday 21/6/67

Dear Merrie-Moo,
I don't guarantee that I will finish this effusion tonight, but will make a good attempt, as I guess it is just about your turn for a letter. How are you and how is 'chicken-chest'? Give him my kind regards and tell him he will get a letter eventually, but I am getting miles behind on my correspondence and this week is (urk!) hygiene inspection week for me unfortunately. All my spare time is taken up with that.

Believe it or not, I have also been busy at the RAP the last few days. Both 108 and 106 batteries are going out on operation in the next day or so and sick parades have been big with a few who try and invent good medical reasons why they shouldn't go out in the scrub. Can't say I blame them, of course! With my 'too full of the milk of human kindness' approach I have given so many 'chits' for light duties for bad skin rashes and ear infections (which are extremely common) that the battery captains are starting to object. But for once I have last say. If I say someone isn't fit, that's that.

Then yesterday I had a boy from the Cavalry Regiment with a nasty cut on his upper lip. No, he wasn't thrown from his horse. He was knocked on the head by the hatch cover of his APC, which the cavalry ride instead of horses 'in this day and age, Nurse Bradford, follow? follow?', as Dr Dougie Piper from Royal North Shore Hospital[1] would say. The Cavalry Regiment are a lot of characters – one of their corporals (Corporal Green) keeps coming week after week with the old prickly heat, because he says I am his favourite doctor. He looks like Uncle Owen and has Uncle Boyd's[2] happy-go-lucky disposition, but sadly he still has prickly heat. I don't think there is a cure for the wretched disease except RTA (return to Australia), or as the gunners say 'a homer'. A 'homer' is a thing greatly to be sought after. The usual thing I am asked is: 'Is it good for a homer, sir?' Or 'What illness can I get that'll guarantee me a homer?' Already we have had to send one gunner back home because of bronchitis. He had five weeks in 8 Fd Amb without any improvement, so they were forced to send him back. Anyway, where was I?

Oh yes, the boy with the bad cut! I sutured it in my usual terrific surgical manner (with sterile technique, etc. – no drapes, gloves or masks) and then had to send him up the road to the Forward Detachment for a day's observation after his bad bump on the head. By the way, they have a small electric sterilizer at the Forward Detachment but as soon as they turn it on, all the power supply in Nui Dat fuses, so it isn't much good to them. So I've been busy with lots of suturing and plenty of blood and gore.

I did my Medcap again this afternoon with a few willing helpers eager and enthusiastic to get out of an afternoon's work by coming with me. Sergeant Allen was in a huff about something or other – the battery captain upset him somehow – and wouldn't come, so Chuck Berry came and did the Castellani's paint and benzyl benzoate (for scabies) dabbing while I did the clinic. One man walked about ten miles to see me, because he heard the Uc-Dai-Loi Bac-si was 'number 1' so my fame is spreading. There was another wretched newspaper reporter from the Melbourne *Sun* there this time, so you never know; I may be featuring down there soon.

I expect I had better get to bed or I'll be no good for looking into showers and down latrines tomorrow.

Love to my silly old sister, Porko,

Dave

PS Keep looking for my 'big' parcel for the family – it shouldn't be too long now.

PPS Has the Pork Publishing Company had any success with a book about snakes? Don't worry too much – it's not all that important.[3]

---

[1]   Professor Douglas Piper, professor of medicine at Royal North Shore Hospital, was a superb clinical teacher much loved by generations of medical and nursing students. He taught both me and my sister. He had a mild speech impediment which he had overcome by stuttering in whole phrases and sentences rather than in single words, and had many phrases like 'Follow? Follow?' and 'In this day and age', which he repeated many times in the course of a lecture.

[2]   Uncle Boyd and Uncle Owen were two of my father's five brothers. Uncle Boyd has a happy, cheery personality and at the time of writing is a semi-retired Baptist minister in Newcastle. Uncle Owen died quite young, after chronic ill health after World War II. He was the most handsome of the Bradford brothers, with blond, tight curly hair. Corporal Green could have been his twin.

[3]   Snakes were very common in SVN and soldiers were always coming across them. They expected the RMO to be an expert on snakes so I enlisted my sister's aid in hunting for a book about snakes with tips on identifying them. Being colour blind didn't help the situation!

Nui Dat
Wednesday 21/6/67

Dear Mum,

Just a line or two – hope you are better now and over your upset tummy. No letters tonight. Wednesday night is always a bad night for letters because of the weekend back home when the letters are posted, but Thursday is usually pretty good in contrast.

I haven't any exciting news to tell you as things are pretty quiet. 106 and 108 batteries are off again on operation. 108 Battery is going to a place called 'the Horseshoe' about 6 miles [almost 10 kilometres] from here, which is a pretty strongly defended place like Nui Dat only smaller. There are six big guns there all the time, which the gunners from 108 will man. The Kiwis have been there the last six weeks, but they're back in base now. I will probably get a trip in a helicopter out to the Horseshoe soon to check how they are getting on as they will only have their medic, Private Williams, to look after them and they'll be out six weeks or so.

106 Battery and Chuck Berry will go off in another direction (not to the graveyard this time), so things will be quieter here at the base. The big American guns will still be just down the road to wake us up at night with their big bangs, although I must confess I sleep through them OK now.

My practice is much the same, although we are beginning to get a bit of 'home sickness' I've noticed – sick parades are tending to get bigger. But, on the whole the gunners are pretty good and I haven't had many 'lead swingers'. Sergeant Allen tells me it is only 312 days to go, in any case.

No more paper, Mother dear,
All my best love,
David

Nui Dat
Thursday 22/6/67

Dear Mother mine,
I am sitting in my tent doing what I do almost every night after tea, or after I go to one of the exciting movies around the place – writing you a letter.

From where I sit I can hear the Maoris singing in the Kiwi gunners' mess which is only about 200 yards [180 metres] from my tent. A few Kiwis are going home to NZ tomorrow, so there are great celebrations. The Kiwi gunners have a pretty high proportion of Maoris and they are the biggest, toughest-looking characters you have ever seen. But they can certainly sing! Apparently they all sing around the bar – old Maori folk tunes mostly and they harmonise very well – it's far from being like the drunken songs Aussies sing, if they ever do sing. I was invited across to the Kiwi sergeants' mess tonight with Sergeant Allen and Sergeant Wittmer for a barbecue tea to farewell the Kiwi medical sergeant whom I've been working with since I arrived up here. He leaves tomorrow for NZ too. It was a terrific meal – steak and chicken barbecued really well – goodness knows where they got their meat from – it certainly wasn't our normal rations. It was the best meal I've had over here. It was rather funny really. Quite a few of the 4 Fd Regt sergeants were there and, as usual before the meal, they were all drinking beer and Sergeant Allen and myself were the only ones drinking softies. Apparently Sergeant Allen hardly ever drinks – when he does it's only gin and orange. But the Kiwis talked him into having one and from then on he had one after the other and he certainly was getting very merry. Gin and orange must be very potent! He is one of those people who get really funny when they are drunk and you couldn't help laughing at his antics. The other sergeants told me they had only ever seen him drunk once before. I just hope he isn't going to make a habit of it now – it would be bad having a medical sergeant who got drunk every night. I am sure I don't need to worry though, as he is very reliable. It just seems to be a common army (fallacious) belief that it does you good to get drunk once in a while – it's supposed to keep you sane. You will be glad to know your son doesn't intend to carry out this particular form of therapy himself – I will just stick to softies and get bloated. Drink is certainly one of the army's big temptations and once again it's hard to see how the average boy escapes – there is little to do at night except watch movies, write letters home or just get drunk, unless you are the reading type, which is a bit unusual here.

It was most embarrassing when Sergeant Allen in one of his lucid moments tonight exclaimed at the top of his voice to the assembled company that 'the MO was a real "gennelman" and the best doc the regiment has ever had'. I packed up and said my farewells pretty soon after that.

Today, as a break from the hygiene inspections, I went out to the big helicopter pad and watched 106 Battery take off for its operation, at 'Eagle Farm'. I took some photos of the gunners setting off to war and of my favourite medic Chuck laden down with his webbing and medical kit – he looked like some sort of pack animal. The great Chinook helicopters were used to move the battery out of its usual site – Land Rovers, guns and all. They are incredible – great huge things with two big rotors. They can hover just above the ground so they can sling the howitzer guns underneath them and then they take off complete with the gun hanging below. I took some slides to show you. Pip and Ian would be interested, even if the ladies aren't. The dust and sticks and stones which the choppers throw up is terrific – you nearly get blown away by the blast. I needed a shower after watching them and had mud, dust and little stones all through my hair and down my back.

Thank you for your little bits about the garden back home. As I look out of my tent at the brittle old rubber trees in their straight rows with their funny big leaves, and the red-brown muddy earth, and the greeny-blue mountains in the distance and the old brown tents scattered here and there through the trees, I often think of the view from our back window and the nice back garden – it would be good to see just one gum tree in the landscape here. It is a popular joke in the RAP that you have really gone around the bend if you say you 'heard the kookaburras in the morning'. Gunners come in and say: 'I heard the kookaburras this morning, sir. Don't you think I deserve a "homer" for that?'

Thank you too for your little sermons. They always do me good. I really am quite happy here and at peace in a strange sort of way. I like the gunners and the way they will talk to me about this and that. I am quite happy in the officers' mess, although they are starting to tease me unmercifully – they think I am a definite crackpot. It is nice to feel that you are needed even when no one takes much notice of you when everything's running OK. I get sad sometimes when I think of so many bright young lives already being spoilt by drink and sin and all that goes with the war. But I am sure the Lord understands them just as He understands all of us, and maybe there are more awful sins like selfishness, hypocrisy and greed, which soldiers on the whole don't suffer much from. After all, 'love covers a multitude of sins', and there is a strange kinship between soldiers. I am sure almost every soldier would willingly die to save one of his mates.

Anyway, as you say, it is being faithful to the work you've been given to do that counts. And, it's of those 'to whom much has been given', that 'much shall be required'.

Keep praying.

Very much love,

Davey

Nui Dat
Saturday 24/6/67

Dear Mum,

A short summarised letter as it's late:

1. I flew by helicopter to the Horseshoe where 108 Battery are, today. Boy! Was it terrific! I love flying in those helicopters – you skim along just above the trees all the way – I am a thoroughly converted air traveller now. I stayed out there all day, looking at latrines and things, toes and tinea, and fixing up all Private Williams' little problems, then back by road convoy through lots of smelly little Vietnamese villages with the kids calling out to us things like: 'hello', 'cigarettes', and 'Uc-dai-loi number 1'.

2. The first edition of *The Baptist* subsequent to my letter arrived today but there was no further comment. I have also received the snake medical book[1] and another letter from Robbie Lloyd in today's post. Thanks a lot, especially for the snake book which will be very helpful – I am always being asked to identify dead snakes and of course I haven't a clue.

3. All my love to my best mother – dear old 'mumma-san', as they call them in SE Asia. And love to all the crazy Bradford family. Please, Mum, no more walking three miles in the rain for that old pharmacy.[2] Actually you are probably all the better for it, like me after a battle efficiency course. But enough's enough!

Must really go to bed.

Nite, nite.

Dave

[1]   Merrie sent me a book called, I think, *Snakes of South East Australia*. It had a good section on the first aid treatment of snake bite, but it was useless for identifying snakes of South East *Asia*.

2   The pharmacy had secured the business of a nursing home in Castle Hill. Every day, prescription drugs for the nursing home's patients would have to be delivered. David, the shop boy, usually did this on his bike after school. It fell to my mother's lot to deliver urgent prescriptions during the day. As she didn't drive, this task required her to walk.

Nui Dat
Sunday 25/6/67

Dear all the family,

Well how do you like the tape recorder? I was nearly bursting to tell you what it was, but I'm pretty good at keeping a secret. The tape I sent was pretty horrible though.[1] The next one, which I am working on now, will be a bit better – I am getting the knack, I think. They are not the most wonderful tape recorders. Wilbur[2] would think the sound reproduction inadequate, but they are quite good enough for the purpose. I'm including a bit of 'the Vietnamese scene' for you in the next tape. Tapes travel pretty cheaply by air mail I'm told.

I went to chapel this morning. Not many there – our sig sergeant (signallers deal with radios and things) is a good Presbyterian and always attends and one of the batteries (108) has another 'Pressy' lance-bombardier who is a YMCA youth worker in civilian life. He has been detached to the Civil Aid Unit by our CO and is to be posted up to Duc Thanh (a Catholic village) about 10 miles away, where he will live and work assisting a warrant officer who's there already. He's a very nice chap and mad keen on helping the Vietnamese help themselves.

My round-up of Vietnamese news:

Me: I have had sore eyes, but now they're better. I feel very well. My usual charming self.

Bob Allen: recovered from his lapse into intemperance. I have threatened him with a special consignment of non-alcoholic 'wines', only to have him exclaim – 'you kill me, sir!' with much mirth. On the night he drank all that gin and orange one of the gunners came up to him later and said he felt sick. Bob had to struggle out to the RAP and take his temperature and said he had trouble focusing on the mercury in the thermometer but otherwise functioned all right. Fortunately he's his old sober self now.

Private Williams out at the Horseshoe: He is very keen at suturing up all and sundry. I have compromised with him a little and told him he can put in no more than two sutures per person and not use any local anaesthetic. If they need more than two sutures he has to evacuate them to me. That should stop any over-enthusiastic treatment I hope. It is awkward though. There are more than eighty blokes in the battery out on operation and he is their only medical help and gunners are always cutting their fingers on their wretched guns. You obviously can't call for a helicopter for every little cut hand. He isn't a bad bloke, Private Williams, just young, over-enthusiastic and a little inexperienced (which isn't his fault).

Chuck Berry: also out on operation and presumably going OK. I may be going out to visit his battery in the next day or so.

Sergeant Murphy: (Sergeant Allen's buddy) has at last finished painting our RAP sign in blue, red and white (the artillery colours) and has gone to Vung Tau to rest from his labours on five days R&C at the R&C centre. I hope he behaves himself down there. Now that R&C leave has started my problems will commence with the old soldier's disease. We have been pretty well free of it so far.

Gunner Lenz: (our mess waiter) – with the other waiter and the two mess stewards tonight caught a snake (about four and a half feet long) [1.4 metres] outside the officers' mess. They had chased it right through the mess and outside, where it dived into the underground shelter (for use by officers in the event of a mortar attack). Nothing daunted, they grabbed an F1 machine carbine and followed it down, blasting away with the gun as they went – the poor snake didn't stand a chance and was brought out triumphantly, riddled with holes. I couldn't find any fangs on it after all that, so it was probably harmless anyway. Still it was much excitement for a time. Gunner Lenz is very prone to excitement. He arrived so late at Brisbane airport coming up here that he almost missed the plane and had to do a week's extra duties for that. I think he was born to trouble, but he's a great character.

My batman: Stolidly goes about his arduous daily duties. He's a fairly uncommunicative guy. Sergeant Allen gives him the rounds of the kitchen and makes him work hard in the RAP, keeping it vaguely clean and tidy.

Gunner Dickinson (the artist): is working on a mural for the sergeants' mess. He had planned a 'religious one' but some of the sergeants objected, so he compromised and did an Aboriginal (Brownie Downing[3] type) scene. It's not bad at all. He also has bad ears at present because he, like lots of others, thinks you have to wash your ears out with soap and water. That's the worst thing you can do up here, but everyone is very surprised when I tell them so. I had to put out special 'Routine Orders' about care of ears in the tropics. At least, I wrote them and the poor long-suffering adjutant had to put them into military jargon for me.

Captain Jones (battery commander of headquarter battery): he is theoretically in charge of me and my doings. He is quite a character with a dry sense of humour and likes to tease the doctor in the mess. He is a very likeable chap and is a wizard at imitating people. He is particularly fine at taking off the 2IC (when he's not there, of course), who remains as pompous and stand-offish as ever. I used to think it was only towards me, but now I find he's like this with everybody, so I don't worry anymore.

Much love to all of you back home,
Dopey Dave

[1] My first tape home would have been similar to my letters – accounts of my days and the people I encountered. They would have heard the background noise of the guns from time to time. Later I got more inventive and taped music from the mess and got other people like Bob Allen to say hello.

[2] Wilbur is Dr Wilbur Hughes, my best friend at medical school, now a haematologist. Wilbur is an organist of note, a composer, and was always greatly interested in electronics and sound reproduction. He would have been highly critical of a tinny little tape recorder like this one.

[3] Brownie Downing, an Australian artist (1924–1995), specialised in painting and pottery depicting 'piccaninnies'. The work tended to be rather on the cute side, but they were extremely popular in the sixties.

Nui Dat
Monday 26/6/67

Dear Porky,

Just a short note to my favourite sister (that's because she's the only one I've got).

I've had an exciting day today. I did my usual sick parade (nothing much of interest) and removed an ingrown toenail under a fabulous local anaesthetic – he said he felt everything but I think he's a bit of a bludger! My anaesthetics are never that bad and, as it was, the toe was so swollen with lignocaine, I couldn't have got any more in if I'd tried.

Then this afternoon I flew out to the famous 106 Battery who are on an operation north of the TFA (task force area) by helicopter for one of my 'sweetness and light' visits. I love helicopters – they're terrific – I think you would like them too, but Pip might be a bit upset – you can just see the whole landscape spread out like a patchwork quilt – it's like being up a high building. It's pretty exciting getting on too, as they don't stop for long – down they come into a clearing – don't turn their engines off and the great big rotors are still churning around – you have to take your cap off or it goes for six (and can actually damage the rotors if they suck it up towards them). Then you run forward from the side and dive in! If you approach from the back you might get your head cut off, they tell me. Then up they go straight away. It's quite impossible to talk to the pilot because of the din, so you just hope you're on the right helicopter and that they'll drop you at the right spot. The gun battery were camped in a little clearing in the jungle that looked terrific from the air, but when you got down, you stepped into thick greasy mud up to your ankles – it is in fact a swamp that most of the poor blokes are living in for a week. But they are a good lot – no grizzles or grumbles – it's Chuck Berry's battery (or should I say, he is their medic) and though I can't say they're all like him (far from it – their language is really something) they all seem to have caught his bright happy spirit. I sploshed around from gun to gun. There are six guns to a battery with about seven gunners on each gun – they live and work around that gun all the time; clean it and oil it when it's not in use and have to be ready at any time to fire it when the order comes over the radio. I talked to all the gunners, looked at rotting toes and skin rashes and sore ears. On the whole they're all pretty healthy though. Chuck is terrific – a real country type – slow and steady and not a terrific education, but he's one of those natural doctors – treats them all the same as though they're all his brothers, and is never shocked or disgusted by anything they do. His motto is, he told me, 'everyone is your friend, until you make him an enemy'. He is a really fine advertisement of what a Christian ought to be, no sermons, no false piety, always cheerful, utterly respectful to his seniors . . . he does me good and not only me either.[1]

Anyway, I was telling you about the gun battery. You really do have to admire them – there they are stuck out in a bog with their guns – with one company of infantry around them to protect them from the VC, and in constant danger at night of mortar attack. There are no showers or any conveniences. Yet they seem quite cheerful and happy. I would like you to meet them all – their comments on the army and life in general are classic. The Australian at his best! So you see, I enjoyed my trip out and back.

How is the hospital nursery? The guns would be bliss compared to *that* noise I would think.

Must close, dear sis,

Much love,

Davey-baby

[1] I have enormous respect and a great regard for Chuck Berry. However it was difficult to have a normal friendship with him due to our age difference and more especially our difference in rank. After I left the army and throughout my time in England, we kept up a regular correspondence and he met up with my family on a couple of occasions when he was passing through Sydney. In the past ten years I have seen Alex once and been in touch by phone and letter.

Nui Dat
Wednesday 28/6/67

Dear old Mum,

I am now finishing off another tape to you which I'll post in a few days when I can think of enough things to say. I'm still as shy talking into it as you people all seem to be.[1]

Nothing very much to report in the last few days. Sick parades are the same. I had my usual Wednesday afternoon trip to Hoa Long this arvo – I am definitely getting quite famous. The army public relations team were there today and took a movie of me and of the dentist (pulling his usual 50 to 100 teeth). Every week I have to give details of my name and where I'm from – goodness knows what for. Today I saw another possible leprosy and some pretty awful deformities, so at least I am seeing some unusual diseases if nothing else up here. Tell Merrie, I saw what I think was a Hirschsprung's Disease in a baby one month old (if she remembers what that is from her paediatrics). I am keeping the Australian Surgical Team busy – there is some talk of them coming up here for lunch one Sunday if permission can be obtained, so that will be a bit of a 'turn up for the books'. Females are a rarity at Nui Dat.

The guns are really blasting away tonight. It is a special fire mission cooked up by the good old 2IC much to the amusement of everyone else. Everyone else seems to think it is a waste of good ammunition! Even the loyal adjutant was heard to murmur that the 2IC must be suffering from megalomania. I think it is just another example of the 'small man syndrome'.

There is a funny story told of the 2IC's visit to 106 Battery out on operation. He demanded to see their local defences and was shown a weapon pit which some poor gunner had been digging all day. All 5 ft 8 in [173 centimetres] of him jumped down into the hole and declared it was 'no b—— good' as you couldn't see over the top. The gunner who had dug the pit asked innocently if he'd like a box to stand on. The point wasn't taken too well by the good major but everyone else in the regiment has been enjoying the joke for the last few days.

Dad's letter arrived tonight and I chased around madly trying to follow his numbering system. I gave up in the end and read each page as it came and got most of the gist of the letter. Merrie's two books[2] also arrived, thank her very much. The book on Australian snakes is a start anyway, but if you can get anything on SE Asian ones I'd be very grateful.

Must really go to bed now mother dear so I will say good night and God bless you all back home. Only 303 days to go now, Sergeant Allen tells me.

Much love from your son,
David

1.   I had received a tape from home, which wasn't very good – everyone was tongue-tied and it proved less informative than letters. It was good to hear their voices although it did make me homesick.
2.   Merrie usually sent me paperbacks which were lightweight and reasonably cheap – detective and spy novels, P. G. Wodehouse, second-hand John Buchan books, etc. I would get three or four per month, usually.

Nui Dat
Thurs 29/6/67

My dear old Mum,

Just a very tiny note to say goodnight before I drop into my bed under the mozzie net and tuck myself up well so the mozzies can't get in. Just to let you know Psalm 91 is still working and I'm still thinking of you all back home.

Thank you for all your letters and thank Porky for the books (very much), but tell her to space them out a bit more or she'll go broke. Or Ian will, which is more to the point.

I would value some more Gamophen some time soon though.

Thanks for sending on the medical journals too – they arrive at odd times brought in special delivery by our happy postie 'Banksy' – at least he is better than your postie from all accounts.[1]

No more time – must go to bed.

Much love,

David

1.   Our house in Castle Hill Road was about midway between West Pennant Hills township and Castle Hill. The postal service in the sixties was poor in this more rural area of Sydney. There is a story that one day the postman had 'had enough' and dumped all his remaining mail in a large private mail box at about 55 Castle Hill Road! However this might have been a myth. Deliveries were uncertain and spasmodic nevertheless.

Nui Dat
Thursday 29/6/67

Dear Dad,

Thank you for your last letter which came last night.

The guns have been very noisy and will be more so in a few hours, but at the moment it's peaceful. They are particularly worried about 106 Battery, which I think I've told you is out on operation north of the task force area – apparently Intelligence reports say the VC are going to have a go at them tonight or tomorrow night,[1] probably with mortars, so every couple of hours we're dropping shells all around the camp from our big guns back here. It sure is noisy! But I would hate to see anything happen to our battery so if it deters the VC from attacking, then that's good. Apparently it's quite an ordeal so they tell me, having shells bursting only a couple of hundred yards all around their perimeter (even if it is our own shells). They are all due back in camp in two days time, so the operation is nearly over. So far they've only had one injury – one of the gunners chopped a couple of finger tips off in the breech of his gun; he was taken straight to Vung Tau, so I didn't see him. He'll be evacuated to Australia probably.

I have been busy with my end of the month hygiene report and end of the month report on sick parade attendances. We have had quite a small record this month for sick parades, mostly because there has been practically no VD. The new arrivals in Vietnam haven't had a chance to get it yet, but I'm afraid things will get a lot worse in the next few months as more and more go on R&R leave. It is a terrible place for ear infections too – and they are awfully tedious to treat.

The Field Ambulance in Vung Tau is proving to be a bit of a problem. The treatment they've been giving some of our patients is pretty bad on the whole. I had one very nice chap – an artillery captain but detached to another unit – come in one Sunday with what I thought blind Freddy would pick as a broken elbow – fractured head of radius to be exact, which can be quite a dicey fracture. Anyway, I sent him down to the 'muddlers' at Vung Tau for an X-ray. They only have a very small machine there and they told him, after taking numerous pictures, he didn't have a fracture, and sent him back with a sling. The poor chap was in agony for the next four days until in the end he went back to them. They at last decided to send him to 36 Evacuation Hospital (US) for further X-rays and sure enough he had a fractured head of radius. When he went back to 8 Field Ambulance though, they wouldn't believe the report and sent him off just in a sling again. After another week of discomfort he went back today and demanded another X-ray and this time 36 Evac sent the films back to the Field Ambulance with him and they at last decided to put a plaster on it. You can imagine what sort of a reputation that sort of thing gets the hospital among the officers up here – everyone you talk to begs you to send them to the US hospital, 36 Evac, if they're seriously ill or injured and I'm sure I will in future even if I get hauled over the coals for it.

I am very popular in the regiment for arranging with the Civil Affairs people to bring the Australian Surgical Team to lunch in the officers' mess here next Sunday. The other officers are all agog at the thought of four females in the mess, and females with 'round eyes' at that, as opposed to the Vietnamese 'slit eye' variety.

I think I will have gained a customer for you by Christmas time. Bombardier Banks (our postie) is going home in mid-November now and I am sure will patronise your shop. He is quite a talker, I warn you, and apparently an old Castle Hill identity – he's married to the daughter of one of those poultry farmer magnates so he may be a pretty good customer if he can drag his in-laws along too. He is a really nice chap and spends nearly all his spare time dropping in to the RAP and yarning on and on about Castle Hill and its residents.

Love to you and all the family from,
Davo

[1] Army Intelligence reports were based on Viet Cong forces' movements worked out from contacts our patrols had with them, results of air surveys from helicopter sightings, and interrogations of captured prisoners of war. Often they were false alarms; sometimes they were accurate (as in the weeks prior to Tet).

Reflections

Human beings are amazingly resilient and can adapt to the most extra-ordinary situations. Once familiar with life in Nui Dat, I settled down to its routine fairly easily. Dr Morrie Peacock, one of the gung-ho young doctors at 8 Field Ambulance with whom I had trained at Healesville, used to quote the line 'every young man needs a war' as if it held some sacred truth rather than being one of mankind's oldest lies. Yet it seems even I was not immune from the excitement of doing 'house calls' via military helicopter and riding in a road convoy heavily protected by armoured personnel carriers. There was always a risk of a helicopter being shot down or a road convoy being blown up by a hidden mine but I don't remember such facts causing me much concern in those early days prior to the Tet Offensive.

Life for all Australian soldiers in South Vietnam was uncertain. It didn't do to have too vivid an imagination. The task force could be attacked any time and, over the years it was based at Nui Dat, the perimeter was probed several times and the base was mortared on several occasions. Our artillery fire support bases out in the field were always potential targets and although no concerted attack on a fire support base happened during my time in SVN, FSB Coral, consisting of two of 12 Field Regiment's gun batteries (including the Kiwis' 161 NZ Field Battery) was attacked by a battalion-strength force of the North Vietnamese Army and risked being overrun early in the morning of 13 May 1968, less than a week after I returned to Australia. For all our active denial – and I think most soldiers, including me, were heavily into denial most of the time – we were engaged in a nasty war. There was no way of knowing whether the local Vietnamese were friend or foe; when you drove through a village there was no guarantee a small company of VC might not be lurking ready to take a shot at you or your vehicle; driving down any road there was always a chance your vehicle might run over a land mine – some-times these things did happen. When we did Medcaps in a village there was really little to stop the enemy attacking us – we were sitting ducks. The fact that they did not attack us and to my knowledge never attacked an Australian Medcap team probably meant it suited the VC for us to look after the medical needs of the villagers even in such a superficial way – there was always the bonus that they could divert useful medication like penicillin, which we might supply to a sick villager, for their own military needs. In all probability we looked after Viet Cong medical needs as well. We did not know who we were treating in all cases. Of course, the infantry men in the battalions (7 RAR and 2 RAR), together with forward observers from our three gun batteries, did not have the luxury of denial because they were regularly out on patrol in the bush or jungle and often came across a platoon or company of VC, whereupon a fire fight might ensue with a high chance of one or two soldiers being wounded or killed.

For most of us, the twelve month tour of duty in SVN was a stressful time.

One of the more irritating aspects of the letters, at least for me now, is my youthful tendency to moralise. I am critical of the padre's sermons because I think his theology is not up to scratch; I bewail the sinfulness of the Australian soldiers and their lack of knowledge of the Christian faith; and I engage in discussions with my father over biblical texts and stories (e.g. Daniel in the lion's den). The letters are liberally sprinkled with impromptu sermons about the questionable morals of the Australian Army and the dirtiness and laziness of the local Vietnamese. Many of these observations were for the benefit of family at home and were not a true reflection of my feelings even then. I must confess too there was considerable hypocrisy in my attitudes, particularly in my stand against Bob Allen adorning the RAP with female nudes. Female nudes did nothing for me, but it was hardly fair of me to ban them when they would probably have cheered up most of my patients. If he had wanted to put up pictures of VFL footballers baring their manly chests I might not have objected. It is worth noting that over the course of the letters, although my moralising continues, the tone of it changes considerably and becomes less hard-line.

My serious discussion with the brigadier of the Medical Corps was about VD (now called STI) and about not notifying to COs the names of soldiers and officers who had contracted such infections. It was encouraging to find that official policy specifically prohibited RMOs from divulging such information to senior officers and COs, despite the fact that COs thought they had a right to such confidential information. My own CO, Reg Gardner, thought I should tell him if any officer developed an infection. As I had already treated two or three junior officers for VD, I was particularly pleased that the brigadier upheld confidentiality so positively. My CO readily accepted the brigadier's ruling; other officers were not so willing to do so, as will be revealed in a later letter.

I can't remember if I ever donated a pewter mug to the 4 Field Regiment's officers' mess for use by all future RMOs as I promised the CO I would – I hope I did so, even though I was not a beer drinker in those days.

The doctors 'at the sharp end' in Nui Dat had concerns about some aspects of the administration and medical management at the Field Ambulance at Vung Tau. There are references to these differences scattered throughout the letters. I hasten to say that the Nui Dat doctors never had problems with the management of major life-endangering injuries at the Field Ambulance. Despite the comments on this subject in the letters, most of our grizzles and grumbles were about minor matters and were a reflection of the usual tension between 'hospital' medicine and 'coal face' general practice which frequently emerges even in everyday civilian practice.

It is probably apparent that my practice was very much a general practice rather than an emergency medicine practice. Much of the work I did was very mundane – treating ear infections and skin rashes, dealing with sexually transmitted infections, and doing minor operations, particularly for foot conditions like ingrown toenails, plantar warts, corns etc. But as well there were a great many psychological problems, some of which presented acutely – a few of these are documented in future letters. I suppose if I had sat down and thought about it, I could have predicted that the sort of stresses the soldiers were living under for a year might have long-term repercussions for their mental health. There was little reason I would have done so, though – I had not worked in psychiatry since graduation; I cannot recall any lectures on army psychiatry at Healesville; and the concept of post traumatic stress disorder (PSTD) had not been recognised at that time. I don't think I was altogether useless in this area of medicine though, as the teaching of psychological medicine at medical school during my time there had been exceptionally good under Professor David Maddison and we had a solid grounding in the subject. I had a natural interest in my gunner patients; during consultations I let them talk, if they wanted to, about their day to day worries and concerns (thus earning myself occasional reprimands from the 2IC for letting sick parades 'go on too long') and I let them know I didn't believe it unmanly or un-soldierly to acknowledge apprehension and fear, but that this was an entirely normal reaction. With hindsight, I was meeting my needs as much as theirs.

The fact was I was settling into my job. I was enjoying what I was doing and was probably becoming a more effective army doctor. And slowly I was becoming aware and testing the limits of the independence I now had as a free agent beyond the reach of church and family.

3

JULY 1967

```
Letters
```

Dearest old sausage (Mum),
My letter writing seems to be getting less reliable I'm afraid – I never seem to get enough time what with looking after 'sickies' and upholding unit morale.

Look at today:

Sick parade and then a visit to the Cavalry Regiment to see a bloke with burnt feet. My favourite Cav Regt patient, Corporal Green, a jolly fair-haired rascal who is always coming over to the RAP with minor ills, real and imaginary, caught sight of me and showed me over one of the APCs. That took about an hour, and then I met the Cav Regt officers at morning tea. After that I had to rush away and do a dreadful FFI (free from infection) inspection at 108 Battery – their battery commander is a real old tyrant who believes no soldier ever reports sick unless found out, so he insists on a compulsory parade once a week where you check them for tinea etc. It's a lot of rot but an RMO does what he's told. After that painful ordeal, I had to see the adjutant to hear about a possible new operation[1] coming up when headquarter battery will move as well, so I'll be moving too. He just wanted to warn me to get supplies ready – this operation may not come off but you have to be prepared just in case. Don't worry, by the way – it's no more danger-ous than Nui Dat if we do have to go out on operation.

. . . Interrupted by a sick Kiwi at 10.30 pm.

Oh – big excitement yesterday – my batman was scrabbling around in a tin we keep our International Health Certificates filed in, looking for someone's certificate when suddenly he jumped about six feet and yelled 'There's a f—— snake in it!' It's only a small tin on top of a shelf in our nice clean sterile RAP. Sure enough, curled up in the bottom was the nastiest looking little snake you ever saw. A sergeant in the RAP at the time obligingly killed it for me (you know how brave I am with snakes and spiders). We identified it as an 18 inch [45 centimetre] long, black with yellow bands, krait (a yellow-banded krait) – one of the deadliest snakes in SE Asia. I took a couple of colour shots of it for your delight. It now resides in a bottle full of metho on the shelf with all our drugs (in true Asian fashion) for all the regiment to see.

I sure look carefully in my bed now before getting in each night.

Lots of love,

David

PS (for Pip) – 'the little man will now walk three times around the tent and retire behind the . . . mosquito net (curtain)' Dickens C.

PPS (also for Pip – applies to the girls in the UNSW library) – 'they drill 'oles in yer 'art, Toby' also Dickens C.

Enough said – 'To bed, to bed, doctor' as my neighbouring tent mate, the AcAdj (assistant adjutant) is shouting out in his usual uncouth manner.

PPPS I miss you all a lot!

[1]   This did eventuate, and was Operation Paddington.

Nui Dat
Sunday 2/7/67

Dear crazy brother, Pip,

I will try very hard and make this letter a literary masterpiece but I'm afraid I'm rapidly getting like all doctors – completely uncultured.

I've just finished tape number two so will send it off tomorrow – packed with exciting news for all the family.

You have scored at last, as the Peter Rabbit joke actually caused a smile to cross my wan countenance (how's that for grammatical construction)? Sorry, I still don't know any jokes. The army isn't strong on good jokes, I've found.[1]

Well, my news: today was an exciting Sunday. I think I told you I casually remarked to the WO (warrant officer) of the Civil Aid Unit at Hoa Long on Wednesday that if the Australian Surgical Team, the civilian one from RPA Hospital in Sydney who are working in Vung Tau, was visiting the area on Sunday then they would be very welcome at the officers' mess for dinner. He jumped at the chance but I little realised how it would go to the heads of the female-deprived gunner officers. They became quite maniacal at the thought of four 'sisters' in the mess (with dresses on – not with army uniforms like the army sisters wear), so soon it was all arranged that they should come. Operations went into full swing at once – the 2IC, who is president of the officers' mess committee, issued invitations to all officers remotely connected with the regiment and to many who weren't. All the kitchen staff went into a huddle and managed to produce a number of fish dishes bought at Baria, so a big buffet was planned. More mundanely, all urinals in the area around the officers' mess were screened with very high hessian walls so female eyes would not be shocked. And a special order went out that no one near the area was allowed to go wandering over to the showers with nothing on, as so often happens in most of the soldiers' 'lines', all quite visible from the main task force roadway.

But everything went wrong! At the appropriate time (12 noon) most of the officers had arrived and the mess was packed with men all getting stuck into their pre-dinner beer (or ginger beer, as in my case) including my two colleagues whom I'd specially invited, Tony Williams, my old Concord mate and the present RMO of 7 Battalion, and Graham Maynard, RMO of 2 Battalion, whom I met at Healesville School of Army Health, but no sign of the Surgical Team. At about 12.15 they arrived and I went out to meet them, all of a twit as I usually am at introductions and oh horrors – four male surgeons but only ONE sister (in a dress to be sure) but only ONE FEMALE. An almost audible groan was heard from the mess.

The poor girl was a bit overwhelmed – a very nice girl she was, by the way, from Cheltenham (small world isn't it?[2]) – but she bore up nobly and met the colonel and the 2IC and the American artillery colonel without batting an eyelid. Anyway, I thought everything was going to be OK when a terrible thing happened. The captain from the Civil Aid Unit who was conducting the Surgical Team around beckoned me in a conspiratorial manner over into a corner and wildly whispered, 'The sister wants to go to the toilet. What are we going to do?'

Now this was NOT my fault as we had thought of this and told the CA people to make necessary arrangements for them somewhere else before the sisters came to the regiment, as there are certainly no ladies' toilets here; but the dopes had forgotten and the poor sister apparently was all uncomfortable. So, valiant as ever, I hurried out – got the battery sergeant-major to clear the sergeants' latrines and the area around it and then came back and in my most tactful manner (you can imagine me, now all the colours of the rainbow) asked the sister if she would care to have a wash before dinner. Then came the big ordeal – I had to conduct the poor thing through all the sergeants' lines and down to their delightful 'little house' and then 'stand guard' at a discreet distance. It was awful, and I hate to think what my RAP sergeant is going to say tomorrow – will I ever get teased? Fortunately the poor long-suffering sister took it all very well and had a good sense of humour. Just as well.

The buffet dinner was a great success and I think we all enjoyed ourselves. A funny Sunday dinner party for me. But everything is funny and different up here and it is no good trying to live as you do at home all the time – it would just be impossible. The 2IC reckons I should 'shout' the whole officers' mess a beer each, for failing to get the four sisters along, but I'll get out of that somehow. It was a good party in spite of all the mix-up. The other sisters didn't come, by the way, as they were up until 4 am this morning operating on a case (or assisting at the op) and were too tired.

How is the Mighty Austin Lancer going? On two or four cylinders at present?

I saw a tiny little transistor radio for only $6 in the PX store yester-day so I bought it and sent it to the 'little creatures'. I didn't think you, Merrie or Ian would like one, but if you do just let me know and I'll certainly get you one and send it home.

Well, that's about it, Pip. There's no further news of headquarter battery and the RMO going out on operation yet. Will let you all know when I hear.

Love to all the family,

Dave

---

1 I can't remember the Peter Rabbit joke. Army jokes were not so much poor jokes as jokes unrepeatable to the family – dirty though they were, some were quite good!
2 Cheltenham is a Sydney suburb very close to Pennant Hills.

Nui Dat
Sunday 2/7/67

Dear Mum,

It's been a big day – the day 4 Field Regiment officers entertained the Australian Surgical Team, all arranged by the RMO, thinking of officer morale as usual. Anyway, it's all in Pip's letter when you get home tonight. A funny Sunday, but I *did* go to church this morning – quite a good service too; but though I would never dream of going to a Sunday party at home, it seemed the right thing to do here, and I guess a party is one way to rest and relax. I had a good chat to Tony Williams and it was good to see him again.

How are you, dear old thing?

Congratulations on the first birthday of Bradford Chemist, Castle Hill, run by the two 'dear old souls' and David, the terror of all chemist errand boys.

Sorry no more time tonight, or I'll never get to bed.

Very much love,

David

PS How are all your funny doctrines?[1] Mine are as funny as ever, but not as funny as Padre Wellings's.

PPS Another tape recording on the way. Am eagerly awaiting yours.

---

1 My mother is a strong-willed woman and frequently expressed her views on various subjects with a cavalier disregard for orthodox Christian

doctrines. As far as church people were concerned she was often not what we would now call 'politically correct'. My father, as the upholder of orthodoxy, would gently chide her but she remained unrepentant. This is not to infer that she had differing views on Christian fundamentals – her rebellions concerned minor matters of Christian behaviour and practice.

Nui Dat
Monday 3/7/67

Dear old Porky girl,

By now the exciting parcel which I sent you for your glory box should have arrived. I hope you don't think it's too awful and that you find some use for it.[1] Anyway it'll be something to show all your nursey friends. My atrocious sergeant, Bob Allen, talked the shop keeper into selling it to me 50 piastres cheaper so you have a bargain.

I have been wicked again tonight and went to the movies and saw *Song Without End*, the story of Franz Liszt. Very good. Not at all wicked and lots of good music. I do miss the piano. The organ in the chapel is little better than a mouth organ with a keyboard. I am pining away for some good old Bach too, although the Far East Broadcasting Company often has some good music when I can pick it up on my set.

There's no more news of the big operation that the valiant 4 Fd Regt RMO might be going on. The political situation in Saigon is all up in the air at present.

Mum and Dad sound bright and perky, don't they? The shop sounds a bit of a future gold mine from all accounts.

Tomorrow I am going down to Vung Tau to 8 Field Ambulance with Tony Williams (7 RAR doctor) to try and iron out all the terrible mix-ups in diagnosis and treatment that have been going on down there. We're going to 'wait' on the CO and try to find out just what's wrong – typical Bradford – will probably get myself into a fight. But there's no excuse for poor medical care even in the army. Tony is as mad as a hornet about the way they've treated some of his patients.

Lots of love, Porko,
Dave

1   A week or so before this letter, Bob Allen and I had a trip to Baria. We bought a fluorescent light for the RAP and an article of night attire (nicely embroidered) for my sister. It might have been a Vietnamese version of a kimono. Bob bargained for everything!

Nui Dat
Thursday 6/7/67

Dear Dad,

I think it must be about your turn for a letter, so here goes. I posted my slides home today – they turned out pretty well – I guess they should have as the new Yashica camera is practically fool-proof.

I have had no letters from home for three days now – there must be some hold-up I think because of the postal officers' strike in Sydney[1]; but tonight it is raining too hard for the mail plane to land so that's why we missed out this evening.

Today was pay day. Pay parades are always fascinating – all of headquarter battery congregate at the orderly room – march in (in turn), sign their name, salute the paying officer, and pick up their money. I only draw about five to ten dollars a fortnight and that's only to pay my mess bill[2] and to buy stamps. Some cartoonist from the Melbourne *Herald* was up here today and drew sketches of the various soldiers at the pay parade with their weapons. He was very quick and quite clever at sketching. I took some photos as well which I'll send when I finish this film.

We had heavy rain today and the ground is very muddy – it seems to be working up to be VERY wet for our big operation, which is rumoured to start on Sunday. The rain doesn't really upset you here as it's so warm all the time. I quite like the climate really and am very used to it by now.

How are all the Penno people? Do thank them for their continued interest and prayers.

Life is pretty much the same here. I've put in my monthly hygiene report and my sick report. I also put in a special hygiene report condemning the regimental command post (a dug-in hole in the ground, which is very stuffy and oppressive). The blokes do eight-hour shifts on the radio sets there and I've had a lot of complaints about it.

Today was spent in packing up stuff to take out on this operation that's coming up. I am taking one of those A-frame haversacks – it seems pointless to take too much, as if anyone needs prolonged treatment we would chopper them back to base or hospital at Vung Tau.

I was reading an article in the *BMJ*[3] today by some English cardinal or other, which was the text of a speech he made to the BMA. He says, amongst other things, that the medical profession, with the present loss of confidence and trend away from 'religion' on the part of modern people generally, has become 'the new clergy' and the modern priests. I am sure he is right. People barely know the church exists except as a place to be buried and married in. I think people do turn to doctors but the tragedy is so few doctors have anything to offer other than medical science. It's a big responsibility, all right.

My love to you all,
Davo

[1]   There were many strikes in Sydney through 1967 and 1968, including several mail strikes. The worst and longest occurred over Tet 1968 and caused great anger amongst soldiers serving overseas. Daily mail deliveries were really regarded as a life-line to home and family.

[2]   We paid for beer, wine, soft drinks and cigarettes in the mess. Officers could also purchase spirits at the bar. Stamps had to be paid for. Other items (stationery, soaps, shampoos, and all electrical equipment) could be bought at the army PX store. The US PX at Vung Tau was the best, with the biggest range of goods.

[3]   *British Medical Journal.*

Nui Dat
Friday 7/7/67

Mother mine, and all the family,
As I write I am listening to your tape (for the second time). I did enjoy your piano playing, Mum, but it made me feel sad as it usually does. I am not sure these tape recordings are a good idea – they have made me feel very homesick for the first time today. You made no mistakes

at all on the piano – what was the piece? Tchaikovsky wasn't it? Apart from a few pauses, it was terrific. Thank you so much.

The lovely biscuits[1] arrived this morning. They are really scrumptious and I enjoyed them. We all sat around in the RAP eating them – even a couple of patients got one each and my old Castle Hill friend, Bombardier Banks, got one for bringing the parcel in. He also gave me a copy of *Farm and Garden* which informed me that my Castle Hill 'duty chemist' for this weekend was Mr C. D. Bradford MPS.

I have been busy tonight as the poor old CO has come down with some wog or other. It's awful just at the moment as he is busy with preparation for this big hush-hush operation that's coming up. I had to go over to his tent and give the poor man an injection for his nausea while he was trying to give the adjutant and the 2IC a briefing. It was most embarrassing for him. It would be no fun being a commanding officer up here. Anyway, I am quite worried about him tonight.

Merrie's letter came tonight. I am relieved to hear that Ian has decided to go on and finish his chartered accountancy exams. I am sure it is always the right thing to finish what you've started doing and go right through with it, even though it seems awfully difficult at the time. This is from my own experience as you poor long-suffering parents no doubt remember – you were both right then, weren't you? How anyone can be anything else but a doctor amazes me now.

What is this rumour about choir stalls at Pennant Hills Baptist Church? It's amazing. You will be telling me the venetian blinds have come down next!

The medical and hygiene supplies would be fine just in bulk, I think. The little bit of soap we have distributed already nearly caused a riot amongst the village kids, so it has to be done carefully.

Much love to my dear old mother and all her bairns aboot her!

David

---

[1] Mum made the biscuits, so they were genuinely home-made and of the cookie variety, i.e. full of butter. The National Heart Foundation would not have approved.

Nui Dat
Saturday 8/7/67

Dear Pippo,
Thanks for the latest piece of trivia from one of UNSW's proud but modest members.

News bulletin (in brief):

Nui Dat: Seething with excitement about the coming big op which starts tomorrow. Top Secret of course but if the VC don't know, there must be something wrong with them. The number of Americans that have been pouring into the place in the last day or so . . . !

My batman: Upset because he can't come out on operation with me and so can't 'kill a VC' for his girlfriend.

Sergeant Allen: Cheeky as ever.

The 2IC: Bursting with importance about the big op. You'd think he was the brigadier himself.

The CO: Recovered from his sick attack last night, thank goodness (my injection did it of course).

Me: My charming, friendly, over-kind self (and modest too).

Well, bye for now,

David (your esteemed brother)

Nui Dat
Saturday 8/7/67

Dear Porky,
Fancy that you met a girl from Concord Repat Hospital who didn't know about me. So passes the fame and glory of the hour! But she loves the good old hospital, does she? Well, it's not a bad place looking back I must admit.

So you want me to come home for your wedding? Do you realise I am only entitled to five days R&R (that means outside Vietnam) and five days R&C (that means at that tropical paradise, Vung Tau) in my twelve months stay over here? Some people do manage to wangle two R&Rs, but not those invaluable people the RMOs. Anyway, I'll do my best. I'll apply to my Senior Medical Officer (SMO), the CO of 8 Field Ambulance, for R&R in Australia for the first week of November as soon as I get back from this exciting op which starts tomorrow. It apparently rests with him when the Nui Dat doctors go on R&R, as he has to arrange alternative medical services for the various units. Our local COs have nothing to do with it.

Today I had a little boy from Hoa Long with an acute asthma attack brought up for me to treat by Peter Angus, the warrant officer. You know how much paediatric experience I got at Concord (i.e. nil). I didn't know what to give him – I've got IV aminophylline but it would have been a battle getting into a vein as he was crying and carrying on. So I gave him adrenaline subcutaneously. I didn't have a clue about the dose but diluted it down and hoped for the best. Fortunately he picked up quickly and 'mumma san' (his mother) was bowing and scraping thanking me. 'The bac-si from Hoa Long has scored again' as my incorrigible sergeant said later.

Tomorrow at 0830 hours we set off for this big op. I'm only taking a big haversack full of medical stuff like tetracycline, penicillin, a few drips (Ringer's solution and albumen) and so on. The hygiene sergeant, Fred Wittmer, is coming with me and Sergeant Allen and my batman are holding the fort at home. We leave by helicopter from Nui Dat. There are about a million Yanks (not literally, but it seems like it) and several US artillery units joining us, so we won't be on our own. It's one of the biggest ops ever in this province, I believe. All it means for me though is seven days with no showers, eating 'hard' rations and endless tinea to treat. At least that's all I hope it means! I'm out there in case any of the gunners get wounded.

Anyway, much love – I agree with your decision[1] about next year, by the way,

Davey Boy

---

[1]   Ian had decided to battle on with his chartered accountancy course despite having failed an examination – it meant having to repeat it, after further study.

Nui Dat
Saturday 8/7/67

Dear Mum,

Well, tomorrow we go out on this big op that everyone's been talking about for the last week or so. We fly in helicopters about 20 miles [32 kilometres] to a place called Xuyen-Moc ('Swan Mock') where 4 Fd Regt will be establishing a fire support base (FSB) with two batteries of guns (and regimental headquarters to command them) and of course the ever faithful RMO to look after their health. It lasts about six or seven days. The two infantry battalions will be deploying through 'the scrub' and to help them there will be a whole division of Yankees and several US artillery battalions. It is the biggest op in this province for ages and they are expecting great things.

We'll be well supplied with home mail by a resupply helicopter every day, so it won't be too bad.

Must get to bed now, mother dear. Don't worry! Operations are not very bad. Apparently I will be camped practically IN the regimental command post so you couldn't be much safer than that. And Psalm 91 is still in the Bible.

Much love,
David

Somewhere near Xuyen-Moc
Tuesday 11/7/67

Dear family,

A somewhat messy and scrappy letter from the big op in time to catch the resupply helicopter.

I am well and quite safe and doing nothing much except digging weapon pits and things. We had an unfortunate accident yesterday when an engineer was killed by a tree falling on top of him when he was trying to bulldoze it out. When I was called to him it was too late, but there wouldn't have been anything much I could have done. Otherwise there have been no accidents or casualties at all in our area, but I don't know about the infantry battalions. The brigadier has strained his back and being the only Aussie doctor in the area I was called to treat him this morning, but apart from rubbing him with Dencorub I couldn't do much for him either. I am sworn to secrecy so don't tell anyone he's done his back in or the Enemy might find out.

Much love and more news tomorrow,

David

from Operation Paddington

Xuyen-Moc

Wednesday 12/7/67

Dear Mum,

The latest news from the war zone: I am sitting in the 11 ft × 11 ft [3.3 metre × 3.3 metre] tent that serves as the RAP, nearly up to my ankles in mud which lies thick everywhere. It has been raining hard on and off over the last few days so things are pretty sticky under foot. We are all smelly and messy by this time but fortunately a new set of 'greens' for each of us is coming out by chopper late this afternoon. My pants are practically standing up on their own at present.

Last night we had an engineer with the Kiwi gun battery blow his foot off with one of those wretched mines which he'd been laying outside the perimeter. It was about 7.15 and pretty dark so I had to put a drip up by torchlight, which is no easy feat, and get him to the chopper landing pad on a stretcher to be 'dusted-off' in a helicopter. They had already put a tourniquet on and stopped the bleeding before they carried him back into camp so I didn't have to worry about that. He was in a lot of pain but should be OK. It is a little different trying to care for a shocked patient in a muddy field in the rain than in the nice sterile wards of RGH Concord.

Much love,

David

PS Only two more full days to go here. It's back to Nui Dat on Saturday most likely. You'll get a good letter then.

Xuyen-Moc
Friday 14/7/67

Dear Mum,

My last letter from 'the Combat Zone'! Tomorrow the big op winds up
and we should be back in the (relative) comfort of Nui Dat. It has been
quite an eventful stay from our (i.e. headquarter battery's) point of
view. Just after I wrote my last letter a small patrol from HQ battery
went out around the perimeter to clear the area and one of the
gunners trod on a VC mine. Fortunately it wasn't a very powerful one
but it peppered his leg with little bits of shrapnel and also a bit went
into one wrist. He was a bit shocked but was quite OK otherwise and
from latest reports is doing well down at Vung Tau. We had to get a
'dust-off' helicopter to take him out.

Then last evening they had to send out a patrol to fill in some pits
that had been sighted and looked freshly dug. All our gunners were
a bit apprehensive by this time and went out rather worriedly, as you
can imagine. We were equally worried back at base. I went and sat
in the command post so I'd know what was going on. They hadn't
been gone long when we heard a barrage of small arms fire from
their direction. Then the gunners on the perimeter of the Kiwi
battery (which is right next door to us) opened up with their
machine guns in the direction our patrol had been going! The 2IC
leapt onto the radio and ordered the Kiwis to stop firing straight
away but it was five minutes before they finally stopped. It was
certainly a relief when our patrol came on the air a minute or two
later and said there were no casualties. What had happened apparently was that the patrol had had a contact with one VC and had
fired at him and he'd responded. His fire had gone into the Kiwi
battery who'd thought they were being attacked so they 'opened up'.
The only trouble was they were firing straight at our patrol. The
patrol all hit the ground and bullets whistled both ways over their
heads for a few minutes but no one was hurt. It certainly was a
miracle they weren't all wiped out. A pretty shaky lot of gunners
came back into camp after that. They have had their share of war
now after that little episode. And to think infantry men accuse the
artillery of never seeing any action! At any rate we will all be glad to

get back to camp tomorrow. What with the mud and the few accidents and the VC not far away, it's not the best place to be in. It's safe enough here in the base though and tonight we have the infantry camped all around us and we aren't right on the edge like we have been so far. I have seen more casualties in base camp on this op than the battalion doctors out in the field. The infantry battalions hardly found any VC at all and the op on the whole has been a bit of a failure. It will be interesting to see what the newspapers back home say about it.

Anyway, much love and I will write a long letter tomorrow night.
David

Nui Dat ('Home')
Saturday 15/7/67

Dear family,
Hi! Well Op Paddington is over and we are all back safe and sound in 'civilised' Nui Dat. Someone said this morning as we landed here in the Chinook helicopter, 'I never thought I'd call this place home'. It's certainly nice to be out of the mud and back in my own friendly little tent with all my usual mess about the place. As you have probably gathered, it was quite an eventful trip – all my patients are doing well though, I heard today. The boy with the foot blown off is much better and our gunner from HQ battery with the shrapnel wounds has very minor injuries really and is up and about, so I feel relieved. Another one of our regiment from the survey troop was injured two nights ago when he was surveying an American battery position. The VC chose the night he was there to mortar the position and he got a bit of shrapnel in his buttock but is otherwise OK. So 4 Fd Regt has really had its first taste of the war. I didn't see the last case – he was about 10 miles [16 kilometres] from us, but the others were all my patients. I must stop this recounting. It's called 'spinning warries' and is much frowned on, especially by the blokes who stay behind at Nui Dat. It was quite an experience though and I personally was in no danger all the time I was there.

I find you get to know the blokes much better out on an op like that. I used to go around the battery every morning and talk to them all. I met one of the HQ battery gunners who comes from St Clements Anglican Church in Mosman. He is a nice chap called David Thomas, a special friend of Gunner Dickinson (the artist).

Bob Allen stayed back at Nui Dat, as you know. They were so short-handed he had to do duties on the wireless set in the command post (he tells us now, 'The medics were controlling the war').

So Pip is a great criminal and was apprehended at Redfern Station of all places. I bet he was all the colours of the rainbow – bad enough to run for a train, but to actually miss it and get caught.[1] Typical UNSW student! What will the 'little creatures' say? I've had another two letters from Rob and Ian 'to keep my morals up'. Ian, in his latest, comments on the weather thus: 'I am just looking out of the window now and see a wind of five knots blowing big dark clouds east.' He is a real character, that child.

Bombardier Banks was talking to me today (as usual – he can't resist a long chat to anyone willing to listen) – he said his aunt was one of your foundation customers at the pharmacy. He thinks Mr Ford, your opposition, is losing his business because 'he is too slack and has lost interest'. I hope that cheers you up.

I am sorry my slides upset you all.[2] Really Nui Dat is safe as houses or at least as safe as anywhere in SVN.

I hear that Len Miller, from Pennant Hills Baptist, is at Healesville School of Army Health and enjoying it. I am sure the army must do you good, for a short time like two years, although as Gunner Thomas says, 'It's not much of a life really – when you're just a humble gunner you're on the receiving end of all the worst as well as the best in the system.' Gunner Dickinson, for example is a regular soldier. He signed up on the spur of the moment, for six years, when a romance fizzled out and he's only done three of the six years. Of course now he wants to get on with his art and study it. He should too, as he has a real gift, but he's tied to the army for another three years. It's rather a shame.

Love,
David

---

[1]   Sydney electric trains in the sixties had no automatically closing doors – people could jump on or off a moving train in a platform at will.

Presumably Pip was running to catch a train home to Pennant Hills at Redfern station but realised it was going too fast to risk the jump and was caught and given a lecture by the station master.

2   The slides would have been of Nui Dat, my sandbagged tent, helicopters, and rolls of barbed wire which separated various army units from one another – to slow the enemy down if they ever got inside the base. They would have looked very war-like back in suburban Sydney.

Nui Dat
Sunday 16/7/67

Dear old Dad,

Thank you for your letter last week which arrived at the height of Operation Paddington and promptly succumbed to the ever encroaching mud after I'd finished reading it.

Today I have had a nice restful Sunday recovering from the week in the bush – only a short sick parade; then a foot inspection of all HQ battery to see that foot rot hadn't set in too badly; then chapel – rather a solemn service today as it was one of our 'OPD' members who copped the shrapnel in the buttock when the American FSB was mortared. Even Padre Wellings seemed to sense it and excelled himself. After that I went up to the Fwd Detachment for lunch with Jack Blomley – turkey and cranberry sauce (typical American rations and not nearly as good as it sounds). He then took the opportunity for an afternoon off and shot down to Vung Tau via chopper and I took his calls. I spent most of the afternoon just talking to the diggers at the Fwd Detachment – they are a nice chummy lot, although pretty rough. Then I went across the road to our gunners' mess, as I had been specially invited to a little ceremony in honour of the signals officer (Peter Harnwell). It was quite a humorous performance, the opening of 'Harmful Fort' as they called it – a few were half 'under the weather', Sunday being a 'stand down' day (i.e. half holiday). One of the sergeants became very confidential and told me I'd made a 'big hit' with the gunners out on the op and they all thought I was 'terrific'. I don't quite know how to take that as he was pretty 'under the weather' himself! After that I scooted back to the Fwd Detachment hospital until Jack came back in time for the Sunday night BBQ.

I'm now in my tent with all my letters – there's one from the 'little creatures' – you'd think I'd bought them a million dollar stereogram instead of a tiny little US$6 transistor radio, the way they go on.

Much love, Dad,
David

Nui Dat
Monday 17/7/67

Dear old Porky girl,
So glad you liked the *kimono* (or whatever the Vietnamese equivalent is called).

You should have seen me putting a drip up in the mud. Sterility went by the board, I'm afraid, but the patient looked bright and perky when I saw him today in hospital at Vung Tau, despite his recent below-knee amputation. He was a New Zealander and a really tough egg. I said brightly, 'Do you remember me?' when I saw him today. 'Now why should I remember you?' he responded. 'Don't you remember the bloke who patched you up?' said I, still bright. 'Oh,' he said with a wicked gleam in his eye, 'so you're the bloke who gave me that weak injection which didn't ease my pain?' (I had given him a quarter grain of morphine, but I didn't reckon on a really tough old Kiwi.) It was somewhat deflating, but then we docs never get our due reward. But I think he was only kidding me, as we parted good friends – he is going back to NZ this afternoon.

My other patient with the shrapnel in the leg is doing well too and being of continental extraction is quite the opposite – nearly killing me with grateful thanks. At least that dumb Field Ambulance in Vung Tau hasn't mucked up this lot of patients so perhaps Tony's and my little pep talk to the administration did some good after all.

Anyway must go to bed, sister Suzy,
Much love from your crazy brother. Hope your exams go OK,
Dave

Nui Dat
Tuesday 18/7/67

Dear Phil,

I am just back from the movies, recovering, you see, from my war experiences last week. It is a bit late but I thought I'd better churn you out one of my shortened abridged versions. The movies were a failure anyway because the task force generator is playing up and kept going weak and the poor old movie operator had to keep turning his machine off so it wouldn't blow up. Finally the power cut out altogether right in the tense and dramatic middle of the last reel so I don't know how it finished.[1] When I left the TF officers' mess, one of the American officers was telling 'you guys' how it ended as he'd seen it before 'Stateside' but I couldn't be bothered waiting. Yanks speak a different language and are harder to understand than Vietnamese sometimes.

Unfortunately I have no rhymes for you tonight except perhaps the artilleryman's (unofficial) war song which is heard many times (unofficially of course) but which is unprintable as there are really only four words in it which would not bring 'a blush to the cheek of the young person'. It's a shame I can't sing it to you, as it's certainly colourful and so rather interesting to an English II student, but suffice it to say it goes to a well known band tune and commences with 'we're a pack of . . .' and ends, with '. . . for liberty'[2]!

I am deeply shocked that you were hauled by the ear into a certain station master's office for the horrifying crime of running down the platform after a departing train. Oh the evils of today's university students. There was a time when they were all gentlemen (or was that only the medical students)?

Latest news, now – people who matter at Nui Dat:

1. Sergeant Allen – a bit obstreperous at present, mainly I think because he didn't go to the 'war' with me and is a bit jealous that he can't 'spin warries'. He's now temporarily one of the despised breed of 'base wallahs'.

2. Gunner Fernandes – my ever faithful batman, ruined a pair of boots of mine yesterday with a famous new leather preservative. They look like nothing on earth at present. He's known generally as 'José' – something to do with Mexicans and bullfights, I gather.

3. Chuck Berry – rather upset as his battery didn't go out on op and had to provide accommodation for about 100 Yanks who moved into Nui Dat while the op was in progress. Chuck was all excited hoping to swap notes and equipment with a Yankee medic, but unfortunately they had no medic with them and Chuck spent the whole week looking after grizzly Americans.

4. 'Banksy' the postman – has been here six months today, which makes him a 'clanger', i.e. entitled to wear two ribbons (you get one after twenty-four hours in country and another one after six months). Before becoming a 'clanger' you are called a 'swisher'. He is his usual cheery, chatty self.

5. Private Williams – my other medic – has just been made a corporal and is still out with 108 Battery at the Horseshoe. He is always sending me little notes, 'RMO, Please send out 1 box tinea ointment, 3 scalpel blades etc' – usually ordering about four times more than he needs. Still, he's enthusiastic and that's the main thing.

6. The 2IC – 'Little Toot' he is known clandestinely (what a good word!), among the other officers. Still fingering his moustache disapprovingly at everything and everyone.

7. Craftsman Dowling – our regimental electrician, at present engaged in putting lights, at last, in the RAP. He is a nice kid and looks like all electricians seem to look – you know, sort of bright-eyed and eager to get a bit of wire in their hands? He was telling me about himself out on the op – he's only twenty but has already been married (because he had to, of course) and is now getting a divorce. He was brought up in an orphanage and then joined the army at seventeen. Some of these kids are old by the time they're twenty. But, he's a good bloke at heart.

Anyway, must stop or I'll go through the whole regiment. Time would fail me to tell of our noble CO, who has a rash on his hands that I can't cure (as yet), but he has recovered from his gastric wog; Jack the Quack from Nui Dat, whose prickly heat is in a state of regression at the moment; our artist Gunner Dickinson and his friend Gunner Thomas; and many others too, whom I meet and doctor every day.

Keep out of the long arm of the law's reach, my son!

Your old brother,

Dave

PS Give my love to Mum.

[1]   The movie was *The Collector* (1965) with Terence Stamp and Samantha Eggar.
[2]   'We're a pack of bastards, bastards are we; We're going to fuck and fight for liberty' – I think the band tune is the Radetsky March.

Nui Dat
Wednesday night 19/7/67

Dear old long-distance hiker mother,
It sounds pretty definite now that R&R in Australia as a general rule will be happening soon unless the army changes its mind all of a sudden, so if I can organise myself on R&R for the first week in November I may even manage Merrie's wedding. Of course, the trouble is you can never be sure as they cancel officers' R&R (or rather, postpone it) if an operation like the last one happens to come up. I will make tentative arrangements with the SMO next Monday when I go down to Vung Tau to the Field Ambulance. He wasn't there last Monday when I called.

I am back in the old routine now after the week away. I didn't do my Medcap at Hoa Long this afternoon, though, as Jack the Quack wanted to do it. He is a rogue because he's never wanted to do it before (reckoned anywhere outside the task force area was too dangerous). But on his way back from Vung Tau last Sunday he stopped at Hoa Long and talked to some of the kids and got all enthusiastic. He then asked if I'd mind him doing the Medcap this week. I let him, of course, as he doesn't get out much, being tied to the phone at the 'dust-off' pad pretty well all the time. I must confess I missed it though, as I haven't been for two weeks. My batman and Sergeant Allen went with Jack today and came back, the batman's Spanish blood boiling and Sergeant Allen full of righteous indignation, as they reckon Jack will try and 'steal' our Medcap. 'Let him find his own village and not steal ours!' 'Don't you give it up, sir; you've done all the hard work down there at Hoa Long.' So you see I have raised a hornet's nest – my batman left me tonight with the dark threat, 'I wouldn't give it up, sir, without a good fight.' They really are funny as I am sure Jack hasn't the smallest intention of 'stealing' Hoa Long, but he has certainly upset my staff. At least they are loyal. Nothing has come of my offer to do another Medcap yet, but I am to see Major Fox (the Civil Affairs doctor) tomorrow and see how his plans are going.

I hope Uncle Bill[1] gets into Katoomba Council – the boys will be bitterly disappointed if he doesn't, I think.

No more news, old thing. Much love from your son,
Dave

[1]   Uncle Bill was a watchmaker and jeweller in Katoomba Street, Katoomba, and had wanted to serve on council as his father had done before him. He was successfully elected and subsequently became mayor a few years later.

Nui Dat
Friday 21/7/67

Dear family,

A very busy day today – sick parade dragged on nearly to lunchtime, with wretched ear infections which are so tedious to treat. Every day this week I've had a minor op to do too, so I am having quite a 'slashing' time!

I managed to get hold of a book called *Snakes of the World*, put out by the US Army, which is pretty good. In fact it's so good and technical as to be nearly unintelligible! So the Pork Publishing Company doesn't have to search any further. Seriously, Merrie, you shouldn't have gone to all that trouble, but thanks a lot. You should just spend your time studying for exams! Dear me! I must stop using exclamation marks – Stephen Hampson said I used eleven in the letter I sent David his brother,[1] so I really must be more careful and less like a Frenchman gone mad.

I hope my latest tape arrives safely – it's quite terrific this time (I hope anyway).[2]

No further news yet about R&R in Australia, except that 'marriedies' will have first preference and poor 'singlies' like me probably won't get a 'look in'. I'm sure it will all work out for the best.

Mum dear, you are not to work too hard; so don't worry if the shop is in too great a mess. Though it is good you are busy there now.

All my love,
Dave

1   The Hampson family attended Pennant Hills Baptist Church. There were
     two boys, David and Stephen. David, the elder of the two, was Pip's age
     and they became good friends. Both of the boys very kindly wrote to me
     while I was in Vietnam.
2   My tape contained music from the officers' mess including Bob Dylan's
     'How many times must the cannon balls fly before they're forever
     banned', suitably embellished with the resounding booms of the
     Americans' 155 mm guns firing!

Nui Dat

Saturday 22/7/67

My very dear Mother,

How are you? Still d.t. ('desperately tired', as Auntie Jean would say)?
I will be relieved when that 'girlie' (as Dad calls her) starts work in the
shop and relieves you of some of the burden. Did I tell you the fruit
cake arrived safely and so did the David Jones biscuits, the Gamophen
and the Tabac deodorant?

No real news tonight, except 106 Battery is going out for a one-day-
only operation tomorrow. Also a concert party is hitting Nui Dat
tomorrow for a big show at 10.30, so I might toddle along after chapel
just to get some photos.

Guess what? I have hit the news. Brian Mitchell's wife sent
up a newspaper clipping (probably from the *Australian*, Brian
thinks) with a big picture of me with a stethoscope on a Vietnamese
child's chest. I look quite dreadful – hair everywhere as usual
and bent over as if I've got a hunch back. I don't know whether
anyone's shown you a copy. It may well have been a Brisbane paper
and not the *Australian* at all so don't get upset if you haven't seen
it. I will ask Brian for it when he's finished with it and send it
down if I can. 'It's nothing to write home about though', to use a
weak pun.

I am really quite destitute of news tonight. The RAP now has
electric lighting throughout, which makes things much easier if I have
to see anyone at night. I will have to get the 'Mexican bandit' (my
batman) to paint all the windows black, so it's blacked out from the
outside at night.

All my love, mother dear; look after those chilblains – I can't imagine such a disease existing up here.

Davo

Nui Dat
Sunday 23/7/67

My dear old sis, Porky,

Here is a big cheery letter for the girl with 'big black circles'.[1] Mum says in her latest letter that you are all 'down in the dumps', so I realise you are missing your kind, sweet, understanding, handsome – need I say more – brother. See enclosed newspaper picture as proof of above – have you ever seen a finer portrayal of 'the hunchback of Notre Dame'?

You would have loved our Australian Forces Overseas Fund Concert today. There were two performances – the first one this morning and the second one this afternoon. I didn't go to the morning's as I wanted to go to chapel, but of course, someone came into the RAP at 0955 hours with a 'gangrenous'-looking toe and I had to do a wedge resection on it then and there, so I missed chapel anyway. Everyone seemed to be going to the afternoon concert so I thought why shouldn't I? I went with the adjutant after lunch. It was a scream – pouring with rain as it does every afternoon now – and they had organised the concert out in the open at 'Eagle Farm' helicopter pad. Typical army! Thousands of miserable-looking troops standing, or sitting on camp stools, in the rain waiting for the concert to start. But, of course, it couldn't be held there as it would have ruined all the electronic equipment so the organisers had a brain wave and decided, owing to the rain (which they knew would happen anyway), they would hold the concert in a big army hut half a mile away. Everyone picked up their seats and set off though the drizzle to the new location. Then everyone (there must have been 500+) crammed in any old how and they backed a truck inside the front door and the entertainers performed on the back of the truck. John O'Grady, author of *They're a Weird Mob*,[2] was the compere – clad in a blue and white Hawaiian shirt, sports pants and sandals, with a wispy goatee beard. He was weak – he didn't even crack any jokes; just said things like, 'Ow ya goin'? The first item will be Sharon O'Brien.' The latter turned out to be a singer – she was the best and had a really good (microphoney) voice. She sang usual pop stuff well, then tried 'Climb every mountain', fairly unsuccessfully, the height proving a little steep for her. Then there were two not-so-young blokes who sang little ditties with a guitar; they had reasonable voices but only sang trash and they told several 'blue' jokes, only one of which I could understand, and I've been in the army five months now. Everyone else seemed to appreciate them, though, I'm afraid. There was also an accordionist, called, if you please, 'Mario Banano', but he was really terrific – played some good pieces and played very well. Sharon O'Brien then sang again and John O'Grady recited a little C. J. Dennis poem about 'b—— Australians' and they finished up. Sharon, by the way, had on a loose nylon maternity frock outfit, no stockings and white gumboots.

It really was all pretty trashy, but I'm glad I went. It was quite an experience being one of a great crowd of soldiers. I'm sure most of them really enjoyed it, mainly because it was someone from home up there on the stage. It was rather moving in an odd sort of way, if you can understand what I mean. I think the soldiers deserve better than that sort of fairly second-rate show, though. I am probably getting all patriotic and unnecessary – but I am really proud at times to be an Aussie soldier.

Anyway, I promised to cheer you up with this letter. Did I tell you that little Ian wrote thanking me for the transistor and started his letter, 'Many unspeakable thanks, Dave!' He is a scream.

Every day there are new rumours about R&R in Australia. One day it's all on; the next day it's all off. It's very unsettling. Don't fret about it, though. Your black circles will entirely engulf your face if you do.

Love,
Dave

---

1 When Merrie was tired after hard work at the hospital, according to Mum, she would develop 'big, black circles under her eyes'.

2 *They're a Weird Mob* was a classic and very popular, extremely funny, Australian novel published in 1957. John O'Grady wrote under the pen name Nino Culotta, who was also the main character, an Italian immigrant, in the novel.

Nui Dat
Monday 24/7/67

Dear old Mum,

Just a short note before I hit the sack. Today I went to Vung Tau, as they elected me to a 'board of survey' on 18,000 fibreglass ear plugs at 8 Field Ambulance which have 'gone off' in the climate. A board of survey consists of a president and a member (I was the member) and they sit in judgement on some article which has 'had it' and write it off so that it can be legally destroyed. We duly wrote off all these ear plugs and successfully cost the government about $400. It was all conducted very solemnly – we had to decide on a day 'three weeks hence' when the offending ear plugs would all be destroyed. In typical army fashion, we had to sign our names about ten times. A fascinating day's work!

No other real news except that sick parades are getting bigger than ever – a lot of nervous-type problems are developing. You have to be psychiatrist/physician/surgeon/padre all rolled into one to be a good army doctor.

Last night I had to certify a man drunk – it would have been obvious to a half-wit but apparently I am the only one qualified to say whether someone is drunk or not for an army charge. The poor kid was all upset and told me he's only started to drink up here because the war worries him so much; he's been drunk every night except when on guard duty. Last night was the first time he'd got drunk on duty. It's all rather sad, as I think there are quite a few like him. I felt a heel having to say he was drunk as he'll get a fairly severe charge, but of course you can't have drunk pickets. I had a good long talk to him this morning when he was sober, but goodness knows if it was any help.

No new war news – 106 Battery got back OK from their little one-day op on Sunday, except that the Chinook dropped one of their precious guns from about six feet [1.8 metres] when taking off with it. That has caused much sadness in the regiment.

All my love to all at Penno,
David

Nui Dat
Tuesday 25/7/67

Dear Philip Pirrip,

Twelve weeks today since I arrived 'in country', so I am nearly half way to earning my second ribbon and a quarter way through my tour of duty – time goes pretty quickly.

I hope the History and Philosophy of Science exams went OK last Saturday and all those long hours of study paid dividends. Have you decided what you're going to do next year yet? Of course, I still haven't the foggiest notion what I'll be doing when I get back from here – one of the other CMF FTD doctors has already teed up a job somewhere, but I still don't know what I want to do. I guess a step at a time is the best policy. Anyway I have a great career in the army stretching before me if all else fails. My CO put in a confidential report to Army HQ about me (along with all the other officers of course). Apparently when a CO does a confidential report on one of his officers, it is the officer's privilege to read what he's written before it goes off to headquarters; in fact, you're obliged to initial it to show that you've seen it. The CO showed me it this afternoon and it's really pretty good – says all sorts of nice things about me. It's very like a school report – they comment on your neatness, conduct and interest in your work and all that sort of thing; the army is just like a sort of grown-up school.

No, I have not seen the PA girl again, she of the embarrassing latrine story. Vung Tau township is still officially out of bounds, so apart from going to army establishments like 8 Fd Amb, you can't see anyone else in Vung Tau at present. I guess the ban on the township and so on Le-Loi Hospital, which is right in town, will be lifted soon, so then I'll go visit the surgical team again. Until then, I'd better be good and not break any rules.

Did the Mighty Austin Lancer get through the petrol strike without running out on you? Sydney seems to be going mad with strikes since I left. As soon as I leave a place, it goes to rack and ruin.

Work hard; stick your nose to the grindstone; put your hand to the wheel; put your best foot forward etc! And with all this helpful advice I finish on a grand flourish from Shakespeare:

'To thine own self be true . . .

Thou canst not then be false to any man.' I forget the middle bit.

Remember me to all my old friends,

Your ever faithful brother,

Dave (Would you believe twenty-five-and-a-half years old – I don't sound like it, do I?)

Nui Dat

Thursday 27/7/67

Dear Mother ('my inspiration'),

How are you? You sound a bit down in the dumps in your last letter.

It is, as you say, three months since I left home – sorry it's going so slowly for you – in some ways it seems an absolute eternity to me and in other ways not long at all. Still, it's a quarter of the way through and I am still well, fit and happy. In fact I seem to be thriving on it. I feel pretty tired tonight but then this week is hygiene inspection time and I hate that! As you know I hate most of all upsetting people and telling them they're not doing things properly; the trouble is most of the cooks, for example, are flat-out, overworked, and do the best they can. Once a month I have to come around and point out all the things that ought to be fixed up, while I know full well they, poor things, are doing their best. It's awkward – I don't think I make a really good army officer – I'm just not firm enough and I guess I never will be. I'm always feeling sorry for people; it's hopeless trying to be firm and cross with someone when you're really on his side. As Sergeant Allen keeps telling me, 'you're too kind-hearted.' But the CO, in a report about me, said I would 'probably, in time, make an effective CO of a Field Ambulance'. So he can't think I'm too bad an officer.

I went out to the Horseshoe today in the road convoy and back this evening. It's a terribly dusty trip out in the convoy and you go through some typically dirty untidy villages with unkempt kids all over the place. It really can be a depressing country – all the adults have expressionless faces as if nothing more would be any surprise to them. The kids are bright and smile and wave at the vehicles, but the adults, mostly women, rarely look up. You wonder what hope there is for the poor country – the people themselves seem completely indifferent and not to care much who rules their land as long as they're left in peace. Of course, too, some of them are pretty shrewd business people and make as much as they can out of the Allies and probably out of the VC as well.

Thank you so much for all the goodies you sent up and thank Merrie for *Witch Wood*[1] which arrived tonight. Tell her I'll guard *Witch Wood* with my life – my other poor books didn't take too kindly to Op Paddington and now have thick layers of mould all over them. What a country! I'll keep *Witch Wood* in plastic – it's the only way to conserve anything here.

No more news on R&R in Australia yet I'm afraid.

Love,

David

[1] This is a little known book by John Buchan, the popular author of *The Thirty-nine Steps* and *Greenmantle*. All the family loved John Buchan's works but *Witch Wood* was definitely our favourite.

Nui Dat
Friday 28/7/67

Dear Sis and all interested nurses,

Only a very short note tonight as I want to get to bed early after a very frustrating day – I have been cross and cranky all day, which, as you know, is most unlike your kind, sweet, adorable, friendly bro' Dave. It is hygiene inspection time and to cap it all today, one-third of the HQ battery came down with vomiting and gastro so I have been doling out Stemetil and Kaomagma all day – it's most depressing and I haven't a clue what caused it. And, it's been unbearably hot and sticky, so I'm not real happy tonight. I will be right after a good night's sleep. At least I didn't get the 'wog' – fortunately.

Sorry for such a short letter.

Lots of love from your old brother,

Dave

PS Enclosed is my copy of the Conference Notes for yesterday[1] – Gunner Dickinson got hold of it and suitably embellished it before I got it though, as you can see – I didn't know my knees were so bad!

¹ The adjutant put out 'Conference Notes' each evening – a one-page sheet handwritten with news from the daily task force briefing – for each officer in the regiment, containing intelligence briefings and details of enemy contacts by patrols, etc. Gunner Dickinson must have been involved in the production of the roneoed copies on this occasion and had drawn a picture of my legs and knees on the back of my copy.

Nui Dat
Saturday 29/7/67

Dear Mr Personality,

How is my kid brother? Not impressed with big brother's kind thoughtful gift of an American helicopter pilot's uniform? Well – I can't say I blame you, but I thought you might at least find it interesting. I couldn't use it up here, so thought it might as well go home.

Thank you for your lucid exposition of Situational Ethics. They sound fairly 'old hat' to me. I am sure there is truth in the statement that what is wrong in one situation may not be wrong in another, e.g. like your own brother at a party on the Sabbath amongst a lot of beer swillers – something I would never dream of doing at home in Australia, but which is just part of daily life here at Nui Dat. But, of course I know that statement can be carried to an extreme. I do think that St Paul's statement that 'where the Spirit of the Lord is, there is liberty' is sometimes forgotten by us Evangelicals and we tend to become a bit legalistic. (I must stop this discussion or Dad will be getting worried and thinking I am getting off the 'straight and narrow').

I miss being able to talk things over – do you remember all our heated debates over the 'washing-up', with you, so intense and white about the gills, me raving in my usual fashion and Merrie putting an occasional 'spoke' in just to help the argument along? Well, I miss that – I cannot imagine discussing Situational Ethics in the officers' mess at all.

Now for Nui Dat ditties:

1. Me: need I tell you all my virtues again? Time is against me I fear.

2. Sergeant Allen: has prickly heat, poor boy, but the Bac-si is curing it for him with good old Whitfield's ointment and alcohol. He's

most unhappy at present too because the 2IC (Little Toot) has curtailed his TAB 'book-making' activities. The general feeling in the regiment is that this is not a good thing as a lot of betting is bound to go on anyway and it is better to have it out in the open and controlled by two trustworthy sergeants (e.g. Sergeant Allen and his buddy, Sergeant Murphy) rather than have it going on, on the sly, all over the place. But the 2IC has decided otherwise, so that's that – more situational ethics, you see. They are all around us up here.

3. Chuck: has recently invested in a camera but is finding it hard to find enough things to take photos of – I think there is some Scots blood in Chuck. He doesn't like wasting anything. He goes on R&R to Bangkok in about ten days, so already my irrepressible sergeant is giving him lectures on VD prevention – he takes it all well though. If there is one person in the regiment I won't have to worry about getting that particular disease on R&R, it's Chuck. (I hope you are not too shocked by all these doubtful stories I am telling you – if I didn't know my family was fairly unshockable, I wouldn't tell you all these things.)

4. Gunner Dickinson: I expect Merrie will show you the somewhat cruel picture of my legs on the back of the nightly Conference Notes that Gunner Dicko did the other day. He paid for his sins though by developing the gastric wog yesterday; he and twelve others from HQ battery. Then, into the bargain, he was nearly squashed by a rubber tree which fell down right on top of the tent he sleeps in with Gunner Thomas. Rubber trees get very brittle as they get older and a bit of wind will sometimes make them break and fall over. So poor old Dicko had a bad day yesterday.

5. Bombardier Banks: liked your 'kind regards' greeting on the back of your last envelope. He says 'his missus' will be coming into the shop 'for sure' now to say hello to Mum and Dad.

6. Jack the Quack: he is same as ever. He said he had to have a night off tonight so has gone to Vung Tau. His excuse is that the new Kiwi nursing sister at 8 Fd Amb (recent addition to the four Aussie sisters) hasn't had anyone take her out yet and show her the VT night life. She is fat and jolly and thirty-five-ish and Jack is fat and jolly and forty-five-ish and he has never seen VT's night life himself, so they should have a funny night. He is no saint, old Jack, although he goes religiously to Mass every Sunday. You can't help laughing at him and

liking him. He really has a heart of gold underneath his rough exterior. I am doing his calls for him tonight.

Anyway I had better stop waffling so I will say goodbye until next time. I hope you didn't get too bad a mark for the English essay.

From your old pal, buddy and friend to the last,

Davey Boy

Nui Dat
Sunday 30/7/67

Dear Dad,

You certainly sound pretty busy in the last few weeks judging from Mum's letters, what with stocktaking to finish, all the scripts you're getting now and all your meetings. Don't go overworking, Dad!

No real news at present. A lot of boys are going on their five-day R&R now – mostly to Hong Kong. They come back laden down with stuff they've bought there. There must be more electrical and electronic gear in this task force than anywhere in the whole of SE Asia. Everyone has their own radio, tape recorder, camera and movie projector. Of course, R&R brings the usual unpleasant medical problems as well, but fortunately our regiment is doing pretty well and we haven't got too much VD. Maybe it's because of our Routine Orders which state that anyone going on R&R must call at the RAP before leaving to pick up: 1) a printed instruction sheet by the RMO on how to avoid VD, 2) a packet of rubber contraceptives. Regardless of age or rank, everyone must go off with them in his pocket. It really is ironic, isn't it, that the son of that notorious chemist who refuses to sell those things has to issue them like lollies to the whole regiment? VD is an awful problem but it has its funny side. I hope you don't mind my telling you all this; but I decided I might as well tell the family all about 'my strange life', as Granddad Lloyd[1] calls it, as long as you don't go telling everyone else. I don't think that last bit of news would go too well in the church newsletter. At any rate, so far our policy is paying dividends, so I suppose the ends justify the means.

The only other piece of news is that I am getting a new batman. The Spanish blood of Gunner Fernandes proved too much for him. Yesterday he went and got very drunk and missed a parade so the battery sergeant major (BSM) told him he didn't deserve to have such a plush job as the doctor's batman. So poor old Gunner Fernandes goes back to being an ordinary gunner and I get another prospect. I don't hold out too much hope for him either, as he has only been here eight weeks and already has spent two weeks in the MCE (Military Corrective Establishment) at Vung Tau for some minor crime or other. Looks like I get all the criminals as batmen. That's the army!

Anyway, Dad, I might have more exciting news for you next time. Thank you for all your prayers.

Much love from your son,

David

---

¹ Granddad Lloyd was a wonderful man. After his retirement from being a watchmaker and jeweller in Katoomba, he moved to Caringbah and devoted his life to looking after his handicapped wife. Every Christmas during our childhood, he would take me and my siblings to see the Christmas pantomime at the Tivoli – quite a treat for children who had never been to the movies!

Reflections

My first military operation was Operation Paddington. I had to leave the relative safety of the task force area and endure six nights with the men of headquarter battery camped in a muddy bit of bushland. My recollections of the operation are that it was highly uncomfortable, it rained almost all the time, there was mud everywhere and everything seemed totally chaotic. All my belongings got wet and coated with mud as did all the medical supplies. There was a very definite feeling that the enemy was very close at hand. For the first time for me, it actually felt like I was taking part in a war and the reality dawned that this was no Boys' Brigade camp. It was an unpleasant experience overall and I think I successfully managed to downplay the impact it had on me in my letters home so as not to unduly worry my family.

Operation Paddington made me realise that being a doctor did not guarantee me special treatment. On military operations in the field I had to 'muck in' like everyone else and I was expected to be cool and competent enough to provide medical care wherever it was needed, whatever the circumstances. This was a good lesson for me and it has stood me in good stead over my years of practice. Learning to cope with just what you've got is never a bad thing. However it was not an enjoyable experience – I hated the general messiness of the operation and the feeling you were never quite in control of the situation and had no way of knowing what was going to happen next. The constant rain, the mud, the low cloud and the poor visibility combined to create an atmosphere of gloom and foreboding. I don't believe I was ever scared, but I did feel a great weight of responsibility weighing me down. I was aware all the time that people were depending on me and, as I had never been in a position like this before, I didn't know how well I would respond to some emergency event should it occur. This was my greatest worry and I never felt it to the same degree in subsequent ops – even during Operation Coburg at the height of the Tet Offensive. In fact when tested with the real-life incidents that transpired, as opposed to the imaginary ones playing around in my head, I think I managed as well as any other doctor would under the circumstances.

I was quite proud that I managed to cope. Fred Wittmer was an excellent hygiene sergeant but not as competent as Bob Allen as a medic, yet together we dealt effectively and efficiently with our casualties. The death of the Australian Army engineer killed by a falling tree on the first day was sobering and upsetting, especially as he was dead by the time I reached him. It was my first medical challenge in the field when I was called urgently to the other side of the camp to examine the engineer. All the way over as we bounced down the track in our Land Rover ambulance I was thinking what I should check first and what I mustn't forget to do. I was really distressed when I arrived and found him beyond my help. He must have died instantly the tree hit him. It was such a let-down after gearing myself up psychologically for a major resuscitative effort. I felt a tremendous sense of failure and genuine loss as though one of my closest friends had died suddenly and left me bereft.

I certainly got to know the headquarter battery men better and for the first time I really felt that I was accepted by them and that I belonged as a vital part of the regiment.

My July letters home are less serious and there are some funny stories – when I recall the visit of the Australian Surgical Team to the officers' mess for Sunday lunch, when only one female member showed up, I still blush at my youthful embarrassment and social ineptitude. And despite my rather scathing dismissal of the touring concert party as 'trashy', the deeply felt emotion of being part of a big crowd of Aussie soldiers on duty overseas, listening to performers from home, lives with me to this day. It's stating the obvious that the various performers who toured Vietnam on concert parties during the war were great morale boosters for the soldiers, but they really deserve far more praise than I was prepared to accord them in those long ago letters home.

Readers may be puzzled by the reference to *Witch Wood*. It tells the story of a young minister of the Scots Kirk during the time of the Covenant, whose first parish lies on the edge of a great wood in Scotland. Despite his preaching and his pastoral care of the parish he seems to make no headway and he gradually becomes aware that most of his parishioners, while professing great piety, are in fact devil worshippers and on high and 'holy' nights in the Satanic calendar they 'take to the wood' and participate in obscene rituals in its dark glades. Inevitably the young minister finds another side to the wood and espies and falls in love with a young woman there who, although a friend and supporter of Lord Montrose, an enemy of the Scottish Kirk, epitomises youth, innocence, beauty and all that is bright and fair in life. The book's theme is the triumph of life and love over the life-denying forces of dogma and cheerless religious observance. It says much for the underlying philosophy of my family that, with the possible exception of my father, who saw some cause for concern in the book's central theme, we wholeheartedly embraced its message.

After three months in Vietnam, my religious and spiritual perspectives were changing. My belief in a personal, caring and loving God, concerned and intimately involved in His creation, had not shifted at all. I now believed with passion and fervour that people mattered far more than things and that we are placed on this earth to love and serve our fellows, especially those less fortunate than ourselves, with all the strength and ability we can muster. Doubtless this was an extremely youthful and idealistic perception and, surrounded as I was by an all-male set of 'fellows', it was fuelled not a little by homoerotic desires and longings – I can see this clearly now, but it was not apparent to me then. I had become at the same time totally intolerant and highly critical of anything I deemed unreal and not consistent with the heart of the Christian message of unconditional love. Things many Evangelical Christians set importance on such as not drinking alcohol, not smoking, not swearing, not becoming over-friendly with worldly or non-Christian people, avoiding secular activities on Sunday and so on, now seemed to me to be a positive hindrance in our engagement with the non-Christian world. Even sexual 'sins' I now saw as being very minor in the overall scheme of things – compared to 'real' sins like hatred, unkindness, cruelty, intolerance, prejudice and being unfair or unjust in our dealings with other people. In effect I was becoming a wishy-washy liberal Christian! I suppose, to be fair to my youthful self, it was one way of coping with my background and with my new environment, which was harsher and less forgiving than any I had encountered before. Whenever I felt guilty about my new more radical way of thinking and how fellow Christians at home might view my lapses from orthodoxy, I could always console myself with the thought that 'it's OK for them – they're not living and working in a war zone'. It seemed to be working for me anyway, because by the end of July I was actually faring rather well emotionally and if I had been asked then if I thought I would complete my twelve-month stint in Vietnam successfully and without major mishap I would have replied unhesitatingly in the affirmative.

4

AUGUST 1967

Letters

[Letter to mother Tuesday 1/8/67 – first page missing; it continues:]
The last two days have been pretty hectic – needle parades are due again, which is an awful bother for us, so the whole regiment is going around with sore shoulders tonight.

2 Battalion had two soldiers killed yesterday and some casualties from booby traps – they were out on patrol on a short operation. One of our gunners had his fingers jammed in the breech block of a gun yesterday, but apart from that, things have been quite quiet.

No more news, I'm afraid, Mum.

Very much love to you and all the family.

David

PS: My new batman is not a bad kid at heart and might be a bit easier to manage than the Spanish bandit.

Nui Dat
Thursday 3/8/67

Dear Dad,

Thank you for your letter which arrived today, together with Mum's. You certainly must have been busy over the last few weeks, so if that happens again, don't worry about a weekly letter – just when you can manage it will be fine. I didn't mean to sound so critical of your letter writing efforts; my handwriting is if anything worse than yours lately.

I hope Mum has thrown off her cold by now and that the new shop girl is good. My new batman is very good anyway. His two weeks down in the military gaol have made him a model soldier. He cleans my boots much better than the last one. We even had him giving needles today at needle parade, much to the dismay of the battery sergeant major when he fronted up for his needle, as he was the person who charged him last time and got him his two weeks in gaol.

Sorry I have no real news tonight except that the CO has fixed up another Medcap for me soon. I am to carry on with Hoa Long once a week, but another day I'll go to another village which the CA people have decided, in their wisdom, will be the responsibility of 4 Fd Regt. There's nothing definite yet though. The CA people are muddlers, I'm afraid – a bit like 8 Fd Ambulance. It's funny how the army seems only able to run corps like armour, infantry and artillery efficiently, but anything like medicine and civil affairs always seems to get muddled up. I suppose armies are really only geared for fighting and get lost with anything else.

Much love, Dad, and thank you for your prayers. The CO seems pleased with me – he says there isn't a soldier in the regiment doesn't know me. That must mean I'm notorious!

Bye till next time – I hope, by the way, you get a nice presentation from the Pharmacy Guild – you deserve one.

David

PS: I was sorely tempted to write again to *The Baptist* last week to refute the pacifist anti-Vietnam views, but managed to overcome the urge.

Nui Dat
Saturday 5/8/67

My dear Mother,

I have just been listening to your tape. I don't think you people should make any more tapes – it sounds like you'll have nervous breakdowns if you do – the strain is so obvious. Just tell me simple things or tape an evening meal conversation – just hearing your voices is enough.[1]

I hope all your colds are better now. We have had a few up here – mostly brought back from R&R in Hong Kong and then they do the rounds of a battery. I saw my first malaria today, or at least I think it was, in a soldier – one of the 'tankies' i.e. boys from the Cavalry Regiment (or 'Calvary Regiment', as Margaret Wood on Radio Australia[2] always irritates me by calling them).

Today I had an opportunity to talk with one of our bombardiers who had the usual old disease after R&R in Hong Kong. The poor boy is married and a Catholic into the bargain, and the old story – he got drunk and 'didn't know what he was doing' – and now of course he's so guilty and upset about it. I told him I could arrange for him to see the Catholic padre if he would like, but he didn't think he wanted that, so I just told him I was a Christian, although not a Catholic, and that, after all, we believe in a God who understands our frailties and can forgive our sins. I don't know if it helped much, as he was quite 'cut up' about it all.

The Baptist as usual has made me boil. A report of some Baptist 'bigwig's' visit to Sth Vietnam prompted an editorial on the Vietnam War, running down Australia's participation, as usual. They especially stress the bigwig's statement that the Vietnamese 'are greatly offended by the behaviour of some Americans who ride roughshod over their customs and lead the way in blatant immorality'. What a load of rubbish! As if the Vietnamese are poor innocents being led astray by the wicked Americans. In actual fact the Vietnamese don't need any 'leading astray'. Prostitution is a completely acceptable part of their way of life and it is nothing unusual to see an old Vietnamese woman quite openly offering her daughters 'for sale' and little brothers are always offering their sisters as 'number one girls' in all the village streets. I agree this is because they are so poor and literally any little money helps, and to make ends meet they use their every 'asset', but this is no real fault of the Allies. The most well paid job in all Vietnam for a girl is to be a bar girl and you can guess what that means. Actually, far from being 'poor innocents' it seems to me a lot of Vietnamese are exceedingly crafty. They make all the money they can out of Allied soldiers, pay lip service to the SVN government, get all the help they can out of Civil Affairs projects and send their sons to fight for the VC! I make no excuse for Allied soldiers – they ought to know better, but then again they are in a strange smelly land, far from home, fighting a war that isn't a war, and on every hand there are opportunities for 'blatant immorality'. Sorry for this tirade but I wish some of the 'know-alls' would join up and come over here as private soldiers and see how they would like it for twelve months. I don't really think the Vietnamese are as awful as I make out either – but they are no more 'innocent' than we are.

Well, all my love, mother mine,

David

1   The exchange of tapes was good in theory but didn't work out too well in practice. The tapes took time to prepare and inevitably sounded staged and unreal. The only advantage was actually hearing familiar voices.

2   Everyone in the task force area had a battery-powered multi-band radio receiver, purchased at the army PX store. Radio Australia, the BBC Foreign Service, Radio America and numerous other radio stations were available on short-wave. Reception was usually good as most radios available to soldiers were state of the art. I don't recall seeing television in SVN – perhaps there was a television station in Saigon but I never saw a TV program during my twelve months in the country. There was an American forces newspaper, *Stars and Stripes*, which we saw occasionally. Copies of Australian newspapers, two or three weeks old, were available in the officers' mess.

Nui Dat
Monday 7/8/67

Dear family,

Quite a hectic two days since I last wrote to you – Sunday started very quietly, in fact the smallest sick parade I think I've ever had; but 7 RAR went out on Operation Ballarat on Sunday supported by Chuck's battery (106) which also moved about 5 miles [8 kilometres] north of Nui Dat and set up a fire support base. I went to chapel as usual and all was well until lunchtime when all our guns back here, including the big American guns, started firing and gradually reports filtered through that one of 7 RAR's companies had had contact with a large enemy force[1] – they tried to disengage and draw back so that they could call down artillery fire effectively on the enemy, but the VC would not break contact. We were placed on two-hour notice to move and the Kiwi battery were moved out practically straight away to give more fire support with their six guns. This meant a mad panic – all our RAP gear had to be assembled, ready to leave in two hours if necessary, so I was busy organising that – then we heard that 7 RAR had quite a few casualties but the situation was such that the 'dust-off' choppers couldn't safely land to pick them up. The poor company couldn't withdraw from the VC, apparently – the VC just followed them every time they tried to move away, which is quite unusual tactics for them – the VC usually 'nick off' pretty quickly. After about an hour and a half, the choppers at last got in and picked up the first wounded. Five were killed in action straight away, but there were many more wounded – some were taken to Vung Tau direct while eight, all told, were brought in to the Forward Detachment here. I went up as soon as possible to help Jack, who was 'flat out'. One of the medics who went out in the chopper to help pick up the wounded had a bullet (only superficial) wound across the scalp and an RAAF pilot got injured in the foot and the 'dust-off' chopper had bullet-holes all through it. Well – at least eight holes! The two patients I saw were really bad – we put drips up on them but the one I was looking after died almost as soon as he reached Vung Tau, making the total six killed in action. It was a pretty awful mess – they should have gone straight to VT, but the chopper pilots were so intent on getting them out they thought it was quicker to drop them here at Nui Dat where there is some form of resuscitation equipment, and go back for more. In all, fifteen were wounded plus the two in the chopper mentioned above.[2]

A pretty black Sunday all around; I guess you have read it all in the papers by now, and a pretty garbled account it'll be too. After two and a half hours the fight was over and the enemy drew off – it was decided then (fortunately) that we in HQ battery wouldn't have to go out as there were good radio communications between our command post here and the two fire support bases (106 and the Kiwis). So the op is going on – there is a feeling that at last we may be on to something big. A pretty big price we paid yesterday, though. Just as well I don't have to talk to any of those 'pills' back home, like Alan Walker, the Editor of *The Australian Baptist* and Ian's cousin and her Melbourne

Uni friends, in my present warlike state – it's a great encouragement to the troops up here to know there are such helpful 'encouragers' as those people back home.

Then today I went out with Major Fox, the doctor from the Civil Affairs (CA) Unit – the mad enthusiast, to Ngaio Giao ('Ni Jow'), a cluster of villages north of Nui Dat which are provisionally 4 Field Regiment's responsibility. We left here at 8 am in two Civil Affairs vehicles with about seven medics and two interpreters. Because of this I had to miss sick parade, but the CO decided I should go because Ngaio Giao is our responsibility. The CA people don't worry too much about little things like security precautions. We just went along the north road with our weapons (normally people go with APC escorts) and into the bargain the Land Rover I was in had no brakes to speak of and very little oil, so you can imagine I felt quite at home – reminded me of Dad's Mayflower[3] in her latter years. Still, we arrived safely.

We split up on arrival at our destination – I did the Medcap at an ARVN (Army of the Republic of Vietnam) compound, i.e. SVN soldiers, where they and their families live, just like the one at Hoa Long and just as clean and tidy. This was at Duc Thanh ('Dook Tane'), which is the centre around which all the little hamlets which make up Ngaio Giao cluster. That took all morning – about eighty patients. Then after lunch we split again and I and half the medics did a Medcap at one of the small villages called Moa. The people are incredibly primitive and poor but it was quite an interesting day. The major has it all quite well organised; the doctor sits at a table and sees the patients and writes the treatment on a card (e.g. half a cc of penicillin; Antepar syrup etc.) and the medics then give the treatment from their little medicine chests. It was terrifically hot and I got quite sunburnt. I was glad to get back to good old Nui Dat for a shower, I must confess.

Bed calls now – I have just been called to patch up a broken finger – the dopey soldier was evacuated from the Horseshoe with it this afternoon but instead of seeing me then, thought it would be OK and tried to take the pain away with alcohol. I have just given him a shot of pethidine and he has rolled off to bed a very groggy soldier. But at least his pain is fixed temporarily.

Much love to you all and thank you for your thoughts and prayers,
David

[1]   This fierce battle became known as the battle of Suoi Chau Pha; my
      'unedited' recollections appear in the Reflections at the end of this
      chapter.

[2]   The fact that I described this situation in such detail indicates the impact
      it had on me; I was unable to conceal it from my family, despite my usual
      inclination to protect them from the realities of this war.

[3]   The Mayflower was described by the unkind as a butterbox on wheels
      but my mother thought it looked 'very English'. It was the first family car
      and Dad bought it brand new in 1952 and used it until at least 1963. It
      was made by the Standard Car Company and its fellow, and much more
      popular, small car was the Vanguard.

Nui Dat

Wednesday 9/8/67

Dear Mum,

A little letter for all of you. Thank you so much for all your bits on the
tape including, 'Oh! What will I say?' I think you all need something
to give you Dutch courage when making a tape – you sound as if the
tape recorder will bite you. I think you should play some more
Tchaikovsky on the piano next time, or if you get stuck, tape me some
of the latest World Record Club album[1] which Merrie says recently
arrived.

Do look after yourself and don't fret! I am quite OK over here.
In fact, I feel extra strong and well although I was a bit tired on
Monday after all the excitement on Sunday. On Monday night there
was a big panic because they thought someone was cutting the
barbed wire outside 2 Battalion on the other side of the TFA. We
all had to get out of bed and 'stand to'. It was a lot of nonsense
of course. I went to the command post with my little 'black' haversack but nothing was happening. It just disturbed all our nights'
sleep.

This morning a poor boy shot himself while cleaning his weapon.
It was really his own fault, as even I know you don't clean your weapon
with a full magazine loaded, but it's very sad following straight after
the other casualties on Sunday. He wasn't a 4 Fd Regt boy but was
geographically close to us – just across the road, in fact. It was just
one of those very sad accidents.

I am flying out to the Horseshoe by chopper tomorrow morning for more needles for 108 Battery. Great fun!

Much love, dear Mum,

David

[1] The World Record Club provided a range of classical and light classical records for its members. They were excellent recordings with good artists and orchestras and were substantially cheaper than records for sale in retail stores. Each month one or two new records became available. A prospectus for the coming six months came out regularly, whereby you could decide what you wanted and could afford. I first heard most well known classical music pieces courtesy of the World Record Club – Beethoven's symphonies, Bach's 'St Matthew Passion', Mozart's Jupiter symphony, and many more.

Nui Dat
Wednesday 9/8/67

Dear Uncle Phil,

It's a long time since I wrote to the future garbologist brother of mine. I have no excuse except the pressure of work, worries of the regiment, war neurosis, shell shock, trench feet, cerebral malaria and general psychiatric deficiency. Here at last is a letter all for you.

You are an absolute failure as a tape recordist. However you are not alone – all at 75 Castle Hill Road are pathetic at it – even Kay Patterson. Ian is best, with Dad second best, but you would all miss out on a prize for Proficiency in Tape Recording Stage I. Still it was nice to hear your voices.

I agree you *should* do honours. By the way, what do you mean, 'I'm not really suited for ordinary school teaching'? I suppose you mean 'I am suited for *extra*ordinary school teaching'.

Now for some regimental news:

The CO: has got over all his little illnesses and is his usual genial self. He brought a tape down to play in the mess the other night which he said was to 'educate' me. It proved to be quite awful and I must have looked rather disapproving as he got all embarrassed and said he wished he hadn't played it. I certainly wished he hadn't either. They were called 'Rugby Songs', so if ever anyone wants to play them to you, find an excuse to escape. He said it came off a record he bought. I didn't know they made such records. Officers are funny people – they seem to enjoy sixth class primary school humour sometimes. I can't understand it at all!

The 2IC: no better, I fear.

The adjutant: he's on R&C in Vung Tau which is very much deserved as he is a real hard worker and a very nice bloke.

Sergeant Allen: still getting over his prickly heat, but otherwise his old euphoric self.

Chuck Berry: out on operation at the fire support base, code named 'FSB Giraffe'. They are in support of 7 RAR. I went out by road to visit them yesterday. The poor things are tired out – they fired some fantastic number of rounds of ammo on Sunday in support of the company being attacked. When necessary, Chuck of course pitches in and works as well as any gunner on the guns, even being unofficially attached to one gun crew – Delta gun. He had great delight in having to give one of the gunners a penicillin injection for an ear infection when I went out to see this bloke's ear. It caused the rest of the battery great delight too and they all flocked around and took photos of the poor fella getting a needle in his behind. Soldiers are awful – they have no modesty at all. Anyway Chuck is as well and cheerful as ever.

Gunner Scroope: my new batman – very likeable, with a really innocent baby face, which quite belies him. He comes from Ballina in northern NSW and his father owns a big sugar cane farm there. He is a good drinker, somewhat reformed since his little stay in the gaol at Vung Tau, but can apparently 'sink' eighteen cans of beer without turning a hair. If he is to be believed, everyone in Ballina can do the same. He works well though and seems to enjoy being an 'almost' medic.

Gunner Lemm: at nineteen years of age, the youngest gunner in HQ battery. He was itching to get out on operation last Sunday. His very words (after it was decided that HQ battery wouldn't move) were, 'We should 'ave went, sir – we should 'ave went. We should 'ave got those f——s'.

Lance bombardier Banks: counting the days to RTA (return to Australia), Castle Hill and his 'missus'. At least he will be a good customer for Dad in the future, I'm sure. He tells me (with a knowing wink): 'Ford is losing all his customers – he's too impersonal and takes it easy too much – a lot of people are browned off Ford.'

Gunner Avery: a new addition to Nui Dat news and is one of Chuck's gunners who comes over to the RAP quite often (for nothing very much). He has a slow drawl, an incredibly sad expression and never does his hair. He is a nice boy and not at all sad really. He is a 'nasho' from WA, an only child, but 'I'm not a bit spoiled – you should meet my folks', he says.

Well, no room left – I'd better finish,
From,
Unca Dave

Nui Dat
Friday 11/8/67

My dear old Mother,
It's been just a usual day today except I got into a fight with the most unpleasant officer in charge of the Cav Regt squadron. He had been badgering the Cav Regt medic to give him the names of blokes with VD and the medic very rightly refused. So I rang him up and told him it was against DGMS (the Director General of Medical Services) policy to give out names to COs and I wouldn't on any account allow the medic to do so. He hit the roof! Told me I was trying to usurp his authority and that the rule was only made for 'idiot' COs. I nearly said, 'Well?' but fortunately remained my usual tactful self. I am getting better at handling difficult army types lately. I am beginning to realise that an army doctor has quite a bit of authority in the system, which I am only picking up bit by bit. The Cav Regt OC says he is going to 'take the matter further', but he won't get far. He can't gainsay the major general's direction, fortunately.

Then this afternoon I went on convoy out to Chuck's battery (which is undoubtedly my favourite battery although they are always in trouble – 'not enough discipline' people say, but at least they are a happy battery). The mud is if anything worse out there. I had no sooner started going around the gun positions with Chuck than it commenced absolutely pouring with rain. They are a most indecent battery too, because, not having had any showers, a downpour is a good opportunity for a clean up. Wherever you looked there were naked bodies in the rain soaping themselves. Then in the middle of the pouring rain they had a fire mission – it was the funniest sight – like a nudist colony manning the guns in the rain. The only thing anyone had on were their ear muffs for hearing protection. I took some photos which the Kodak labs may refuse to print as being too pornographic. I was completely soaked too but it soon dried off when the sun came out. I think Chuck and I were the only ones with our clothes on!

When I got back I found that my ever-ready-to-tease staff had stuck up *Playboy* pictures all over my office walls[1] and when I got back to my tent, pinned on my mosquito net (on the top leering down at me) was one of the worst 'rude nudes' I have ever seen – I have enclosed her for you in this letter but you had better not let Pip see her.[2] Sergeant Allen is quite incorrigible but it's no use getting upset about it. I must admit it was rather funny.

Much love,
Dave

[1] The teasing was related to my apparent unworldliness more than anything else, and to the Australian soldier's love of provoking fellows and superiors. I don't think it was because they suspected I was gay – Bob Allen might well have had suspicions about me, as he was very shrewd and missed nothing; but if he had such thoughts I'm fairly certain he kept them to himself.

[2] I cannot imagine why I would send a female nude photograph to my mother, of all people. By today's standards it was probably fairly soft-core porn but it still seems odd and potentially upsetting for her.

Nui Dat
Sunday 13/8/67

Dear family,
Just a short note this morning enclosing this glorious photo of me returning from the shower one afternoon. Ian Yerbury, one of the other officers, took it. What a torso! 'Like a horso, only more so'. Do you like the background view of the latrine and urinal? Pretty delightful scenery, isn't it? I thought you might like the photo.

I have just got back from chapel. I didn't write last night as I went to the movies instead. It was a really funny film called *The Russians Are Coming*. It's all about a Russian submarine which accidentally gets grounded on the beach of a little remote American fishing village. There's resultant panic as the people think the Russians are invading. We all enjoyed it. I went with one of the other officers and Don Harris, new American liaison officer from the American artillery battalion, who is a nice chap.

All being well I am hoping to have a restful afternoon (not like last Sunday afternoon). There is a cricket match on today (sergeants vs gunners) which would be interesting to watch, but I think I might just sleep.

Anyway, much love to you all.

Will write again soon,

David

Nui Dat
Monday 14/8/67

Dear family,

Just to thank you so much for your tape which I enjoyed immensely. The biscuits[1] arrived too and were demolished at lunch time today at our Medcap at Ngaio Giao. Anh, the Vietnamese interpreter, who is a Buddhist with a bright sunny face, and always full of fun said they were 'Uc-Dai-Loi biscuits – Number 1'.

Last night I had five letters and the tape. I will never catch up writing back to everyone. I didn't get a chance to read any of them until about 11 pm as one of the gunners in 108 Battery chose last night to put a bullet through his big toe, which of course is a classical way of getting an SIW (self-inflicted wound). There was the usual panic; some officers have no common sense: 'Come quickly, doc – one of our men is suicidal!' – which he wasn't; just a bit drunk. Also angry that he had lost two stripes only the day before for some reasonably major crime and shooting his big toe was his way of attracting attention to himself. There was much kerfuffle and I eventually took him up to 8 Fd Amb and Jack and I straightened him out a bit. Afterwards I had to go and report to the CO. All very involved and full of military legal implications, which of course box me up. The toe wasn't much hurt by the way, but I expect there will be all sorts of nasty charges resulting for the poor bloke. SIWs are pretty serious military offences if they can be proved, which they generally can't be.

I've had an exhausting day at Ngaio Giao and saw 100 patients – all smelly, unwashed and demanding. But it's good fun really and I do like the little kids. I wish there was more you could do to help them rather than just a few pills which won't go far in fixing their problems. We won't be going next Monday but will change the day next week in case any suspicious VC try to set a trap for the Medcap team. I am sure this is only a theoretical security measure.[2]

106 Battery are still out on Op Ballarat supporting the 7 RAR infantry. It should finish in a day or so. I will go and visit them tomorrow afternoon to see they are OK. They presented me with a special badge the other day, as I am their doctor, which I am very proud of and have sewn to my cap. It's a green tortoise carrying a big shell on a red/blue (artillery colours) background and nicely embroidered. They chose the tortoise as their mascot ('slow but sure'). The other battery (108) are much faster at firing their guns than 106, but 106 claim they are more sure. So I am proudly wearing a tortoise on my cap – the only non-106 battery officer to do so except the CO who has a little metal badge with the tortoise on it.

I am well and safe, so don't fret. Things seem to have settled down to relative normality again for a time. Pip, please tell that friend of yours I haven't found the few American soldiers I've met at all arrogant. On the contrary, they kill you with kindness. The American artillery battery (A Battery of the 2nd 35th Battalion[3]) here at Nui Dat love Aussies. They have a photo of the Queen and Prince Philip in their officers' club and plaques of all the Australian regiments on the wall. LBJ doesn't get a look in. In fact when their general came to visit them last year he was most upset because all the gunners were wearing Aussie bush hats instead of the horrible regulation Yankee peak cap. Since his visit, they don't do that anymore.

I may be biased (in fact I'm sure to be at the moment) but all the nasty things said about the Americans and their handling of the war over here are not true. They are hopelessly idealistic and sentimental, but they do seriously want to help the South Vietnamese overcome the communists and get on their feet as a nation.

Our soldiers' morale is pretty good on the whole. No one is wildly enthusiastic about the war; everyone hates Vietnam and wonders why on earth anyone should want to fight for it, but they are resigned to being here and most want to help if they can and make a reasonable job of it. I am surprised how many want to come on Medcaps with me, to help me treat the locals, not just to get out of normal routine work. I don't really think the war is hopeless. I have met some keen and intelligent South Vietnamese soldiers who really want to make SVN a safe and peaceful nation free from communist aggression. They are not all indifferent by any means.

Much love,
David

---

[1] The biscuits were probably 'coffee creams', one of my mother's specialties.

[2] Anywhere outside the task force area involved some element of risk, but in fact, in hindsight, Australian Medcap teams were never attacked. We didn't know that for sure in 1967!

[3] There were two co-located American artillery units at Nui Dat – A Battery 2/35 Battalion, with six 155 mm self-propelled guns, and 1/83 Company, US Artillery, with two 8-inch self-propelled guns and two 175 mm self-propelled guns.

Nui Dat
Thursday 17/8/67

Dear family,
I must apologise for not having written for the past two days, but I was too tired last night. I think I owe you all letters and a tape too now, but that will have to wait until Sunday.

I have thoroughly enjoyed playing the third tape. It is very good. Uncle Bill does sound aldermanly. Everyone comes over very well and, Mum, you are much better on this tape. I knew the best actress on the Blue Mountains (circa 1939)[1] would not let a little thing like a tape recorder beat her for long. I do think letters are much better in the long run though. Six o'clock in the mess when the mail arrives is still the most exciting time of the day for everyone. The CO gets his mail up at the Task Force HQ but he nearly always has tea with us at the regiment, which means he doesn't get his mail until later. He looks at the pile on the table and says, 'Who do I hate tonight?' meaning the person who scores the most letters – (that is usually me)!

Thank you for your letter which arrived tonight, Mum, with more of your nice home-spun Christian philosophy.[2] What a shame more people don't have mothers with your wisdom (like Monash University students, for example). As you can imagine they are 'hung, drawn and quartered' in every mess in Nui Dat from the brigadier's task force mess down to the gunners' mess (or as it is known in army slang 'the Snake Pit'). You wonder if any would change their minds if they saw the casualties we had ten days ago.

I guess wedding preparations are really getting under way, with Ken and Jennie's[3] wedding next week; you must be getting into 'the Wedding Spirit'. It seems very unlikely though that R&R in Australia will be possible for me. Only about one person each month will be eligible from each battery and I would feel badly standing in the way of a married bloke going home. There's always a chance, but not a big one. The CO is unhappy about officers going home too, as they will be away at least eight days from Nui Dat (allowing for travelling time), which he thinks is too long. It's all up in the air at the moment and seems to be creating many headaches deciding who can actually go.

Nothing else to report,

Much love to all,

Davo

[1] My mother enjoyed taking part in an amateur dramatic group in Katoomba from the age of fifteen until she married seven years later. She did have quite a flair for it and successfully directed several plays staged by the church youth group at the Baptist church in Seaforth when we lived there (prior to moving to Pennant Hills).

[2] My mother's home-spun philosophy would have been along the lines of the need to fight to defend a Christian way of life against the forces of Godless communism.

3   Ken Hawley was the son of a previous minister of Pennant Hills Baptist Church and was a friend of mine prior to my joining the army. He married Jennie, another minister's daughter, and later he became a Baptist minister himself.

Nui Dat
Saturday 19/8/67

My very dear mother,

How are you and all your famous family?

How did your day off in town go? Did the transport strike eventuate and hold you up? You have had endless strikes in Sydney. As you say, the 'commos' seem to be arousing trouble everywhere at present – Monash Uni students, strikes, riots in Hong Kong, civil unrest in the USA.

No real news from Nui Dat at the moment – there are no new operations involving the regiment just now. Chuck is going on R&R to Bangkok next week; his last one was cancelled at the last minute because of the op and he couldn't be spared. My R&R request for the first week in November has gone in now with my first preference Uc-Dai-Loi (Number 1) Australia and second preference Taipei, so I will just have to wait and see what happens. You never know your luck in a big city.

Merrie's time at Hornsby Hospital must be drawing to a close? Next Tuesday I will have been here sixteen weeks – in fact, in six weeks our first lot of 'nashos' from 4 Fd Regt will be going home for discharge from the army (their two years completed) and this will go on right up until the time the regiment itself is replaced. Of course, we will get replacements in due course for the 'nashos'.

All my love,

David

Nui Dat
Monday 21/8/67

Dear family,

Thank you for forwarding up the black and white photos I took.[1]
The Vietnamese lady in white is the midwife at Hoa Long dispensary
and the little boy next to her had quite bad burns on both hands. He
caused quite a stir by fainting when we were dressing them. The two
blokes wrestling together are Mick, the dentist's driver, and Sergeant
Anh, our usual Vietnamese interpreter, outside the dispensary block
at Hoa Long. Notice how tiny Vietnamese men are – very slender
limbs and small bones. No wonder they can glide through the jungle
and no one sees them.

It was quite an eventful day at Ngaio Giao today. This morning
while I was at the Duc Thanh Vietnamese Army compound
they brought an old chappie in from the village outside with gun
shot and shrapnel wounds. It apparently happened last night at a
more distant village. It was impossible to know if he was friend or
foe, but we patched him up as best we could. I put a drip up on
him and we got a 'dust-off' helicopter out by radio to fly him to
the Vietnamese hospital at Baria. He was amazing. He had some
pretty bad wounds and must have lost a lot of blood but was still
reasonably conscious and not groaning or moaning at all. It is
astonishing how much pain the local people can stand without
complaining.

A little parcel from the RSL arrived for each soldier today –
two cans of beer, two small packets of tea and coffee, a tin of
Johnson and Johnson's baby powder, a carton of cigarettes, a tin of
apricots and Nestlé's cream, a writing pad and envelopes and some
boot polish. I will be having a gay time, won't I? I have already
given the cigarettes away but will probably keep the beer for a
rainy day!

. . . I was just called away to see a soldier from HQ battery who
'cracked up' and started shooting his weapon indiscriminately
around the place (luckily, no one hurt). The 2IC and I had to disarm
him. This poses a problem. Tomorrow I have to decide if he is
psychiatric and ought to be medevac-ed as such, or whether he

should be charged and sent to detention for forty-eight hours at Vung Tau.[2] I think you need the wisdom of Solomon to be an army MO.

Anyway, much love to you all and sorry I haven't had time to do a tape yet.

David

[1]   I always sent my black and white film home for my father to get processed through his pharmacy. Slide film, however, went direct to Kodak in a provided post packet as the cost of developing and mounting the transparencies was included in the price of the film.

[2]   Although I argued that the soldier was suffering a psychiatric breakdown, it was deemed important 'for good military discipline' that he be charged and court-martialled. He duly was court-martialled, but ultimately he was medevac-ed home for discharge from the army, as described in a September letter.

Nui Dat
Thursday 24/8/67

Dear family,

I couldn't write last night as there was one of those Nui Dat 'panic nights'. Someone in Intelligence had it 'on good authority' that we were going to be attacked last night. There was much excitement and typical military nonsense. Everyone spent half the night in their weapon pits and it was such a lovely moonlit night. You could see everything nearly as bright as day – the VC would have had to be halfwits to attack. Of course, nothing came of it. I believe it's on again tonight so I prepare for another uncomfortable time. Have you ever tried sleeping with your boots on in case you have to get up in a hurry? It's not recommended!

I've got a trip with the CO tomorrow to Saigon, which should be quite fun. I'm a witness in a big trial. Gunner Curd vs half the Vietnamese in Saigon. Gunner Curd is an engaging character from 106 battery who tried to go on R&R but was robbed by a bar girl, who stole his wallet. Gunner Curd, being a good Aussie soldier, did not take this lying down and proceeded to wreck the offending bar, pretty effectively by all accounts. He suffered a cut lip when some person hit him with a stick and I have to testify that his lip was in fact cut as he said. It should be quite a funny court. The CO is hearing the case actually in the bar. I fear he will be all on Gunner Curd's side.

No more time if I'm to catch the mail today.

All my love to you all,

David

Nui Dat
Saturday 26/8/67

Dear old sis,

Well, how is Ken Hawley's wedding going? I expect you are all there right this moment and Dad is probably in one of his wedding misbehaving moods.[1] I feel quite envious that I am not there.

I made another tape for you all yesterday in which I told you about my exciting trip to Saigon and the scary helicopter flight home at dusk. My task at the actual court case was very arduous. I had to testify in the trial and say I examined the accused and found he had a cut lip consistent with an injury sustained as he described. I carried it off with a flourish. I had to swear an oath on the Bible to 'tell the truth, the whole truth and nothing but the truth' in time-honoured fashion. Gunner Curd was found guilty by the CO of a fairly minor charge and was given twenty-eight days 'field punishment'. The CO and I then had an excellent lunch at the Rex Hotel (the famous senior officers' quarters in downtown Saigon).

How are you? Still got black circles, nervous rash, dyspepsia, tummy aches, restless legs? Uncle Ross tells me in his latest letter that you and your bridesmaids had caused your dressmaker to go demented – I can well believe it. How about the venetian blinds in the church? Any brain waves yet? Have you got your exam results back?[2]

No time for more tonight.

Much love from your old brother,

Dave

[1] When my dad was comfortable with people – those who were like-
   minded in their Christian faith – he would relax some of his shyness and

reserve and become witty and funny. This often happened at Christian weddings. He would make jokes, make funny speeches and even at times, if it was someone he really liked who was getting married, he would compose several verses about them which were very apt and extremely amusing. Mum used to complain that he got out of control at weddings.

2   These were my sister's final midwifery exams at Hornsby Hospital.

Nui Dat
Sunday 27/8/67

My dearest old Mother mine,

Just a very few lines before I go to bed to say I am well, strong and happy. How are you all? The mail has been most erratic this week what with your mail strike, our poor weather and general mix-ups with mail planes this end. Still, I expect I will get an extra big heap in a day or so.

Today has been a quiet restful day. I spent the afternoon being a good soldier, cleaning my weapons (which is supposed to be done every day, but which I do about once a month) and darning my socks. Then this evening Jack had to go urgently to Long Binh (a US base) by chopper about something or other and so I am taking his calls again. We had a fever brought in from 7 RAR but observations, a few aspirin and a cool fan are all he needs tonight. I spent about two hours just talking with one of the medics up there – an angry young 'nasho' (he doesn't really appreciate the army), who rejoices in the nickname 'PJ'. What 'PJ' stands for I don't know. They may even be his initials but that seems too easy an explanation. He is a good kid.

Went to chapel this morning – only three of us there today, but I had a long talk afterwards to one of our bombardiers who goes to church (he is a Presbyterian). He is contemplating marrying a Catholic girl. I just listened and said 'um' and 'ah' very wisely – I am getting good at that. I don't know if it helped at all.

We had a nice lunch today in the mess with some of the gun battery officers there because it was Sunday. I drove Peter Harnwell home to the American 1/83rd afterwards and saw Tom Sullivan the doctor there. I had a Coca-Cola with him and some of his fellow officers. Many of them are soon to return to the States.

Time for bed.

Much love,

Davo

PS: I am listening to classical music over the Armed Forces Radio Station – very good.

Nui Dat

Monday 28/8/67

Dear Dad,

Just a short note, as I haven't written to you for so long.

More excitement! Did I tell you about the HQ battery gunner last week who got a bit drunk and depressed and fired a few shots around the place, fortunately not hurting himself or anyone else? I have to appear as a witness for his defence in a court-martial at Vung Tau next Wednesday. I am getting very legally involved one way or another recently. Some of the gunners really get themselves into problems, mostly from drinking too much. They are just like kids – I feel quite sorry for Brian Mitchell, our poor long-suffering adjutant – every week there is some gunner or other in the regiment who does something wrong. Like two tonight; they went on the swimming trip to Vung Tau today (a weekly Monday 'treat' for a carload, supervised by an officer) and these two didn't come back, for some reason. They 'got lost' on the beach after drinking a fair bit and turned up at 8 Field Ambulance tonight acting strangely. The Military Police think someone must have drugged them. So 'Mitch' has to organise yet another endless army investigation. This sort of thing is always happening and the swimming trips are sure to be stopped for a while now – it is hard on the rest of the law-abiding blokes, for they get little enough time out of Nui Dat as it is. So many of the soldiers are awfully likeable, good fun and fine characters in many ways but they seem to lack an 'anchor'. It is nearly always the HQ battery boys who get into most trouble, too – 'base camp neurosis', the other task force area doctors call it. They aren't actually doing anything conclusive – just manning radio sets and phones, filling sand bags, tidying up the area and other soul destroying things like that; whereas the boys from the gun batteries at least have their guns to fire and maintain all the time. They have more purpose, I suppose.

Enough philosophising!

Much love, Dad,

David

Reflections

Sections of my letter of Saturday 5/8/67 deal with issues of morality and prostitution during the Vietnam War. The letter is an important one for me because it contains the crux of what I believe today about STIs, prostitution and sexual morality in general. My anger at the visiting Baptist bigwig's report and his views on 'blatant immorality' in Vietnam show how far out of kilter with orthodox Christian belief I had strayed.

Firstly, my attitude to STIs – I actually believed then (even though I did not voice it in my letters), as I believe now, that STIs are *not* a punishment for sexual indiscretions – they are merely a subset of infectious diseases which are spread in one particular way, i.e. by sexual contact of one sort or another. As such they are morally neutral, and people with STIs or at risk of STIs should be medically treated according to the same principles as people with cholera, influenza, typhoid or bird flu. There are sensible measures that can be taken to prevent the spread of most STIs and people have a right to know what these measures are, preferably *before* they begin to be sexually active. Public health authorities have a responsibility to ensure that good preventive education happens and they have neither a mandate to lecture consenting adults about their sexual behaviour nor an obligation to be advocates for the 'moral majority'.

Second, as to prostitution – back in 1967 I was slowly edging towards the conclusions I have now held for a couple of decades – that prostitution has existed since time immemorial and having survived countless savage attempts to suppress it through the ages, will continue to exist, simply because it fulfils a vital need. Attempts to eradicate it through Draconian laws have not worked and never will. It is an area of life where the law should bow out, with the sole exception of ensuring that exploitation of under-aged and marginalised or helpless individuals does not occur. Many people, both women and men, who work in the sex industry provide an invaluable service both in peace time and in war – some of my best and most memorable patients have been sex workers and I have learned a great deal from them. Of course, it is totally unacceptable that young women, or young men for that matter, are constrained to resort to prostitution because of extreme poverty or social dislocation, as was the case in SVN during the war. In an ideal society, options should be available for sex workers to leave the industry to take up other work should they wish to do so. It has to be said, though, that some people actually enjoy the work during some period of their lives, that they are good at it and will choose to follow this ancient profession. I have always remembered the description one of my SVN army medical colleagues gave me – quite laconically and rationally, without boasting or embarrassment – of the encounter he had with a female sex worker in a massage parlour in Bangkok where he went on R&R. He described how special she had made him feel; what an extraordinarily sensual experience it had been; how open and friendly she was and how unlike a business arrangement it had seemed and how he had welcomed the chance to take her up on the offer of spending the remainder of his leave with her. It had shocked me at the time, but I've never forgotten the impact his utterly candid confession made. In my honest moments then, it did not seem a particularly wicked arrangement for either of them. It had certainly made him happy and eased his frustrations after six months in the war zone and it had probably paid her bills for a few weeks to come – and he was a nice honest young Aussie man who would have treated her well and with respect.

Finally, I was developing a new outlook on sexual morality – an outlook of my own, not one inherited from church or family. Being homosexual inevitably alters your perception of sexual laws and customs. I realised in 1967 that if I ever acted on my homosexual desires and needs, quite apart from any religious scruples I might have about it, I would be breaking the law in most Western countries – certainly that would have been the case at that time in all Australian states and territories. Despite myself, I felt angry about this – it seemed irrational, unfair and discriminatory. At the time I had no intention of acting on my desires but I couldn't help feeling that a non-Christian soldier who happened to be gay like me had as much right as any of his heterosexual comrades to relieve his sexual frustration when he went on R&R with someone of the same sex who was willing. Perhaps it wasn't surprising that the Baptist bigwig's inflammatory comments aroused such passion within me. Beneath the meek exterior lurked a sometimes angry young man.

But sex, prostitution and VD were not my main preoccupations in August. On Sunday 6 August, the battle of Suoi Chau Pha took place in thick jungle beside a stream bearing that name, some 18 kilometres north-west of the Australian Task Force base. My letter written on 7 August describes the scene back at Nui Dat. While not as well known as some of the other battles involving Australian troops, for as long as it lasted, Suoi Chau Pha was a fierce action between A Company of the 7th Battalion RAR, supported by the guns of 106 Battery RAA, and C12 Company 3rd Battalion of the Vietcong 274 Regiment. It resulted in six Australians killed in action and another nineteen wounded, with five Vietnamese proven killed, another ten suspected killed and at least twenty-five wounded.

From 4 Field Regiment's viewpoint, the battle was notable for two reasons: the sterling performance of 106 Battery and the competence, coolness and bravery under fire of the forward observer from 106 Battery, Lieutenant Neville Clark, who was accompanying the 7 RAR officer commanding A Company at the time. Neville was subsequently awarded the Military Cross for his part in the battle. The official army analysis of the battle states:

The Forward Observer did an outstanding job in getting fire on the ground where it was required. As mentioned earlier in this report, he brought fire for effect from one gun to within 60 m of our own troops with the result that the VC were forced to withdraw, and must have taken casualties. The close support fire from 106 Bty was extremely accurate. In all, 106 Bty fired over 800 rounds.

All I remember now of that terrible Sunday is the chaotic scene in the small hospital area at the Forward Detachment. In the very short time we had before 'dust-off' helicopters returned to take the most badly injured on to Vung Tau, the three Nui Dat doctors and a handful of medics did what we could for the shocked and severely wounded soldiers from the battle. The sight and smell of mud and blood, caked on sodden army greens, came back to me vividly as I read the letter. The A Company medic on the ground had managed to apply shell dressings to the worst of the wounds and we succeeded in getting some IV drips running, but the first soldier I attended had bullet wounds to his chest and was practically pulseless when I examined him. There was little chance that he would make it, and he died shortly after I examined him. We all had a sense of helplessness and a realisation that the little Forward Detachment was ill-equipped to deal with real battle casualties. The severely wounded needed blood and lots of it and we had none.

War results in death and cruel physical injury for some but it has other substantial costs. The psychological stress and trauma of living and working in a war zone on active combat duty is far more pervasive, subtle and potentially just as damaging in the long term as physical war wounds. In the short term such psychic trauma shows itself in resort to alcohol, seeking solace wherever it might be found − often in the arms of a bar girl, suffering the physical and psychological consequences of contracting a sexually transmitted infection and finally for some, in desperation, attempting a self-inflicted wound. For the Nui Dat doctors, it was these psychological sequelae of war which occupied most of our professional time, far more than the time we spent dealing with acute battle injuries.

I don't have access to official statistics but, in my twelve months in SVN, I came to know about and saw or treated self-inflicted injuries and accidents, including wounds produced by 'friendly fire', as often as I encountered injuries attributable to the enemy. In any place where a large body of young men is camped for any length of time, where firearms are readily accessible, where heavy machinery is used and where alcohol is freely available, accidents are bound to occur and of course they do with great frequency despite good military discipline being exercised. I am sure more thought has been given to these issues over recent years and just as workplace health and safety has become an issue in the civilian workplace, so, too, preventive activities in the Australian Defence Forces have been stepped up to decrease these unfortunate and often needless losses of life and limb.

The activities of anti-war protesters back home in Australia and on American campuses caused the soldiers in Vietnam much grief. The average Australian soldier had a fine nose for bullshit, especially when delivered in spades by military authorities back in Saigon. And so, by August 1967, a significant number of soldiers considered the war a hopeless case. But anger at the protesters seemed to be one thing that united us all whatever our private views about the war. It seemed a paradoxical opinion but the line of reasoning went something like this: we at the coal face were entitled to a dissenting opinion if we wanted one – we could see first hand what was happening; 'long-haired' university students back home didn't have a clue what was going on and as they, the male ones anyway, had either missed the draft or been granted a deferment, they should have the grace to keep their mouths shut and just be grateful they weren't here. The perceived – and as it subsequently turned out, actual – lack of support for the armed forces slogging it out in Vietnam was the hardest aspect for the soldiers to come to terms with. The situation was manifestly unfair – two boys roughly the same age, who had sat together and been best of friends all through high school, because they were born on different days, had different outcomes in the national service lottery. One boy could coast through university or do whatever else he wanted, forever out of the army's reach; the other boy might have been one of those killed at the battle of Suoi Chau Pha.

I wrote to my mother in August, 'I am well, strong and happy,' and it was the truth. Although I only dimly appreciated it then, in taking on a 'counselling' role I was at last practising the sort of medicine which suited me best. While most around me were very far from their comfort zones, I was actually settling well within my own.

5

SEPTEMBER 1967

Letters

Nui Dat
Friday 1/9/67

Dear family,

Thank you for all the letters and the news of Ken's wedding. Thank you too for the talc, Mum, which arrived tonight. I opened it in the mess when the mail arrived and all the officers reckon I am now a *real* artillery officer – the next thing I'll be getting is a lace handkerchief, which gunners are traditionally supposed to carry, they predict.[1]

We had a sad event tonight. While sitting in the mess we all heard a shot fired nearby and soon after I received a phone call to say someone had been shot accidentally in our neighbouring unit (ARU). I rushed over but, by that time, they'd put him in a vehicle and taken him to the hospital. I ran up there to find the medics in a panic as Jack couldn't be found. Just as well I arrived! The poor kid had been shot through the abdomen and the bullet had come out through his spine with almost certain spinal cord damage. Anyway, I set to, patched him up, gave him morphine and organised a 'dust-off' chopper immediately. Jack then turned up most upset – he'd been asleep in his tent all the time – the only place the dopey medics hadn't thought to look. Sergeant Allen had run up with me to help, so once again it was 4 Fd Regt to the rescue. I just hope the poor boy pulls through all right and hasn't any severe spinal injury. His best pal shot him (by accident, cleaning his weapon with a full magazine attached). The unfortunate soldier who had the accidental discharge was more shocked than the wounded one. Wars are wretched, aren't they?

I went to Vung Tau last Tuesday with the regimental sergeant major (RSM) and the padre for the court-martial of the soldier who started firing his weapon around the place. Legal delays meant I had to have tea and stay overnight at 8 Field Ambulance, so I shared a tent with the pharmacist, Wally Williams. There was the most amazing wind and rain storm that night and I slept really badly as my cold was developing. Next morning I had to go to the MCE (Military Corrective Establishment) to see the gunner and certify him fit to stand trial. The court-martial wasn't to start until after lunch, so Peter Grainger (a doctor who used to be at Concord) and I went over to see the big American 36 Evacuation Hospital and then I had lunch with him at the Army Transit Centre. The court-martial was a bit of a muddle. There was much indecision about the actual charge and whether the gunner was pleading guilty or not guilty. I was summoned for a long confab with the judge associate and then I was allowed to testify that, in my medical opinion, the soldier was not fit to undergo detention and punishment. I then was able to leave, so I hope it means the poor gunner will get off and be medevac-ed back to Australia.

On a lighter note – old Chuck got back from his R&R in Bangkok and the usual irrepressible RAP staff (mainly Sergeant Allen) began teasing him about how soon he would be needing penicillin injections. Chuck was very funny with his descriptions of the Bangkok girls. He apparently used to go at night with his friend to one of these little bars and sedately drink Coca-Cola. The first night, the girls came and talked to him and told him what a cheap price they were. Chuck listened patiently in true country fashion, consistently declined their offer and carried on talking with them. The second night the quoted price was a lot lower. The third night all the girls eagerly told Chuck they were 'for free' and the last night they were offering to pay *him*. That's a disreputable story no doubt, but it has its funny side. Chuck said to me afterwards, 'You know, it's funny, sir; I guess they were really just prostitutes, but nothing like prostitutes at home.' I doubt Chuck would be much of an authority on prostitutes at home either. 'They were so friendly and nice to talk with and weren't at all upset when we turned them down.'

It does give you some idea of the sort of temptations the army boys face. Eastern values and Eastern standards are just not our standards. It's no use saying the soldiers ought to avoid the bars – where else is there for the chaps to go at night in a big Eastern city when they're on leave? You can't expect them to sit in their hotel room reading a Gideon Bible! Anyway, Chuck says he enjoyed himself thoroughly the five days he was in Bangkok. I would love you all to meet him – he is a real inspiration.

I must go to bed and get my aching head and stuffy nose clear.

Much love,

David

PS: I had a nice long talk in the mess last night with the 2IC and Major Jenvey, the battery commander of 108 Battery. We talked about the army, how officers manage soldiers and their different management styles, what the place of a medical officer should be in a regiment and so on. It revealed the 2IC in a much more human and friendly light.

[1] This was a longstanding army joke with some basis in tradition – that artillery men (particularly officers) carried lace handkerchiefs, being considered somewhat 'precious' by members of other corps. It had nothing to do with any perception that I might have been gay.

Nui Dat
Sunday 3/9/67

Dear Mum and Dad,

A joint letter for the two of you tonight, as I'm too tired to write separate letters. It has been a busy day with a long and involved sick parade this morning so that I wasn't able to get to chapel. As it was Sunday, we had a buffet luncheon in the mess with a few visiting officers from other units. I had a great chat with Don Harris the American liaison artillery officer. He is a very pleasant chap and comes from Baltimore, Maryland. Also a good talk with a bloke I like very much from 3 Cav Regt – one of that unit's nicest young officers. It was a good lunch too with some excellent barbecued meat – I am never sure where they dig up these special cuts of meat which appear only on the rarest of occasions – I suspect it's deep-frozen American meat supplied especially for officers.

Yesterday I spent the afternoon lying down trying to overcome my cold, but then Tom Sullivan, the American doctor from 1/83rd, came visiting. He is counting the days until he gets out of the army. He is to go home very soon so this was really a farewell visit. He was drafted into the army (most reluctantly) and for the period he is in the forces his medical career is really on hold. He says the lucky ones are the doctors who get drafted into high-powered medical or surgical army medical units, where they can get some real experience. He finds being the doctor for an artillery unit very unsatisfying medically. We ended up going to the movies at the task force officers' mess and saw *Gordon of Khartoum*.

This evening I had a bit of drama too. A young HQ battery gunner had a sort of breakdown and became quite hysterical. He was so panicky and in such a state that it was nearly impossible to hold a coherent conversation with him, much less find out what was wrong. He'd had a few beers during the day but didn't seem to be particularly inebriated and was continually crying and moaning and throwing himself about restlessly. It took several of us to get him loaded into the RAP Land Rover and I had to sit in the back with my arms tightly around him (which seemed to calm him somewhat) just to restrain him until we got to the Forward Detachment. Jack and I tried to calm him until a big injection of valium had the desired effect. I hope he's OK by morning – who knows what might be behind it all – bad news from home? A 'Dear John' letter? He is a lovely chap and normally very calm and sensible.

My best love to you both,
David

Nui Dat
Monday 4/9/67

Dear family,
It's been a funny old day, so this letter will be very short. I had to tell you about how I pulled rank on a major, though. This morning I was called to visit 106 Battery as their battery commander (BC), a major,

was sick. He had clearly been sick for a couple of days but refused to see a doctor. He's a wonderful chap, but ultra stubborn. Eventually Chuck persuaded him that I ought to have a look at him. When I got to examine him he had classical signs of pneumonia, which I told him in no uncertain terms. I said he would have to go to hospital in Vung Tau and said I would go and arrange his transfer by chopper with Jack Blomley at the Forward Detachment there and then. He could follow on at his leisure and his driver could drop him at Jack's place opposite the helipad. I did this and the hours ticked by but he didn't arrive at the helipad and I heard later from the battery he was refusing to go to hospital. I tried gentle persuasion by phone, but in the end I had to tell the CO and the CO simply ordered him to go.

While we were having drinks in the late afternoon before tea, a crestfallen major arrived in the mess, still very disgruntled that he would have to go to hospital. So I phoned Jack and he came down to see him to provide a second opinion. Jack totally agreed with my diagnosis and so together we finally got him 'dusted off' to Vung Tau.

I've more packing to do for the planned op[1] which is coming up, so must finish.

Much love,
Davo

[1]   Operation Ainslie.

Operation Ainslie
Duc Thanh
Friday 8/9/67

Dear family,
It is Friday morning and we have been here since Tuesday – I am so sorry I haven't written to you before this, but really there's been either no time due to all the military operational rubbish (packing up to leave Nui Dat, then digging weapon pits and sandbagging the RAP tent here), or else it's been raining too much and it's been impossible to get a dry bit of paper to write on. Today however the sun is shining, the RAP has a substantial sandbag wall all the way around it and inside the floor has been dug down to about two feet deep, so it's as safe as

houses if the 'funny little men' take it into their heads to mortar this fire support base one night.

I have done my morning rounds to both gun batteries (108 and the Kiwi battery) who are out with HQ battery on this operation. Everything has been very quiet so far on the op. The villagers in the suspected VC-sympathising village have all been moved out and settled into their new army-built hamlet about 5 miles [8 kilometres] south. The infantry are now searching the area. Back here everything is quiet too; no casualties except the usual fungousy feet.

The position is a nicer one than on Op Paddington – not quite so muddy, but still pretty bad after the rain. It's good having Sergeant Allen out with me this time, as he organises everything very well and makes things comfortable.

I had one letter last night from Mum (the first since I got out here) and one from cousin Robbie (typed this time, as they're 'going through a typing phase'). *The Australian Baptist* came yesterday too – I see I am in print again and they haven't edited the letter this time. The soap, fruitcake and butterscotch all arrived safely before I left Nui Dat, so thank you.

I must apologise very much for forgetting Father's Day, Dad, and say a very belated 'Happy Father's Day' to you. I just completely forgot about it until last Sunday night when the adjutant said he'd sent a telegram to his father that day – I thought at the time I must write and say sorry for forgetting, but I forgot even to do that with this op coming up.

Sorry I won't be able to write individual letters to you all while out on op. It's just hard to organise the time to write – not that there's heaps to do. It's just awkward to get away by yourself long enough to write in peace. At any rate, I am OK; my cold's cleared up and I have a cosy little stretcher – I decided to pack one in with the RAP stores this time – why be unnecessarily uncomfortable? I sleep more comfortably even than the 2IC in my safe fortress-like RAP.

I think you had better tee up another organist for the wedding, Merrie. If I do manage to come home, I certainly won't mind taking a back seat – I'll be so hopelessly out of practice anyway I'd botch it all up.

It'll be lunchtime soon – more American C rations: tinned turkey loaf; tinned ham and lima beans; tinned ultra sweet chocolate biscuits and hot powdered coffee. Oh for a good old cup of Aussie tea. The American packs don't have tea in them at all – only coffee or cocoa. Back at Nui Dat we only get 'instant' tea – you can probably imagine what that tastes like.

After lunch, I will do a foot inspection and daub various fungousy feet with Castellani's paint – what army medicine would do without Castellani's paint, I can't imagine.

At the moment most HQ battery gunners are laying barbed wire around our perimeter. They are working about as hard as council workers back home. Sergeant Allen is down with them spinning jokes, by the sound of the laughter. Others are digging pits in which they will sleep with sandbags around them and their little poncho tents over the top. The remainder are sandbagging the command post. There are no guns in HQ battery and once camp is set up there isn't much to do except routine duties until the op is over.

Anyway, all my love and I will write another of these scrappy letters as soon as I can,

David

Duc Thanh
Monday 11/9/67

Dear old Mum,

Sorry about this awful scrappy paper, but it is difficult out in the bush. It is a nice fine morning and things are having a chance to dry out – the rain will probably be back with us by about three o'clock this afternoon. I even did some washing today – socks and hankies and underpants – they're all about the same colour by this time – a sort of dusty greeny-brown.

I am seriously behind on my correspondence, so apologise to people back home who are expecting letters. I must write to Judy and Brian[1] in Taiwan soon, to find out how far away from Taipei they live in case I'm suddenly told I am to go to Taipei for R&R. It would be nice to visit them, if it's possible.

Bombardier Banks' mother sounds a nice old thing. She has every reason to be proud of Jeff, as he is very well thought of in the regiment as the friendly postie. It's quite a big job and can cause a lot of upset and discord if it's not done properly. There's not much as important as mail up here. Jeff is back at Nui Dat at present and gets all our mail ready for the resupply aircraft every afternoon.

I would like to see one of Merrie's wedding invitations. I am glad they are simple. I do hope Merrie does well in her exams. I have arranged for a 'birthday present' to be delivered to 75 Castle Hill Road on the afternoon of 20th for her. I just hope nothing goes wrong and it gets there OK. You'd better tell her to be home that afternoon, if possible.

The new shop windows sound pretty daring with balloons AND confetti! Weddings are pretty much on all your minds at present, I suppose. And I am very surprised that stubborn old fuddy-duddy Dad has at last invested in a petrol lawnmower. Was he worried that Dr Dick's dire prediction might actually come true?[2]

I am so glad the shop is thriving – 800 scripts in one month sounds quite outstanding to me. Mr Ford must be retreating in confusion.

Everything is very quiet out here on operation. No night disturbances or anything. The gunners have had very little to do. Apart from the mud, we are all well and 'in good heart'.

Much love, mother dear,
David

[1]   Judy Dillon was from Pennant Hills Baptist Church. She and her husband Brian were working as missionaries in Taiwan.
[2]   The dire prediction was that he'd get a 'rupture' if he kept using the 'push-me pull-you' one.

Op Ainslie
Duc Thanh
Tuesday 12/9/67

Dear family,
Thank you for all your letters which arrived today, with news of Ian's South African uncle, Rev. Stephen Bradley, arriving in Sydney. So he is going to take part in the Wedding Ceremony? As usual a Bradford function is going to be a little out of the ordinary with an excommunicated (is he really?) bishop[1] presiding at Merrie's

wedding. Will Mr Logan, our pastor, be upset to be sharing the pulpit with a bishop?

You are picking up army slang well, Mum, calling me a 'stirrer-up'. The correct rendering is in fact just 'stirrer'. Every army unit has its 'stirrers' – they are usually presented at some time with a large wooden spoon to help them with their stirring.

I am dying to hear how the trip to town with Dad and Merrie went – what sort of suit did they eventually decide on for him? Have you persuaded Dad to get a new pair of rusty green socks for the great occasion, or is he still too attached to the 'old pair'? It had to happen, but must have been difficult, for Dad to have to swallow his pride and actually consult a dentist. The pain must have been exceedingly bad for him to do that. But it serves him right for neglecting his teeth so long.

There is no new news to report from Operation Ainslie. It seems to be very quiet. We are supposed to be packing up on Saturday or Sunday night. It will be good to get back to Nui Dat then and have a shower with hot water. Still, it hasn't been too bad so far and I feel very well. I have a good suntan, too, as I've only been wearing shorts (knobbly knees and all) for the past few days.

For Pip – from 'Starlight' (that's my radio call sign, by the way)[2]:

Your taste in jokes has definitely degenerated since I left home – that last cartoon[3] was pathetic.

I had better finish off now and get back to uplifting more morale.

Love from,

David

---

[1]   It was untrue and an exaggeration to say that Rev Stephen Bradley, Ian's uncle from South Africa, was an 'excommunicated' bishop. At the time there were two branches of the Anglican Church in the republic and Rev Bradley was a bishop in the Evangelical low-church branch, but his consecration as bishop was not recognised by the more mainstream high-Anglican faction.

[2]   I had been required to communicate with a medic by radio on Operation Ainslie, so had been using my radio call sign for the first time. I wrote it in the paragraph to Pip purely for interest.

[3]   I can't remember the cartoon now.

Duc Thanh
D+10[1]
Thursday 14/9/67

Dear family and Merrie especially,
('This is Nine Zero; Starlight speaking – Over')

First of all a very Happy Birthday to old Porky girl. I hope this arrives in time, but knowing the mail, it probably won't. I hope the present arrives in time too, but knowing the army PX store, it probably won't either. Still, as Sergeant Allen is always telling me: 'you can't win 'em all sir'. The thought was there. Just think! This is the last birthday before you become an old staid married lady, settle down and become a pillar of society – at 23. And I'll be 26 next birthday – not that anyone will notice my birthday this year – a certain important event on 4th Nov will no doubt overshadow my humble birthday.

Have you at last decided the difficult question of who to invite to the wedding and who to leave out? It must be quite a job. I would rather like a peep at the guest list (when it's final and complete, of course).

As you can see by the letterhead, it is now the tenth day of the famous Operation Ainslie – so far it has been very successful. The village of Xa Bang, once a notorious VC sympathetic village and one on which the local VC depended for their food supplies (as it is the centre of a large dairy farming and pumpkin growing area) is now no more. All the villagers, not without some protest, have been moved 5 miles [8 kilometres] south to a 'new beaut' village built for them by the army engineers, where they can live safely (under the eye of Nui Dat). All the thick scrub from the side of the road to Xa Bang has been cleared for 300 yards [275 metres] on both sides by the engineers' bulldozers and the road should now be safe for army vehicles and civilians. The infantry battalions are at present sweeping through the jungle and rubber plantations on either side of the road looking for any signs of VC activity. So far they have killed about seven VC and captured weapons and things – so all in all it's been pretty good and we've had no casualties to speak of.

Back here at the FSB everything stays very quiet and I have a beautiful suntan from sitting in the sun reading. Apart from the odd stitching up of a cut or two, I've had nothing to do.

I had an exciting ride on an APC the afternoon before last – one of the 'tankies' up at Xa Bang was bitten by a wasp and they wanted a medic to see him before nightfall, so the Cav Regt medic thought it was a good idea to tell them I had to go, so I could have a ride on an APC. So I jumped on and away we went – they are not the most comfortable vehicles to ride, but it was quite a thrill. The medic always rides in the 'repair tank' – the APC whose job it is to go to aid any of the other APCs which are in trouble. We had to help pull another APC out of a bog first, before we got to see the patient. To get it out they needed a specially long tow rope and three APCs chained together all pulling like mad to make it budge at all. We then went and attended to the wasp-bitten one, who wasn't ill at all, as is usual with urgent medical radio messages. On the way back a terrific storm came on and I got wetter than I've ever been in my life. The rain was coming down so hard I thought my face would be cut to ribbons sitting up on top of the APC. It was good fun, though!

I have probably bored you all to tears with these military details, so I had better finish now. It is nearly morning tea time – more American coffee with 3.5 mg ascorbic acid added to each packet. Americans are really mad people.

Much love to you all, and happy birthday again, Merrie,

David

PS to Merrie: Sergeant Allen says to thank you for your kind wishes and he sends his love. He says he hates to think what sort of stories I write home about him. He agrees with you I need bandages to stop my head getting too swollen.

PS to Mum: Thank you for the newspaper cutting about Major James – he was at 2 Camp Hospital when I was there last October – 'Digger' James as he is better known.

---

[1]   D +10 means the tenth day of the operation.

Op Ainslie
Duc Thanh
Friday 15/9/67

Dear family,

Just a little note to tell you about a funny happening yesterday arvo. Seeing things were pretty quiet, they decided it would be a good idea to do a Medcap in the local village. So with the Kiwi battery medic and Gunner Scroope, my batman, supported by the RSM (regimental sergeant major) with his three burly RPs (Regimental Police) we set out to do a Medcap and as soon as we arrived in the village, the locals descended on us in their usual way when we told them the Uc-Dai-Loi Bac-si had arrived.

One man seemed very insistent, pointing at his knee and giving little hobbling demonstrations – there didn't seem to be much wrong with his knee, except some varicose veins behind it, so I gave him a few aspros and put a crepe bandage on the offending knee. He still didn't seem happy but was pushed away by the milling mob – he then went and grabbed Gunner Scroope and led him down the road until suddenly the cause for his worry became apparent – one of his cows had been wounded by a piece of shrapnel (or something like that) in the knee. All he had been doing was trying to show the dumb doctor what was happening. Talk about 'language difficulties'. I didn't find out about this until I got back to camp, so the poor old cow went unattended – not that I could do much to help a cow.

Another dreadful old woman with about a dozen black betel-nut-stained teeth (all loose) and apparently causing her a lot of pain tottered up and wanted them all pulled out. We *have* a couple of dental forceps in our main Medcap supplies but didn't have them with us yesterday for this little impromptu show, so I had to tackle them with a tiny pair of Spencer-Wells artery forceps. One of the little front teeth came out easily enough but the big back ones were no match for the S-Wells. A Yankee soldier (engineer) nearby handed me a pair of pliers and I had a go with those, but it was really too much even for my cast iron stomach. Grinding teeth stained with betel nut are not a pretty sight and certainly no use tackling without proper instruments – even if you knew how to use the instruments correctly.

Still, it was quite a good Medcap – I had no interpreter, but a little bright-faced youngster of about twelve appointed himself interpreter and by showing him figures on my watch face, he was able to tell the people when they should take their tablets. With my limited knowledge of medical terms in Vietnamese (pain, stomach, deep breath, cough etc.) we managed to scrape by. We parted the best of friends, he shaking my hand solemnly and saying 'Uc-Dai-Loi, Bac-Si, Di-Uy, Number 1' when we left – (Di-Uy is captain). Everything in Vietnam is Number 1 or Number 10 – there seem to be no in-between grades.

No other news really. I am very fit now. We are not going back tomorrow, but probably will be on Sunday. The op is going so well they may even prolong it a little further.

Fancy Dad getting a new suit AND two new pairs of shoes. He won't be recognisable at the wedding.

I have been twenty weeks in SVN now.

Much love,

David

PS At least the regiment has me to laugh about – the story of the wounded cow and the bandaged leg is doing the rounds as I write.

Duc Thanh

D+13

Sunday 17/9/67

Dear old Mum,

Just a short note on Sunday morning to let you know we are definitely moving back to Nui Dat and 'comfort' at 1015 hours tomorrow – not that it has been too bad at all out on op this time. The weather has been very kind for the last five days and we are all burnt brown as berries and look very fit and healthy. Op Ainslie has been successful on the whole and has given the old VC a bit of a tough time for two weeks.

I've just been to church! A new Kiwi padre (Methodist) has arrived for the Kiwi battery to take the previous Anglican padre's place (the latter has gone home to NZ). The new guy conducted the service this morning for the whole regiment out here and for the infantry company who are camped around us. It was a very good service too. Apparently in the NZ Army they don't bother splitting up into Anglican and OPDs but have combined Protestant services. He used the Anglican communion service straight today. Apparently he's caused quite a stir back in NZ Methodist circles – they are totally opposed to the NZ commitment in Vietnam (very pacifist, apparently) and were all against him coming over. Nearly all the NZ papers had big editorials about him. The Methodist Conference was even strongly split on whether to send him a letter wishing him best wishes and the assurance of their prayers. Poor man! It couldn't have made his departure overseas very easy. Church people can be crueller than any others when they put their mind to it. Pacifists may be dedicated in their opposition to wars, but they sure cause enough personal wars sticking to their principles.

Yesterday we had a visit from the chief of the general staff (CGS), Sir John Wilton. They call him General 'Jovial' because he's just the opposite. I had to change out of my shorts and put my shirt and long greens on so I could line up with the other officers to shake his hand. He arrived in a chopper with General Vincent, Brigadier Graham, another brigadier, an air force 'big-wig', our CO and numerous photographers and TV cameras. What an opportunity for the VC to attack if they'd only been on their toes. They could have wiped out most of the Aussie Army top brass. The CGS inspected the whole FSB, looking like he had a bad smell under his nose, shook my hand and asked if I was kept busy. I said 'No' and that was the sum total of our intelligent conversation. Anyway he got a lot of mud on his good shiny shoes, much to the gunners' delight, and departed after about twenty minutes.

Much love to everyone at 'Lantern Woods'[1] and I will write again when back in base. Thanks for all the letters which arrived yesterday.

David

PS, for Pip: Joke of the Week – Gunner heard whispering loudly to Sergeant Allen in my hearing, 'Why don't you hide his shorts so he can't put them on in the morning?' Apparently my knobbly knees are a standing joke in the regiment.

---

[1]   'Lantern Woods' was the name of our family home at 75 Castle Hill Road. Mother named it.

Duc Thanh

Tuesday 19/9/67

D + 15

Dear old Mum,

Well, surprise, surprise! We are *still* out on operation despite the fact that we were *definitely* going home on Monday. The Yanks have now stepped into the op and tell us we are *really* going to catch one of the main VC regiments and destroy it this time, so we are all sitting here awaiting the Yanks' pleasure, before they decide we have either caught said regiment or missed them and let us go back to Nui Dat. The weather continues very nice – not too much rain and plenty of sunshine – and by now we are all fairly comfortably installed. I've still had nothing much to do except walk around talking to people, although tomorrow there's another Medcap planned in the afternoon, providing we get some Medcap stores on the resupply chopper today.

I was so sorry one of my recent letters upset you.[1] I certainly had no intention of making you sad, as Dad said it did. I would love to come home for the wedding, but it seems so difficult for it to work out. At the moment it looks like about two people from the whole task force will get home to Australia for R&R each month, so I don't really have much chance. All your talk of wedding preparations is making me wish more than ever that I was home with you, having a share in them, but it's no good getting upset about it. And more than ever as I talk to some of the boys here, I realise how fortunate I am to come from such a happy family, as so few of them seem to. Whether I get home for the wedding or not, at least I'll know you are all thinking of me, and I will certainly be thinking of you. Although it's an awfully trite thing to say, I will be there 'in spirit' even if not 'in body'. But you never know with the army! Things are always 'turning up' – it would have suited Mr Micawber. I may yet get home for that wedding. And now five months (almost) have gone by and I am nearly halfway through my stay up here. It really goes pretty quickly, doesn't it?

We now go back to Nui Dat on Friday, but I'm not counting on it this time – when we actually move, I'll believe it.

Much love, Mother dear, and don't go fretting.

David

PS: Merrie's exam paper was fun to read – what a shocker! I would certainly have failed.

¹   I think this refers to my letter of Thursday 17/8 in which I more or less state categorically that I won't be home for my sister's wedding. My mother seems to have interpreted this as indicating I didn't want to return. A typical misunderstanding in the exchange of mail.

Back home at Nui Dat
Thursday 21/9/67

Dear family,

At last Op Ainslie is over and we are back at base safe and sound once more. Everyone seems to think it was quite a successful op and we (the Aussies as a whole) had very few casualties. One of the infanteers was killed but apart from that there were only minor injuries. Last night I had to treat two infantry boys who had been camped around the outside of our FSB (to protect us). An infantry company had been firing mortars and a couple of rounds dropped a little bit short and these two were injured by small pieces of shrapnel. One had a small piece enter his right cheek, so I didn't like keeping him overnight in case it had penetrated to somewhere vital, so we 'dusted him off' in a chopper to Vung Tau.

Three letters arrived from you tonight – the mail is still crazy as I had no letters the two nights before. I hope Dad's sinuses have cleared up OK.

That trip home from Gran's at Caringbah sounds dramatic. It must have been a shock to nearly run someone over. I know how dark it is in that little hollow at Meadowbank. It's a miracle Pip missed him – the MAL's sudden death brakes came in good use for once.

I am very tired tonight and my cold has freshened up, so I will get to bed as early as I can and write you a longer letter tomorrow night.

I came back to find my sandbagged tent wall had fallen down, my hygiene sergeant has been charged with 'falsifying a hygiene report', by saying there were maggots in one latrine when the officer in charge of that area reckons there weren't any, and that about a dozen people

wanted to see me 'urgently' about something or other this afternoon.
It will all sort itself out, I guess.

Much love to all,

David

PS I am not really miserable even if the last few paragraphs sound
it. I was invited to the gunners' mess (the Snake Pit) this afternoon for
a (soft) drink, which is unheard of for an officer, so they must like me.

Nui Dat
Saturday 23/9/67

Dear Mum,

I am just back from the movies at HQ battery (with all the soldiers)
watching *The Night of the Generals*, which is very good and exciting.

I am totally better but tired after two busy days. Yesterday was a
long and somewhat trying sick parade and there were a couple of
minor ops to do. I was without Sergeant Allen too, as he had to go to
the Horseshoe to see Chuck with the resupply helicopter, but Corporal
Williams was here to assist and of course the amiable Gunner
Scroope. Peter Williams is very efficient and is a nice boy in many
ways – he just has a tendency to want to put everyone right all the
time, but other than this he is an excellent medic and I am lucky to
have him at 108 Battery.

At the end of sick parade, the CO dropped in unannounced just to
see how we were doing. He is a good man and has the happy knack
of setting you at ease. You certainly feel you can talk to him unre-
strainedly about anything on your mind.

This morning was another long sick parade, but quite enjoyable
and I had to do a minor op[1] on one of the cheery HQ battery gunners,
Gunner Galea, who is of Maltese stock and hales from the Gold Coast.
He chatted away happily throughout the whole procedure.

I received the formal invitation to Merrie's wedding in tonight's
post. It's very impressive and extremely tasteful – my congratulations!
What a terrible shame that it looks most likely I will have to apologise
that I can't attend.

Much love, dear old Mum,

David

1   I enjoyed doing minor ops. I can't remember now what procedure I had
    performed on Vince Galea but it would have been either an operation on
    an ingrown toenail, incision or excision of a skin cyst, drainage of an
    abscess, removal of a mole or wart, or incision of a thrombosed pile.

Nui Dat
Wednesday 27/9/67

[First page of this letter to my mother is missing.]
Today I had to go out to the Horseshoe, as Chuck was in difficulties
with a few bad ear infections. Chuck's battery has been at the Horseshoe for about one month now, although they are leaving it soon and
coming out on the next operation with us. I went out by chopper at
0900 and stayed all day. I returned by road convoy tonight. It was
perfect weather today. I really like tropical weather – it was quite hot
but there was a nice breeze from the sea. All the 106 Battery gunners
are as brown as berries, as most of their gun firing is done at night
and they spend the days lying sunbaking on the tops of their little
huts. I treated all the ear infections, looked at all the skin rashes, then
just pottered around talking with everyone from gun to gun with
Chuck in attendance. Chuck is a bit weighed down with problems as
they have put him in charge of the canteen (as an extra duty). He is
happier with skin rashes than he is selling beer and soft drinks and
adding up figures, I think.

I had a happy and restful day listening to all the dreadful stories
about R&R doings and answering questions on every conceivable
medical topic (from LSD, to how you catch tinea). I must admit that
is the part of my duty as RMO that I like most. There are great disadvantages to being in the army and being over here (especially when
I think I might miss Merrie's wedding, for example), but really I am
very happy with my job and I am sure that's how you are meant to be.
As old ministerial Judy Renn[1] said to me when I rang her that last
Saturday night at home, 'If it's the Lord's will for you to be in Vietnam,
then you won't be happy anywhere else'.

My 'tankie' medic (that's the one from the Cavalry Regiment) is a very
nice bloke and pretty shrewd; he prophesies that I am going to feel 'lost'
when I get back to Australia and out of the army. He thinks I regard all

the soldiers with such a 'fatherly' air[2] that I will miss them all too much when I get back on 'civvy street'. He is probably right to some degree, but if I am to get anywhere in medicine, I will have to get out of the army and get back to studying. Army medicine is pretty restrictive. I will have to start thinking seriously about what to do when I get back to Australia – I still want to do surgery, so I guess England is the place to go.

Well, I had better wind up. Peter Williams, the 108 Battery medic, said to me on the last op, 'You have deteriorated since you came into the army, sir – you are becoming very sarcastic.' Perhaps he is right and the army is bad for me. Although Gunner Thomas, who over-heard the remark, exploded and said, 'What does that little pipsqueak mean by insulting our doctor?'

Guess what? I had another letter from my 'girlfriend' (the sister from 2 Camp Hospital) who does the funny drawings. She is now working in Malaya at Terendak in the British Military Hospital. She must still love me. I can imagine Merrie: 'Sergeant Allen, quick run for the head bandages'.[3]

Must finish! We leave for the new op on Saturday morning. The op is on the beach, practically in the sand, so it won't be mud to contend with this time but sand, sunburn, glare, eye infections and heat exhaustion, I suppose.

Much love to all the family,

Davo

PS For my birthday – please no pyjamas or singlets – not used in SVN. Cotton underpants (jockey type of course), black or dark blue, so they won't show the dirt, hankies (again dark coloured) and good old Aussie tea bags would be the best presents.

[1] Judy Renn was several years older than me but we had been great friends at Seaforth Baptist Church. She was a brilliant pianist and organist and married a Baptist minister.

[2] Len Starkey, the medic, was probably just being kind. I was two or three years older than most soldiers but I was hardly 'fatherly'. He was right, though; I did miss them when I got home from Vietnam.

[3] The head bandages were to treat my swollen head. My sister always tried to cut me down to size. The 'girlfriend' was Vicki, who is mentioned in March 1968 Reflections.

Reflections

Operation Ainslie took up most of September. The Fire support base was located right on the edge of another rubber plantation. It started out very wet and the mud underfoot made conditions unpleasant. The weather gradually improved and my main recollections of that time are of sunshine and very little to do. I remember I revelled in my ride on an APC, mostly because I enjoyed the company of the 3 Cav Regiment troopers, and was not entirely indifferent to the fact that a couple of them seemed to enjoy my company in return. I also had fun doing two impromptu Medcaps in the local village of Ngaio Giao, including the amusing encounter with the outraged owner of the wounded cow. The Civil Aid people's contention that 'if the Allies are ever to win in South Vietnam, it won't be on the battlefield the war will be won' had some truth in it. It's certain that visits by army medical teams to local villages generated infinitely more goodwill than search and destroy missions. They also generated far more goodwill than what Operation Ainslie was all about – the total physical destruction of a suspect village and its surrounding farmland, with the enforced movement of all the villagers to a new location, purpose built by army engineers. There was something extremely schizophrenic about the way the Vietnam War was progressed!

A low-key paragraph at the end of one of the September letters documents an event which meant a great deal more to me than I could ever reveal in a letter home. In any case, I would have lacked the words then to say how I truly felt. I was very fond of the young HQ battery gunner who unexpectedly and quite uncharacteristically lost all control and developed a severe panic attack one evening. I had seen him around the base and treated him for minor problems on a couple of occasions. With some difficulty, because he struggled against us, we transported him to the little hospital at the Forward Detachment. I remember my own loss of control, for I found I couldn't stop crying as I literally held him in my arms to restrain him in the back of the army Land Rover. His normal rational mind had been taken over by some terror he could not name. Somehow for me that evening he epitomised all the damage and harm war inflicts and has always inflicted on young men down the centuries. He was hurting but temporarily beyond anyone's help. I don't remember what happened to him afterwards; perhaps he recovered and served his time with no recurrence of his breakdown; but as I have no recollection of him beyond that evening, it's more likely he was sent home deemed no longer suitable for war service.

Peter Williams may have been more accurate than he could have known when he observed that I had 'deteriorated' during those first four months or so in Vietnam. I was certainly changing, but what he took to be 'sarcasm' was more likely a new willingness to speak my mind.

6

OCTOBER 1967

Letters

The Beach, near Xuyen Moc
Tuesday 3/10/67

Dear family,

My first letter from Operation Kenmore. We arrived on Saturday morning by chopper and sure enough, as predicted, we are camped beside the beach about 10 miles [16 kilometres] north of Vung Tau. The area we are camped in is typical seaside country – sandy soil and those sort of untidy fir tree things (like you get beside the Nepean River). The weather has been pretty fine and as hot and sticky as ever. We set up the RAP really well this time – dug down into the nice sandy soil about 2 feet [60 centimetres] with sandbags all around and it looked really nice and clean until the second night, when we had some very heavy rain. I woke the next morning to find water lapping around the top of my stretcher. The water soaked easily into the sandy soil, but unfortunately, anything dug down below the surface collected all the water seeping through the sand and our RAP collected nearly all of it. As fast as we bailed it out next morning, just as fast it seeped in again so we gave up the struggle eventually and suspended sheets of iron across the floor. If we have fine weather from now on, it should dry out. It was such a shame as the whole thing was set up very well. Still, that's typical Vietnam.

Yesterday we all went swimming at the beach – my first swim in the South China Sea – much the same as at home, except that the water is much warmer and seems very salty. The surf is a bit pathetic, like Gerroa. It seems a funny sort of war when you go off on swimming parties.

This operation is very quiet – so far anyway. The battalions are searching an area which is thought to be a VC supply area and so they're looking for stores, ammunition and rice. Nothing has been found yet and the gunners back here (on this FSB) are facing a very quiet time. The whole task force is here with us – the brigadier and our CO, so it's a big show; but there's nothing much to see for all the fuss.

I have had the Kiwi padre camped with me for the last 24 hours sharing the RAP's hospitality. It has been a little wearying. He's a nice chap but like most ministers he's a great old talker – and I feel like having a bit of a rest sometimes, but when you've got someone hanging around all the time it's difficult.

Keep me up-to-date on the wedding preparations, won't you? I'm sorry this letter is so disjointed and poorly written, but it is really hard writing letters out on operation – it's so hot and sticky and you're always being interrupted.

Love to all the family,

David

PS I had another letter from my 'War Correspondent', Frankie Atkinson from Pennant Hills Baptist yesterday. He is really wonderful to write so regularly.[1]

---

[1] Frank Atkinson was about my dad's age with two children about the ages of Merrie and Pip. He wrote very regularly to me throughout my twelve months in SVN and his letters were interesting and most welcome. He was a very fine man.

Fire Support Base
Operation Kenmore
Friday 6/10/67

Dear Mum, Dad, Merrie, Pip and Ian,

How are you all? I'm just hoping that Wedding Fever hasn't made you all sick (or sicker than usual, I mean) and that you're all standing up to the strain. I'm so glad Mum's nightmares[1] have gone now and that you've managed to find a suitable wedding dress, old thing. Promise me you'll send me photos of everyone in their wedding finery. Has Merrie started to get her presents yet?[2] I'll bet the house is in even more of a comfortably untidy mess than ever. Just as well I am not home to add to the confusion. I can just imagine Dad getting worked up for one of his silly moods – he'll be quite unbearable on the Wedding Day, if I know anything about him. And I guess Mum will be too busy worrying about this and that to keep him under control.

The mail has just arrived – one letter today from Mum with the newspaper cutting about the rocket accident – labelled, just as we thought it would be, 'US Rocket Kills Three Australians'. Newspapermen are awful! They never mention how often Australians have been rescued by US helicopter gun ships, or that the whole thing was an accident which could have happened to the RAAF just as easily as to a Yank helicopter. Typical Australian news reporting – it's always someone else's fault. No, I didn't have anything to do with that incident – they were 2 Battalion soldiers who are on the opposite side of the task force to us and that day I was out at the Horseshoe all day. These accidents really are awful, though. We had one ourselves today on this operation – one of our HQ battery bombardiers was wounded when a mine detonator accidentally went off in his hand and peppered him with little bits of aluminium. Fortunately all his wounds were very superficial so Sergeant Allen and myself patched him up and loaded him off to Vung Tau on a 'dust-off' helicopter. Otherwise we have been extremely quiet – still swimming every day and mainly sitting around reading.

Much love to you all,
David

[1] Mum's nightmares were purely about what she would wear; what would be the most appropriate outfit for the mother of the bride.
[2] Wedding presents were mostly delivered to the bride's home in the weeks preceding the wedding. In 1967 the most common presents were casserole dishes, parfait glasses, splayds (a combined knife/fork piece of cutlery), sheets and pillowslips, and towels.

The Bradford family, in a photo I took on a picnic in 1967. *Left to right*: Pip, Merrie, Mum, Dad.

The farewell at Sydney airport on Saturday evening, 29 April 1967, before I flew back to Brisbane to rejoin the regiment. My family members are on the right.

H.Q. Battery.
4 Fd. Regt.
AFPO 4
GPO Syd.
2/5/67

Dear Family,

Here is my first letter from SVN! We arrived here this arvo. at about 2 o'clock at Vung Tau and after waiting there about an hour we flew into Nui Dat by Caribou aeroplane. The flight from Brisbane to Darwin was very pleasant — all mod. cons; air hostesses etc but the flight from Darwin to Vung Tau was altogether different. We were all packed into a Hercules and there we stayed for 8 hours — very little to see and very little space to move about in, so we were all relieved to get here I can tell you. The YMCA had a hot cup of tea at Vung Tau airport which was very acceptable. A great crowd of American soldiers were there too & a funnier looking lot you've never seen. They all seem to have weak eyes — at least 50% were wearing glasses.

My first letter home from Nui Dat.

My tent among the rubber trees at Nui Dat.

The front of the regimental aid post (RAP) for 4 Field Regiment in Nui Dat.

The Australian Task Force chapel at Nui Dat.

Fred Wittmer, Hygiene Sergeant (*right*), and me outside the RAP at Nui Dat.

PREVENTION OF VD

VD is preventable, despite popular opinion amongst soldiers on the topic.

This is how you prevent VD.

1.   DON'T DO IT

Abstaining from sexual intercourse (i.e. NO SEX) for 12 months is NOT detrimental to good health and does not cause mental illness, warped personality, sterility, impotence or atsophy of any vital organs. It is the SURE way to avoid VD. If you will not or cannot stick to this rule though, READ on.

2.   SEX BEFORE ALCOHOL

If you are drunk, you will NOT worry about VD and will not take any precautions, therefore if you must have sexual intercourse, DON'T get drunk before hand.

3.   USE A CONTRACEPTIVE ('FRANGER; RUBBER etc)

These are freely available and if used correctly, will prevent VD in 99 cases out of 100.

4.   URINATE (PISS)

As soon as possible after intercourse and PISS IN SQUIRTS

5.   WASH

Wash your penis and scrotum as soon as possible afterwards in soap and water, (warm if you can get it).

6.   DO NOT ACCEPT PILLS

Do not accept pills of any kind from anyone to prevent VD. The so called "NO SWEAT" pills are extremely dangerous, as they may cover up serious veneral disease (e.g. SYPHILIS).

7.   DO NOT KEEP 'MILKING' OR SQUEEZING your penis for several days after intercourse to see if a 'DRIP' is developing. If it is going to develop, it will do so without your help.

Constant squeezing causes IRRATATION and a slight discharge which can be confused with VD.

8.   GET A BLOOD TEST

Get a blood test done 5-6 weeks after sexual contact of any kind. These are available at the RAP.

9.   See YOUR DOCTOR if in doubt.

A note I wrote on how to prevent VD. A copy was given to all members of the regiment before going on R&R or R&C leave.

A vaccination parade at one of the gun batteries in Nui Dat – Sergeant Bob Allen is second from the left.

A dust-off helicopter on the pad, outside the Forward Detachment of 8 Field Ambulance, Nui Dat.

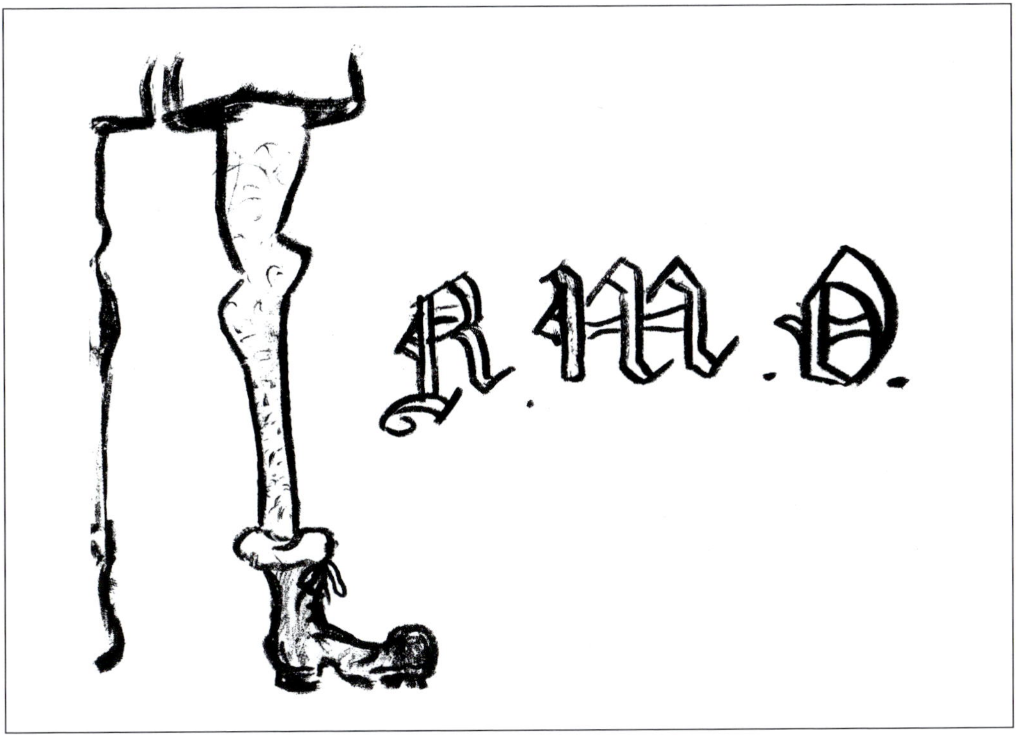

R.M.O.

A drawing of my knobbly knees by Gunner Dickinson on the back of one of the daily conference notes for officers in July 1967.

Jack the Quack from Nui Dat – Captain Jack Blomley.

Private Alex (Chuck) Berry ready to leave on an operation with 106 Battery.

Sergeants Ken Murphy and Bob Allen on Operation Ainslie.

Captain Brian Mitchell, Adjutant of 4 Field Regiment, in his 'office' at Nui Dat.

Three 106 Battery gunners wearing ear muffs, out on operation. Gunner Avery is in the centre.

Lance Corporal Peter Williams (*right*) and me at the Horseshoe.

A group of 106 Battery gunners at the Horseshoe.

A gunner, sunbaking with a can of beer, on top of dug-out sleeping quarters at the Horseshoe.

A snap of me at the HQ Battery farewell party in the gunners' mess ('the snake pit') at Nui Dat, described in my letter of 8 April 1968.

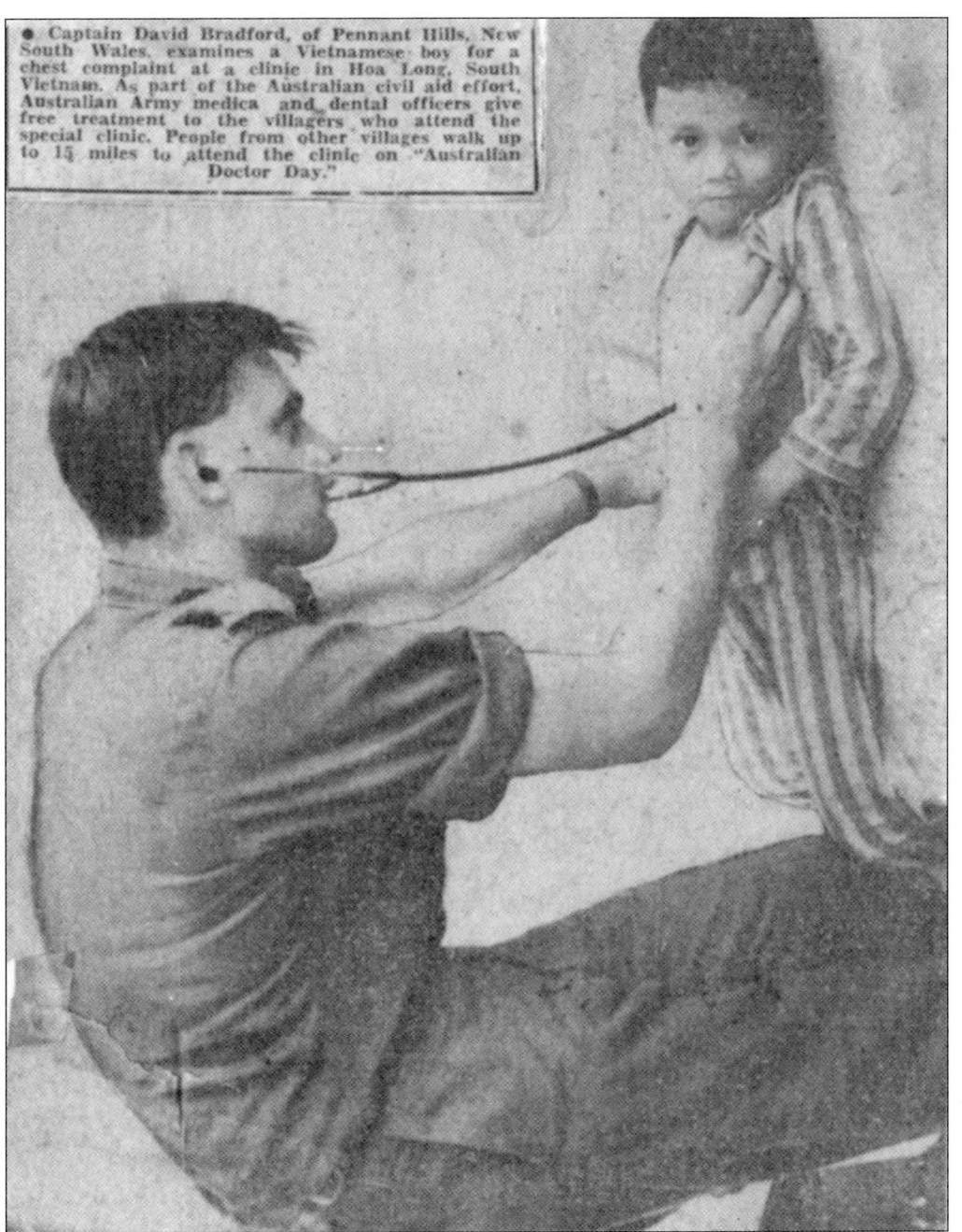

A newspaper cutting of me examining a Vietnamese child on a Medcap in Hoa Long, mentioned in my letter of 23 July 1967.

A Medcap in a village at Ngaio Giao with the Civil Aid team.

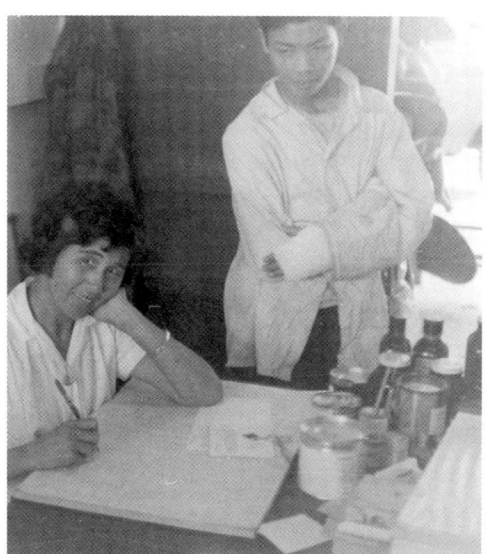

The midwife in the dispensary at Hoa Long on a Wednesday afternoon Medcap. The boy with the burned hands is mentioned in my letter of 21 August 1967.

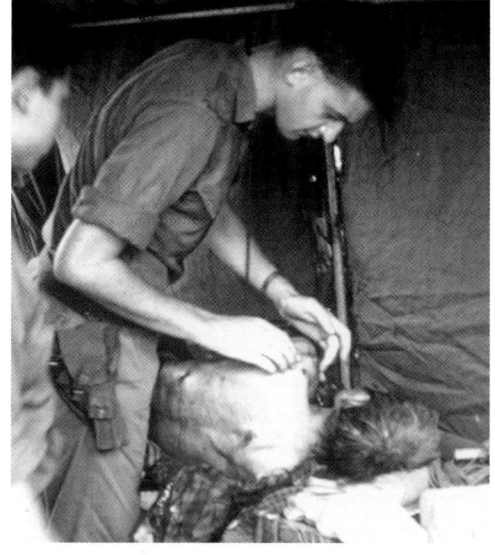

Tending to a civilian with shrapnel wounds on a Medcap in Duc Thanh.

Gunners from HQ Battery about to board a Chinook for Operation Paddington.

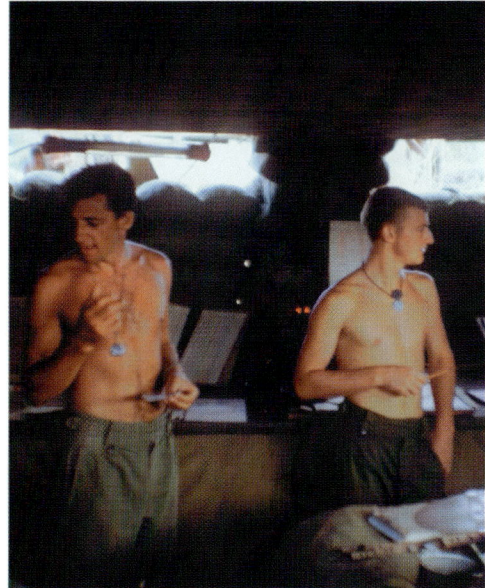

HQ Battery gunners inside the Chinook bound for Operation Paddington.

The underground gun battery command post on Operation Coburg in 1968.

Me, recuperating after my spell in hospital, reading a medical text on Operation Duntroon.

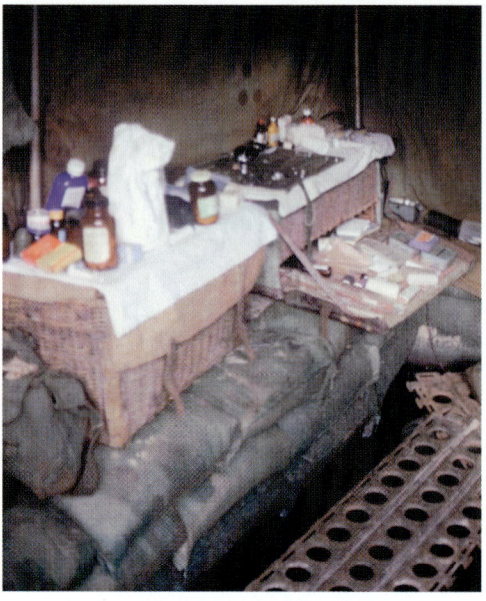

The flooded regimental aid post (RAP) on Operation Kenmore.

The heavily fortified and dug-in RAP on Operation Coburg.

The HQ Battery patrol about to go out with the Regimental Sergeant Major (*far right*) on Operation Paddington, described in my letter of 14 July 1967.

A couple of gunners' sleeping dug-outs on Operation Duntroon.

The view of Taipei from my window in the Ambassador Hotel when I was on R&R leave in November 1967.

A busy Saigon street in November 1967.

Final parade for 4 Field Regiment and hand-over to 12 Field Regiment at 108 Battery, Nui Dat, 14 April 1968.

Farewell champagne for the commanding officer (CO), Lieutenant Colonel Reg Gardner (*left*), and Lieutenant Patrick Thorne (*right*) at Luscombe airstrip, Nui Dat.

The final departure: the CO's party of
4 Field Regiment personnel boarding the
Caribou at Luscombe airstrip, Nui Dat,
April 1968.

Me arriving back at Sydney airport on
8 May 1968.

Me at the site of the old Luscombe airstrip, Nui Dat, in November 2004.

Last day of Operation Kenmore
Tuesday 10/10/67

My dear old Mother and everyone else,

First I must thank you for the photos[1] which arrived yesterday.

Tomorrow this operation winds up and although it's been quite pleasant out at the seaside and I've had more to do the last few days, with everyone from Task Force HQ coming to me for treatment (mostly for bad ears or stingray bites), I'll be glad to get back to the comparative peace of my own tent and RAP. You see, when out on op, the RAP tent seems to be taken for granted, by all who come out visiting from Nui Dat for a day or so (like padres), as the guest house. Sergeant Allen gets most upset about it. For the last three days we have had the padre and the LAD (light aid detachment – i.e. the engineering detachment for the regiment) CO, a captain, eating and sleeping with us and they sure do get in the way. It's hard enough treating people out in the bush in a little 11 ft × 11 ft [3.4 metre × 3.4 metre] tent without several other people living there as well. It would be OK if they didn't try to take over. The padre is a nice enough chap but he insists on getting into arguments with the diggers (like Gunner Scroope, my batman, and Gunner Manning, the hygiene duty man, who both legitimately live around the RAP). I have to keep on trying to keep the peace. And Peter Snowden, the LAD captain, is a lovely guy and easy enough to get on with under ordinary circumstances, except he thinks we don't run things properly – he's been in the army thirteen years and reckons he's an expert on living in the bush, so he tries to organise us. The four of us, (Sergeant Allen, myself, Gunners Scroope and Manning), who make up the RAP contingent breathe rather a sigh of relief when all the visitors leave to go back to base. It's not that we're inhospitable, just that they get in the way. The padre is really pretty good (e.g. doesn't believe in padres drinking, which is a pleasant change) but he has the usual teetotaller's tact and holds forth at great length on the evils of young soldiers drinking. You can literally see their hackles rising. Why can't you get the happy medium – Christians who hold sound views but have a little common sense in the way they put them across? But, back to camp tomorrow and a little privacy for a while.

I have had no more news either of my R&R, or of the four weeks I've been promised afterwards in an American hospital in Saigon. A break from the usual routine would be nice now. Not that I'm fed up or anything (it probably sounds like it on reading this letter) but I do need a short change of atmosphere. Being on call twenty-four hours a day, seven days a week, even when you're not often called out, becomes a bit of a strain. Only the other night one of the gunners woke me at 2 am, with an aching leg after one of these stingray bites he got during the day. One of the RAP 'guests' got upset and told me I shouldn't treat people in the middle of the night but should tell them to come back in the morning unless it was an emergency. People can be funny!

Much love to you all,
David

[1] Photos of home and the garden, and one of Mum's decorated shop windows.

Nui Dat
Thursday 12/10/67

My very best Mother,
Just a little note tonight as I have had one of my busiest days for ages. The first day back after an op is always busy; all the people who have just held off seeing a doctor while their own doctor is away, come out of the woodwork, plus all the aftermath of the op (sore eyes and skin rashes). Today was even worse than usual. I didn't finish sick parade until after noon and we started at 7.45 am. There were twelve 'tankies' from 3 Cav Regiment to be seen as well as all my gunners. Then this afternoon I had to do about thirty medicals on 'nashos' going home to Australia from the regiment. They're not being discharged until April but there are so many in 4 Fd Regt due for discharge over the next year, they have to stagger their times of departure from SVN, so we can get replacements over a gradual period. So I am quite 'wore out' after all that and the RAP looks as if a bomb hit it – still unpacking from the bush, papers and medical documents everywhere.

To cap it all tonight, one of the HQ battery gunners went

and collapsed. He had been sick with 'gastro' for a couple of days and tonight he apparently was so weak that he just fainted away. He created all sorts of drama as he decided to do it right outside the orderly room in full view of the battery sergeant major (BSM), who is a right old panicker. I at last managed to calm down the BSM and get the poor old gunner off to 8 Field Ambulance (the former was by far the harder task).

The adjutant's wife, whom I met at Brisbane airport as you may remember, has been writing to Brian. She has got it into her head that it's a dreadful thing some nice girl hasn't snapped me up yet and has predicted that an English girl will sweep me off my feet the minute I arrive in the country. It's a bit of an amazing prophecy as she only knew me for about half an hour all told.[1] Then I go and read your fears in your latest letter.[2] Have no fears. There is no country like good old Australia, and besides, England is going to be too cold for me after all this tropical weather. I must go to bed now. Much love to you and please don't overdo it in the next few weeks.

David

PS Jack the Quack finished today at the Forward Detachment and returns to Vung Tau. I will really miss him. He has been replaced by a Major Joyce. I met him today and he seems a bit of a pain in the neck. 'Old Mumbles' is his nickname amongst the medics.

[1]   I don't know why I would recount this story, except that it reflected my general anxiety about the family expectations that I would be eventually getting a girlfriend and 'settling down'. I knew quite clearly that this would *never* happen.

[2]   My mother guessed intuitively that I would like England so much I would settle there and never return. In fact, this almost did happen and I stayed in the UK just short of eleven years.

Nui Dat
Friday 13/10/67

Dear family,
Just a short one as I am recovering from a party in the mess tonight. I had a quick trip to the Horseshoe by helicopter this afternoon as

Chuck is weighed down with ear infections amongst the men, all picked up in the sea no doubt during Op Kenmore. So it was a tedious time for me looking into soggy inflamed ear canals.

Then this evening we had a rare visit to the mess of the two forward observers from 106 Battery, Tony Williams[1] and Neville ('Nobby') Clark. They are both extremely nice blokes and it's a shame we don't see more of them. Inevitably they do all their fraternising with 7 RAR and the infantry officers. So a real party atmosphere prevailed tonight. Nobby has an excellent voice and knows all the verses to Rudyard Kipling's Barrack Room Ballad about 'The Screw Guns'. This is a time-honoured traditional song for artillerymen everywhere (well I don't know about the Americans). Nobby has one of those open gregarious personalities and is totally unabashed about singing in public, so easily gets everyone to join in – a wonderful gift to have.

So we are all hoarse from singing:

Smokin' my pipe on the mountings, sniffing the mornin' cool,
I walks in my old brown gaiters along o' my old brown mule,
With seventy gunners behind me, an' never a beggar forgets
It's only the pick of the Army,
that handles the dear little pets!

For we all love the screw-guns – the screw-guns they all love you!
So when we call round with a few guns,
o' course you will know what to do –
Just send in your Chief an' surrender –
it's worse if you fights or you runs:
You can go where you please; you can skid up the trees
but you can't get away from the guns!

There are many more verses but that's all I can remember.

Anyway, it was a nice time and we all enjoyed ourselves.[2]

Much love,

David

---

[1] Not Dr Tony Williams, the 7 RAR RMO. I knew two Tony Williamses in SVN.

2   Parties in the officers' mess were a rare event in SVN, but when they did occur the officers let their hair down. Lots of good stories were told and there was a great sense of camaraderie. I was always sober – most of my colleagues were not, so I was the (usually willing) recipient of many confidences.

Nui Dat

Sunday night 15/10/67

Dear family,

Thank you for the great swag of letters in the past two days. I'm sorry to hear Mum has the gastric flu – she must have it in sympathy with me.[1] I have had dysentery since yesterday lunchtime and have been flat on my back ever since, except for a feeble attempt to struggle through sick parade this morning. Just now I got up long enough to stitch up someone's cut head. I have been 'pretty crook' really – last night I was sure I was going to die and even put myself on Chloromycetin, but I am much better now and should be OK in the morning. So I can really sympathise with you, Mum.

Much love,

David

1   Letters were greatly important for serving soldiers but they had their obvious advantages and their disadvantages. The written word could never be taken back – something written in the heat of the moment or in the depths of a 'down' time could hit the recipient like a blow. The lag time of several days often made things worse. By the time I heard my mother was ill she was probably well on the way to recovery and I would be worrying needlessly.

Nui Dat

Thursday 19/10/67

Dearest Mother (that 'dear, good woman')[1],

Well you certainly have had a bad time in the last week, haven't you? I am so glad you are feeling better now and that the gastric flu has cleared up. I know just how you have been feeling and I know exactly what you mean about the terrible weakness afterwards. For the last four days I have been just pushing myself around and that's the time I feel most homesick (when I'm a bit below par). I am OK again now, as I hope you are.

Merrie sounds a bit 'strung up' at the moment. Both of you must be careful not to overdo it in the next few weeks. There's no sense in you both being so tired on the big day that you can't enjoy it.

I am glad Merrie liked the Vietnamese sheets. I was rather taken with them myself and was sure she'd appreciate the embroidery.

Has Ian recovered from his exams yet? I do hope so – will he have to wait long for the results?

Do take care of yourself, Mum, and I send all my love,
David

---

[1]   A minister's wife at Seaforth Baptist Church had once referred to my mother as 'that dear, good woman'. It became a family joke.

Nui Dat
Saturday 21/10/67

Dear old sister Porky girl,
Well, only two weeks to The Day! I suppose you are getting so excited you can hardly speak. Just as well you don't have any trains to catch or you would be floating off every station and knocking your crazy 'scone' open. I am so glad you liked the sheets. I thought they were rather fetching myself, but there is always the little doubt when I buy something that I have made yet another 'boo-boo' and the colours, to an average person (as opposed to one like me possessing superior colour sense[1]), may seem appalling. I am glad that is not the case with the sheets. Your shower tea sounds like a successful afternoon – quite a 'haul' of presents, I imagine. Who was at the shower tea? Many glorious glamorous 'pieces'[2] from the church or were they all nurses?

It is almost certainly fixed now that while you are waltzing down the aisle towards the assembled choir and clergy (bishop and pastor) ready to take your place beneath the wondrous beauty of the three venetian blinds, your old brother Dave will be on a plane flying towards Taipei for R&R. I commence my R&R on 4th November and instead of flying towards good old Sydney I'm afraid I'll be flying north – farther away. Sad as it is to be missing the wedding, I will really be glad to get away from this hole for a while, especially as we look like going out on yet another op this week coming – a five-week op this time – at least I'll have the break of R&R in the middle of it. Guess who I'm going on R&R with? I had a ring the other day from the CO to say he had heard he was going to Taipei the same day as I and would I like to join him and his friend Lieutenant Colonel John McDonagh (the CO of the Civil Affairs Unit) to see the sights of Taipei. What can one say to such an offer?[3] Knowing me, as you do, you can guess I would be quite happy to potter around Taipei on my own without having two half colonels breathing down my neck, but that's that I guess. I told him I had to call on a missionary friend while I was there, but that didn't deter him – he said he had to see friends too so it would be quite OK to split up for things like that. I won't have to stay at the same hotel, as the colonels are staying at a very posh place. I think I will go to a less imposing more reasonably priced one. They are all supposed to be very modern and clean in Taipei, so it will be good to have a few civilised comforts for five days. I would much rather the somewhat doubtful civilised comforts of 75 Castle Hill Road (bathroom and all[4]) but it is 'not in mortals to command success'[5] (on R&R leave anyway).

I hope Mum is quite better again now. I haven't had any mail the last three days but I suppose there will be a big swag tomorrow. The post office system is all mucked up again – it happens periodically.

I don't think I have any more news of importance. Things are pretty quiet for the present, but with this new operation coming up, things should spark up a bit – I hope not too much.

Anyway, much love, dear old sis – I know it must be an awful blow to you and Ian not having your dear, kind, sweet, terrific organ-playing, modest, handsome, elegant, refined brother and brother-in-law to be, home for the wedding, but bear up there's a good soul. I will write again before the Great Day.

Much love,

Davey boy

PS Alan Begbie[6] is up here as chaplain-general and is taking the ten o'clock service tomorrow – he wants to see me. I must be getting famous, so I had better not miss church this Sunday.

1   Readers might recall that I am red-green colour blind. I once selected some towels for a present, believing they were identical in colour, only to discover one was green and one was brown.

2   This is heavy sarcasm. Many Christian girls in the sixties wore little or no make-up, favoured the twin-set and pearls approach to fashion, were strongly discouraged from wearing shorts or pant-suits ('men's clothing') and looked dreary and dowdy.

3   My heart really sank at this news. I was hoping for the chance to explore an Asian city on my own. I liked the CO, but the thought of spending my precious five-day R&R with him was a downer.

4   The bathroom at home was the size of a large cupboard and had a gas hot water heater over the bath which almost exploded every time it was turned on.

5   Joseph Addison – 'Cato', 1713.

6   Rev Alan Begbie was Chaplain-General for the Australian Armed Forces at that time. He was a very well known Sydney Anglican and my father had met him on several occasions. He knew I was serving in Vietnam, although we had not previously met.

Nui Dat

Wednesday 25/10/67

Dear family,

I'm just back from Hoa Long after a usual busy Medcap afternoon with the expected rush on soap, combs and Band-aids. At least all your soap and other donations are appreciated. I thought I would drop you a line before I have a shower.

I had some good slides back yesterday[1] from Operation Ainslie which you may enjoy looking at in a few days time. Some of them are taken through a telephoto lens which I borrowed for a day or so and they haven't turned out badly. The colours are funny in the film though – I think it's due to the effects of atmospheric conditions on the dyes.

It was very busy this morning, so much so that I couldn't attend the briefings about the coming op and had to send Sergeant Allen for me. We leave early Friday morning. It's a really big one this time – the Yanks are in it again, like with Op Paddington – that's top secret, of course and shouldn't be committed to paper.

Bombardier Banks is all excited, as he goes home in three and a half weeks. He says he'll take some things home for me, so I'll try to send my Christmas presents home with him.

Tomorrow I'm going to Vung Tau to get all the details fixed with the doctor who's replacing me when I go on R&R. I also have to get the new American doctor at 1/83rd Artillery to look after the remains of the regiment at Nui Dat when I go out on operation, as Jack the Quack's replacement 'old Mumbles' at the Forward Detachment says he's 'too busy' to look after the gunners too. Pity about him! Poor old Jack always had to do it on the last three ops.

My grammar seems to be going to rack and ruin. On reading over this letter it sounds 'all peculiar', as Mum says. Tomorrow I have to sign my visa application for Taipei. They had run out of them and they have to be lodged by tomorrow so it looked like I was going to miss out.I thought for a minute I might be able to 'pull a swifty' and get Australia nominated instead, but no such luck. They found some more visa applications so all is well and it's definite that I go to Taipei now.

I'm hoping for a few letters tonight. There's been some major hold-up the last few days in ordinary air mail.

All my love to all at 'Lantern Woods', alias 'that quaint little home'!

Dave

PS: It's excellent to hear you have won Banksy's mother as a permanent customer. That's one in the eye for old Fordy![2]

PPS: I'm glad to hear about the choir stalls and the ivy leaf decorations. But what about the venetian blinds?

PPPS: At last a joke for Pip. Why did Lurch feed 'the thing' with Coca-Cola? Because, things go better with Coke!

---

[1]   Slide processing was prepaid at the time of purchase of the film and the packet contained an envelope for posting the film off to Kodak.

[2]   In fact, Mrs Banks went to the doctor each Monday and obtained a swag of prescriptions each time. She was excellent for business!

[Note written on 'Get Well' card headed:
'Happiness is learning your doctor graduated at the top of his
*   class . . .*
Overpage:
. . . last Tuesday . . . Get well soon!']

Thursday 26/10/67

Dear Mum and others,

Out on op again tomorrow morning and I was hoping to make you a
tape tonight, but no such luck. It is 8.30 and I haven't stopped all day
and still have to pack ready for tomorrow.

I couldn't resist this card from the American PX in Vung Tau today.
A lot of letters and my birthday card arrived – Beaut! Thanks for all
the birthday thoughts, not to mention the presents. Aunty Marge's
parcel arrived too, a lot of paperbacks – terrific – all detective novels.

Boy! Things sound hectic at home. Can you get inside the front
door? Enclosed is an appropriate 'peanuts' note for you, Mum, and a
'mouse for cheering up people' from my 'girlfriend' (the army nurse
in Malaya). She is always dropping me little notes embellished with
similar drawings.

A few words for Pip:

1. Sorry – how could I get a Matthew Arnold quote wrong?[1] You
haven't answered my quotation question yet though.

2. The cheque for the World Record Club's 'St Mark's Passion'? No
sweat, as the Yanks say, which means I'll fix it.[2]

3. Wish Merrie and Ian good luck for their tour to 'Newfoundland'
as some wit dubbed Tasmania.

Signing off and lots of love,

Dave

PS A belated get well wish to the best mother in all the world from
'the Quack from Nui Dat' (or one of them anyway).

[1] Pip and I used to send each other quotes and ask for the author. The
     Matthew Arnold quote he had sent me was: 'The sea is calm tonight, the
     tide is full, the moon lies fair upon the straits', 'Dover Beach', 1867. I
     can't remember what I set him.

2   I was the official family subscriber to the World Record Club and there was a cheque owing for an album of Bach's 'St Mark's Passion' recently received at home. For the musically knowledgeable reader, I know that Bach's 'St Mark's Passion' is officially lost, but various versions have been produced over the years including a WRC one in 1967.

Out on Operation 'Santa Fe'

Sunday morning, 29/10/67

MY LAST LETTER TO A SINGLE SISTER – YOU'D BETTER TREASURE IT!

Dear Sis,

Thank you so much for the flattering portrait of me which you deigned to send me and also for the very life-like painting of 'the weirdly gruesome one', Pip. What a cheerful birthday collection – a real rogue's gallery! Are they from a Flintstone book or something?

But seriously, thank you for all the birthday gifts – the books look very good – in fact I have started reading the spy one already. The tea pot has been put to excellent use, despite many ribald comments from those outside the RAP staff, who are only jealous anyway.

(. . . pause to give someone a penicillin injection for an ear infection).

While I write this I am listening to 'the Protestant Hour' on Sergeant Allen's radio from Armed Forces Radio Saigon – for once a good sermon too (which is amazing – from an American Presbyterian Church). We have already waded through 'Music for a Sunday morning' (which means anything that isn't the 'Top 40') and 'the Catholic Hour'. The radio stays on all day and whatever comes over, good or bad, we get it. The air is filled with the noise of bulldozers pushing down undergrowth. The area we are camped in for this op ('Santa Fe') is very jungley – thick scrub and banana trees. It's a very noisy place at present, what with the aforementioned bulldozers, the clanking sound of the APCs which seem to drive around aimlessly most of the day, choppers whirring in the air, the occasional 'bang' from some of the guns and so on. I'm rather counting the days until Thursday afternoon when I leave for Nui Dat to prepare for my R&R which starts on Saturday.

About the Wedding! Still no news on my obsession – the venetian blinds. As you may have guessed, I think Mr Logan's[1] latest idea for the service is fairly awful. It is hard to imagine Dad in that tender role of joining Ian and your hands in front of the assembled congregation. I await with great interest the account of your wedding rehearsal next Tuesday evening.

You must be scoring well for wedding presents. It makes my humble sheets and as yet non-existent cuckoo clock look very mean and miserable – not befitting a magnate with money-bins at all. I have only written about three cheques all told since I arrived in SVN – I am just allowing my millions to accumulate in my pay book. I only draw $10 a fortnight to pay mess bills and my canteen account (my few soft drinks and all the beer I buy everyone else). Everyone 'shouts' everyone else – the only snag being it's cheaper for them to buy me a lemonade than it is for me to buy them what they're drinking. I even bought a bottle of wine for the evening meal one night, as it was my turn, and consented to a thimbleful myself. I don't really get what people see in wine at meal times – it's so bitter. Someone always says, 'Now doc, I know what would be a good one for you to start on'. They never seem convinced that I haven't any desire to start on any. What are you drinking at the wedding? Apple cider I suppose, or is it just fruit cup?

I had better go and do my duty and visit the batteries, spreading joy and gladness. Love from the money bin magnate.

David

PS: Don't forget to send me a card from your honeymoon. What are you doing? Driving to Melbourne to get across the ferry to Tasmania? I seem to have forgotten the details if I ever knew them. You won't want to visit people on honeymoon but if your car breaks down in Melbourne and you're scared of Ian's 'mad' Aunty Gwen[2] go and see John Moroney, the vicar of Hawthorn.

I gather that renowned mechanic Mr Hughes predicts all manner of car trouble for you. Take heart – the MAL got from Sydney to Healesville to Sydney to Brisbane and back to Sydney again all against his dire predictions.

---

[1]   The pastor.

[2]   Ian's Aunty Gwen in Melbourne was a psychiatrist and a somewhat formidable lady.

Reflections

Operation Kenmore for us gunners was sun, surf, sea and sand. And for the RAP staff it was coping with a medical centre placed only inches above the water table and dealing with guests who soon outstayed their welcome. Despite my complaints about our guests these were only minor inconveniences and probably troubled Bob Allen and the staff more than they did me. I'm afraid I privately thought the teetotaller Kiwi padre a bit foolish for his obvious insensitivity to the feelings of the gunners, even though I had to half-heartedly support him as a teetotaller myself. My 'deterioration' must have been continuing.

There were no battle casualties of any note on that operation and no medical emergencies worse than cuts, sunburn and stingray or jellyfish stings. The wet season was ending and the daily swimming parties were refreshing and highly enjoyable. It indeed seemed a funny sort of war when you could go swimming every day in the South China Sea. There were no women around so few soldiers bothered to wear swimming trunks. I was unused to nudity and it was a disturbing experience swimming beside handsome naked young men. Being subjected to such unexpected visual stimulation made me realise that my gay feelings were not so easily suppressed or sublimated in practice as I thought they might be in theory. I am not aware that any of my fellow officers or soldiers suspected my true sexual orientation at this time. Most just thought I was very repressed by my religious convictions. They all, quite rightly, concluded that I was a virgin and that, as the officers in the mess put it with monotonous regularity, my next fuck would be my first. If Bob Allen had his suspicions, he never voiced them to me or anyone else that I am aware of. I was relieved, but a little sorry, when Operation Kenmore came to an end.

Back home, plans for my sister's wedding were proceeding apace. Despite the unanticipated delights of Operation Kenmore, I felt sad not to be part of the family celebrations, and was very sorry I could not take my R&R leave in Australia to be there on the day. I was just in the wrong place at the wrong time. Six months later, R&R in Australia had become so common and accepted for Australian soldiers and officers that then I would have had little trouble organising my leave to coincide with a family event of major importance. Looking back, I wonder if I could have been more forceful and asked my CO to intervene on my behalf with the SMO in Vung Tau. The CO was a kindly man and had always been helpful and sympathetic with me. But being pushy wasn't really in my nature and consequently I have always felt guilty that I let my sister down by not trying harder to attend her wedding.

Although I was looking forward to a break, even if I had to spend R&R with the CO and his friend, I did feel reluctant to leave the regiment while its members were all out on Operation Santa Fe. The first few days of the operation had been sunny and uneventful but there were strong rumours that things would definitely get more nasty in the second part of the proceedings. Bob Allen and the rest of my staff were vocal in their regret that I was leaving them behind and they were not taking kindly to the prospect of an unknown doctor from Vung Tau replacing me.

So October ended for me with many mixed emotions – sadness that I wasn't going home for the wedding, regret that I was leaving the regiment in the lurch and excitement to be getting away to an exotic Asian city for five days. There was also considerable frustration that my opportunity to explore Taipei alone and have adventures, of whatever kind, would be extremely limited.

7

NOVEMBER 1967

Letters

FSB Wilton
Op Santa Fe
Wednesday 1/11/67

Dear Dad,

Happy Birthday to me! I was awakened at 3 am this morning by the phone in our mice-infested RAP ringing, with the switchboard operator from the command post wishing me a happy birthday. Someone is planning to present me with one of the tiny American ration pack cakes with twenty-six bits of stick stuck on the top of it as a birthday cake, later in the day.

It is about time I dropped you a line. I do hope you managed to get all your stocktaking and income tax[1] done by yesterday. It must have been a trial with all the wedding preparations as well. I suppose you are just about 'broke' now after the big event.[2]

I haven't much to tell you at the moment – the operation is going exceedingly quietly – the weather is very good and I've had little to do. The second phase of the op starts on Friday, when the regiment moves to a new position, and it promises to be more lively. Fortunately, I'll be on R&R then.

Thank you all very much for the cards and presents. The books particularly have been a real help on this operation – I've done a lot of reading. Tomorrow afternoon I will be going back to Nui Dat on the resupply chopper to get ready for R&R – I have to get paid. Then I actually leave on Saturday morning.

It sounds frightening your playing one of my tapes after church.[3] I have forgotten by now all the things I said on that tape. I'm glad I don't have to hear it replayed – how embarrassing!

Well, that's all for now, Dad.

Much love to all,

David

[1]   It was unusual in the sixties for individuals and even small business people to use tax accountants. Most people filled out their own income tax returns. After a few years of marriage, Ian did Dad's tax return for him.

[2]   In the sixties, it was still the norm for the father of the bride to pay for the wedding in its entirety.

[3]   I had made a tape specifically for the church people. I have no idea what I said – it must have been singularly unexciting – but Dad played it to any members of the congregation who wanted to hear it after a service one Sunday evening.

Nui Dat
Thursday 2/11/67

EXACTLY SIX MONTHS IN COUNTRY!

My dear family,

Two days to go to the Big Day. The excitement at 'Lantern Woods' must be well nigh fever pitch. I just hope you have Merrie shut up safely in the house. If she is allowed to wander around the streets, goodness knows what will happen to her. She is bad enough at the best of times but I bet she is so vague now she doesn't know the way from the front door to the lounge room – that's of course if anyone can make that journey without moving great piles of wedding presents.

I am feeling a bit sad tonight – first, because of missing the wedding, but it's no use worrying about that I guess; secondly, even though I should be excited about R&R, I feel sad at leaving the regiment out on operation. Tomorrow is a big day when they move to a new FSB position right in an enemy stronghold area and I would feel really awful if anything happened to them in my absence. The replacement doctor from the Field Ambulance, Morrie Peacock, arrived and is out in the bush with them now, and he's an excellent doctor, but it's not the same. It's amazing how attached you become to your own unit. Another thing I heard today was that I may not be coming back to the regiment until 28th November. Morrie said he was sure I was to stay on in Saigon after I returned from R&R for three weeks working at a US Army hospital. I know this was promised me, but I didn't expect it quite so soon. Of course it will be quite an experience and I'll enjoy it when I get there, but at the moment I just feel upset at leaving 'my practice' here at 4 Fd Regt. I should know for sure tomorrow if this rumour is true and I'll let you know straight away.

I remember Mum saying that when I came home I would be sure to have changed in some ways. I suppose that's true enough – you can't spend a year over here without becoming a little different. The officers in the mess tell me, 'It's becoming hard to shock the doc these days.' Apparently I don't blush as easily, and really after listening to some of the gunners' 'confidences' it's no wonder. The things they tell you! It's especially so out on op, when there's nothing much to do once the camp is established but sit around and talk. And people all seem to congregate at the RAP. I guess I have never really realised until the last few months what a 'sheltered' life I've led and just how much I have to be thankful for that I was shielded from so many pitfalls by a wise father and mother. I have got to like my soldiers so much that it really hurts me to hear how some of them live and how so often they miss out on the best things in life.

I must stop raving, when there are much more interesting things to talk about – like weddings.

Must close for tonight with all my love to you all,
David

The Ambassador Hotel
Taipei
Sunday 5/11/67

Dear everybody,
Now that the tumult and shouting has died down after the wedding, I guess you will have time to hear my news. I arrived last night about

seven o'clock in Taipei after a five and a half hour flight from Saigon, which was pretty good – Pan-Am, with steak for dinner and pretty air hostesses. We checked in at the R&R counter and got the drill on hotels and then we were sent off to the hotel of our choice. The CO and his friend, the other lieutenant colonel, both decided on the Ambassador, the most luxurious of the R&R joints and as the one US officer on the trip decided to go there too, I thought it would be silly not to join them, even though it's US$10.50 per night. It's only for five nights and you might as well be comfortable after six months in rotten old Vietnam! I looked out for church timings this morning but couldn't see anything much, so today I thought I would be a heathen and not worry. As it is, my civvy clothes are all crushed horribly; so badly I couldn't wear them until the hotel had them pressed, so I had to cool my heels until nine-thirty this morning before I had anything other than my uniform to wear. The hotel then brought me my pressed clothes and, with much bowing and scraping Oriental fashion, a tailor to measure me for a twenty-four hour US$40 suit.

'Ah so, captain need suit velly badly – I maka zee fine suits. I number 1 velly fine tailor and use only best quality English wool.' And so on at great length, all with me only in singlet and underpants. I am completely hopeless and have only been 'taken down' about ten times so far today. Anyway, I do need a suit to go out to the officers' club at night, so I gave in and Peter Woo is obliging at ten o'clock tomorrow morning with a perfect high quality suit. I hope I didn't choose too horrible a colour – it's a sort of bluish shade.

The hotel is superb. I have my own shower, bath, hot water, toilet (!), radio, television and air conditioning. And there are no girls knocking on your door at all hours of the night, unlike most of the R&R hotels – which is a distinct advantage.

Today we spent wandering around town. There are some amazing stores with all manner of Oriental 'junk', but also some very high quality merchandise. Everything is open on Sunday; and the traffic – there are millions and millions of little red taxis which zoom around madly and cost 10 NT dollars (about 25 US cents) for most city trips, but it's a hair-raising drive. I bought a lot of reprinted – i.e. 'pirated', there being no copyright laws recognised in Taiwan – medical books for next to nothing.[1]

I must close now and have a big soak in the bath and then to bed in nice clean sheets. We had an excellent meal tonight – proper northern Szechwan Chinese food. It was very hot and spicy but I enjoyed it and even handled the chopsticks OK.

Much love,

David

---

[1]   I still own them today. I certainly got my money's worth out of them.

The Ambassador Hotel
Taipei
Tuesday evening 7/11/67

My dear Mother,

More news from R&R. Yesterday I did a fair bit of shopping – in fact I don't think I have ever spent so much money in my life. R&R is a bit like being a sahib in the East, airily tossing money here and there – taxi men, shoe shine boys, ladies selling red paper button-hole flowers.

I then went to 'Hospitality House', a sort of home from home for servicemen run by an American Christian organisation and had lunch with the manager Sid Hendry, his wife and some 'odd-bod' American servicemen who happened to be there from bases around Taipei. They have Chinese servants and it's all very pukka and colonial. There was a piano so I had a good time practising for about an hour. They have managed to organise a trip for me to see Judy and Brian Dillon in Kao-hsiung – by plane, but it's really quite cheap (NT $634 or US$15 return). I'm going early tomorrow morning and coming back tomorrow evening – 400 miles [645 kilometres] in one day and then the next day it's back to Saigon. It will be worth it to see someone from Pennant Hills.

Today we went on a tour (the two colonels and myself) to an 'aboriginal' (Taiwanese) village called Wulai where we saw native dancing, a waterfall, had a Chinese meal and a ride on a cable car. The two COs have been so good and it's been no drag having to share my R&R with them. They only drink lightly and are really only here for a quiet time, so it's worked out well.

Much love, Mum,

David

Nui Dat (again!)
Thursday 9/11/67

My dear family,

I'm at old Nui Dat again. R&R is over and it's back to that salubrious holiday resort, the Australian Task Force, with shower buckets and deep pit latrines – what a let-down after a lovely big bath with running hot and cold water and a flushing toilet. I am only here for the night to collect some clean clothes before flying back to Saigon tomorrow for ten days or more there. While there, I will work in the RAP in the mornings (very short and undemanding, I believe) and I'll be able to work in one of the American surgical hospitals in Saigon in the afternoons. It should be a little refresher course, although on hearing the news from the operation when I got back today I feel a bit of a 'heel' being away from the regiment any longer.

The FSB has had quite a bit of trouble from the enemy this time, with VC probing the perimeter at night and firing shots into the camp. We had our first 'killed in action' (KIA) too – one of the 108 Battery gunners, Gunner Tregear, was killed by the blast from a Claymore mine. A couple of VC had managed to sneak in and set it up right inside the camp. He was the only casualty – the poor kid was going on R&R the next day and hadn't dug himself in very deeply – just said, 'That'll do; I'll only be here until tomorrow' sort of thing. When it went off he copped a piece of shrapnel in the head. No one even noticed he'd been wounded until someone went to wake him the next morning. He must have died almost instantly. So, the poor old regiment is really in the thick of it this time. It is a bit tough on the relieving doctor as things sound a bit rougher out there than at Vung Tau. Still, there's no sense in my being a martyr and I might as well accept the offer of a stay in Saigon.

I had a very enjoyable day with the Dillons. Brian is a very nice chap, though very serious. Judy looks very well. They have a nice neat little flat with all mod cons. Taiwan is amazing – absolutely different from SVN – the people are happy looking and extremely industrious – not like the poor war-weary Vietnamese. They work in the Presbyterian Church, which is very strong on the island, in the city of Kaohsiung (pronounced 'Gawshung'). We rode around on bicycles looking at temples and markets and saw a full funeral procession.[1] The Chinese are a fascinating people. I never thought the East would appeal to me, but you can't help but be impressed by their resourcefulness and their pride in their great Chinese heritage.

I thought you would like the enclosed leaflet about the Taipei bars. This is a big problem in Taiwan. Immorality is quite legal and the government makes quite a bit of money out of the Prostitution Tax. Each girl has to be registered and 'have a needle' every week to 'keep her disease free' (or relatively so). You can 'buy' these girls for however long you like (all your R&R if you feel like it) and a contract is drawn up with the proprietor and you pay US$15 per day for the pleasure of her company. Most of this goes to the government as tax and the girls live on only a pittance. Of course, it isn't only for R&R soldiers; it's for the Chinese men too. Young people rarely marry before they're at least thirty years old. Brian and Judy told me the 'moral problem' is very great in Taiwan. It's just become an accepted part of Chinese life. Sorry for all the gory details but I thought you might be interested. No wonder the CO took me 'to look after him', as he claimed.

Well, much love to all,

David

[1]   This was a Chinese Buddhist funeral, in a long procession, with clashing cymbals and colourful paper flags and lanterns.

Saigon

Friday 17/11/67

My dear Mother,

I am at present listening to the wedding tapes. What oratory! Didn't your cheeks blush when all those nice things were said about you? I know mine did at Mr Ridley's[1] remarks about 'that brave doctor in Vietnam'. I feel quite a hypocrite sitting here in the comfort of a (virtual) hotel room, even if it is only an army officer's quarters 'BOQ' in Saigon. I feel I ought to be up in the DMZ (demilitarised zone) leading a charge against the VC in the face of tremendous odds. It was a great thrill to hear the tapes. It made me realise what a lot I missed out on, but it was really good to know people were thinking of me.

I had a very interesting day today at the 3rd US Army Field Hospital in Saigon. It is a big hospital situated in what used to be an old school building. I had an interview with the CO who arranged for me to have the morning in the operating theatre assisting in an operation. There is no doubt about the Yanks – they are tremendously obliging people and would do anything for you (and really, there is no reason why they should – all too often the Aussies take all they can from the Americans and give little in return). The resident MOs said I can go back anytime in the next two weeks and assist in theatre, which is very good of them.

I had a big surprise today – a huge parcel of Christmas goodies (nuts, ham, dried fruits, fruit juice, big tin of bikkies) all arrived (from David Jones) from Dr Lew Wheeler, the urologist from Concord whose resident MO I was for a while. I had lunch with him (and Tony Williams) before we both left Sydney. I really didn't know him all that well, so it was a real treat to receive the parcel.

Well, much love from the SVN capital, Mum,
David

1   The Rev. John G. Ridley was a well known Baptist minister and evangelist who had won the Military Cross in World War I. He was an old friend of the Bradfords (my father's family) and participated in my parents' wedding.

Saigon
Sunday 19/11/67

Dear Merrie and Ian,
Thank you for your letter from Eaglehawk Neck – the mere thought of a log fire is utterly repulsive here. I just don't think I could face Tasmania, not until after a period of acclimatisation back in Sydney. I don't quite know how long you were staying down there, so I'll send this letter to 'Lantern Woods'. It sounds awfully interesting, Tasmania, with all the old ruins from convict days.

The wedding tapes were much appreciated but what speeches! With respect Ian, your father and another one of the speakers sounded as though they were definitely on the convention platform rather than at a wedding. I'm glad the car was suitably decorated – I really missed that part most of all – it's a shame you were denied my inventive genius. Still, it sounds as though a second best job was done (as good as could be expected without me there).

For the last two days I have been back in theatre. The doctors at the US 3 Field Hospital have been terrific. They are all young (well, about my age) and drafted into the army mostly (for two years). They greeted me with open arms, sympathised with my plight (being stuck at Nui Dat with no hospital experience to be had for twelve months) and said I was welcome to come and assist in theatre anytime I am in Saigon. One of them took me round the hospital and talked about all his cases. They have some real 'sickies'. There's a renal unit there with two artificial kidneys and they always have people for dialysis – after shock (post traumatic, post malarial, post leptospirosis). Some of the wounds are just terrible. One boy had a shrapnel wound in the back of his neck which took away a great mass of muscle and knocked out his spinal cord at the C4 level so he's quadriplegic because of it. They send their spinal injuries to a special centre in Tokyo for rehab before shipping them back to the US.

It was really good to do some theatre work again. The MOs there reckon I ought to seriously consider going to the US to do my surgical training.

Well, must go to tea, Mr and Mrs Gilchrist (Jnr).

Love,

David

Saigon
Wednesday 22/11/67

Dear Phil (and everybody else),

Thank you for your letter today and the copies of your exam papers. I could have made a stab at the Psych paper, (but would have definitely failed), but there isn't a single question in the English paper I could even have attempted.

Quotations first:

It was Lord Byron who said: 'Be amorous, but be chaste!' and proceeded to disregard it, of course. Fancy you missing that one.

Yours[1] is almost certainly Shakespeare but what character said it I am still puzzling over. I am handicapped in that my little quotation book is still at Nui Dat – by the way, why does Mum persist in calling it 'Nuit Dat'? My writing must give her that impression, I guess.

NB Please excuse water drops on page – I have just washed my hair as miraculously electricity, shower AND toilet are all working tonight.

I am back to 4 Field Regt next Monday or Tuesday and I won't really be sorry. I went out to 3 Field Hospital again today and helped in the theatre. The worst war wound I have yet seen[2] was being patched up but I won't go into details to spare your sensibilities (being a mere Arts student). I do hope your exams went OK anyway – I'm sure you had no trouble.

I am still eagerly awaiting the wedding photos. Are the honey-mooners back? You had better write me a long letter soon with all your plans for the next year.

When does Trevor from Pennant Hills leave for SVN? It's a shame he's going to Saigon. It must be really hard for a soldier in this city. I hope he can find some Christian people in Saigon with whom he can spend his free time, as it can be very lonely here. At least at Nui Dat, even though you can't escape the place, everyone is together and it's not at all lonely. If you're not interested in touring the bars in Saigon, there's not much else to do.

Major James ('Digger'), the army doctor who lost one leg (Korea) and who was at 2 Camp Hospital last year, is coming up in January to the Field Ambulance so that's a good thing. He's a very good and sensible doctor. He may be taking Jack the Quack's place at the Forward Detachment which will be excellent and such an improvement on old 'Mumbles' who's there at present. Jack is now at Vung Tau.

Well Phil, must finish,

Behave yourself,

David

PS a note for Mum: This is just a little note at the bottom of Pip's letter to send you my love. I am so glad everyone enjoyed the wedding. It must have been a real gala day. Granddad Lloyd raved about it in his last letter so he must have heard many good reports. I had to laugh though – he said the wedding was most enjoyable even though 'the speeches by some of the clergy were a bit long'!

D.

1   Pip's test quote for me was: 'A young man married is a man that's marred'
    – Parolles in Shakespeare's *All's Well That Ends Well* (II, iii). However, there
    was a twist to this as Rudyard Kipling had also repeated the same line in
    'The Story of the Gadsbys' – I was supposed to get both correct!
2   Extensive injury to the lower back and both buttocks with amputation of
    one leg. The wound was so deep the sacral bone could be seen. The
    wounds were caused by the soldier stepping onto a mine in his path.

Free World Headquarters

Saigon

Friday 24/11/67

Dear Mum,

Please excuse the notepaper[1] but it is lunchtime and I am writing this
from the RAP at the Free World Building and I've left my writing stuff
at home.

I have just been reading one of Dad's letters (as unintelligible as
usual, I'm afraid). Mrs Banks is not the only mother/wife/relative, I
believe, who has been upset by the little duplicated army note about 'the
homecoming soldier'.[2] Letters have been written by distraught relatives
to the Minister of the Army, I hear, there has been such upset about it.
It is an American thing (or at least adapted from the Yanks) – they have
all sorts of corny notices like that one. I suppose Jeff is safely home
again now and Mrs Banks' worst fears should have been set at rest.

Yesterday we went to Bien Hoa and I saw the hospital the Aussie
Surgical Team are working in. They were 'flat out' when we arrived –
quite a lot of civilians had been brought in that morning with shrapnel
wounds – from American mortars or VC mortars, who knows? – it's
the same with the civilians, no one has a clue whether they are friend
or foe. The injuries were in people of all ages; little babies and old folk.
There were all manner of injuries, face and head wounds – they had
to do two craniotomies that morning and deal with chest wounds and
abdominal wounds. The poor surgeons looked tired out. They spend
hours and hours on the patients in the theatre and then they go back
to scruffy old wards to be cared for by the Vietnamese nurses and
doctors who are apparently not 'too hot' but think they are terrific.
The Surgical Team are really only 'guests' tacked onto the provincial

hospital to do the surgery for the local hospital staff; and the locals won't be told anything about how best to run wards. Serious post-op cases *do* go into one little post-op ward which the Aussie sisters look after, but only during the day. At night they just haven't enough sisters to do shifts and still be able to continue the surgical work next day. Fortunately the Vietnamese are pretty hardy people and seem to do very well after surgery, despite the unsterile conditions and lack of good nursing care, but all the same it must be frustrating for the surgeons. It is not unusual for them to arrive in the morning and find the relatives have taken away one of their prize patients (perhaps someone they've spent all day operating on) because the relatives have decided there's no hope and they're going to die anyway – they think they ought to die at home so off they take them. It must be very hard, working under such conditions – being a civilian hospital patient in Sth Vietnam is nothing like being a hospital patient in Australia – you really wouldn't believe it unless you saw it yourself. I think it would upset me too much to have to work under such conditions.

Well, so much for today, Mum. I do hope you are well and looking after yourself.

Lots of love, and to all the family,

David

PS Tell Dad I don't really mean it about his illegible letters – they are great fun to decode!

1   US Army medical record paper.
2   Unfortunately I don't have a copy of this amazing letter but it was essentially a standard note sent by the army to the next of kin warning them that, on return to Australia, their soldier relative might seem a little odd and take some time to adjust again to normal civilian life. I think it only applied to 'nashos' and not to regular army soldiers.

Saigon
Sunday 26/11/67

Dear old 'marriedies',

By now you must be settled into your little house on the Blue Mountains, with the honeymoon over and done with, and back to humdrum daily living. I do hope you both weathered the crossing of Bass Strait? I have really enjoyed playing the wedding tapes over – it made it seem like you were really married, in my mind at least. No photos have arrived yet so I await them anxiously.

I am so glad you enjoyed Tasmania – it sounds a fascinating place. I might get there one day, you never know – maybe on my honeymoon too? I doubt it – I think I must be a bachelor for life. Aunty Audrey wrote me a short time ago and said I mustn't, on any account, be a bachelor as all bachelors, especially the ones she has met 'on the mission field', are 'old women'.[1]

Today I went to church at a chapel attached to one of the soldiers' quarters ('BEQs', the Americans call them). The 'chapel' was a huge barn of a place with an electric generator just outside which made a very loud distracting noise all through the service – you could barely hear the minister even though he used a microphone. They had quite a nice electronic organ too but you could hardly hear that either. There were about fifteen people there I suppose in this huge space – the singing was slow, dreary and woeful. We had a responsive reading and you couldn't even hear the neighbour next to you reading out the verse, so you can imagine the jumble. Then the minister gave a talk on how we can't help ourselves but need 'Someone Else' to help us, but full of trite little phrases and 'funny' stories about 'a little boy who went to church with his dad' – you know the sort of thing?

I went out into the dirty Saigon streets bustling with poor, equally dirty Vietnamese civilians – soldiers here, there and everywhere – an occupied wartime city in fact, and I was very sad because I felt what a poor sort of show we Christians make to a world in an awful mess. I thought back to the chapel with its rows and rows of empty chairs, dusty floors, dingy walls, languid organist and the handful of bored looking individuals, and it seemed little wonder some crack-pot theologians thought up the 'God is dead' theory. The way we Christians (as a whole) go on, you would think He really was, and Christianity, instead of being God's Good News, has become, for the ordinary man in the street, an empty hulk and a clatter of trite little phrases and stupid jokes. I know I am overstating the case, but as I walked further down the street I passed several American GIs in uniform and they were laughing, smiling and engaging in the usual 'pig' Vietnamese banter with some of the ragamuffin kids on the street and I couldn't help thinking that their friendly cheery faces were a better advertisement for Western civilisation than the glum stuffy lot I had just been with in the chapel. I'm expressing myself badly and you will think I have 'fallen from grace', but there's no one else I can say these things to – being over here certainly does make me rethink things more deeply. But sorry, I didn't mean to write you a sermon and, after all, you've heard this sort of thing from me before – it's beginning to become my hobby horse.[2]

I go back to Nui Dat on Tuesday. Sergeant Allen rang me the other day to say 'hurry back!' – apparently they are getting tired of replacement doctors. My batman handed in his resignation last week. He said it was OK 'batting' for Captain Bradford but he wasn't going to do it for other doctors as they were 'too demanding'.

Well, much love to you both. Hooroo,

David

---

[1] I interpret this as an attempt on my part to get my family used to the idea that I wouldn't be getting married. At the same time, having no real concept of what life as a gay man might be like, I did have a fear, which Aunty Audrey's comment played into, of ending up a peculiar old bachelor.

[2] This is an understated picture of my admittedly confused thinking at the time. During my days in Saigon I had occasional strong feelings about the apparent irrelevance of orthodox Christianity to the war as it was being waged in Vietnam at the time. Temptation had raised its head as well – at the BOQ where I lived in Saigon, I had met a couple of young American officers at the evening movies for officers, who, in hindsight, I am sure were gay. They had invited me to a Sunday party at a private address in the city – of course, I had turned down their invitation because the party was on a Sunday, but I felt a strong urge to go. There was something almost too friendly and too familiar about their invitation and I felt I was getting into dangerous waters. I'm sure there was an element of personal frustration in my dissatisfaction with Christian Witness in Saigon. Sex and religion are always a potent mix.

(Back to) Nui Dat
Thursday 30/11/67

My dear family – everyone,

This letter will have to do you all, I'm afraid. I feel a 'heel' not writing some individual letters after I received a bunch of six letters today, sent back from Saigon where they had been forwarded on from here. Plenty of exciting news, I see.

1. Pip: What a trip you must have had by plane to Canberra and back with Davey Hampson! I'm glad I wasn't on board – even with my vast flying experience (now) I doubt I could have properly handled a situation like that. I bet you were glad to get your feet on solid ground again.[1]

2. I'm so glad Merrie and Ian called in on John Moroney in Melbourne, as he was so good to me when I was in Healesville. He wouldn't have been at all perturbed by their unexpected visit, even if he did have visitors. How are the 'honeymooners' settling into their palatial Glenbrook home?

3. In answer to Pip, my views on birth control are fairly standard medical ones. I do not think 'the Pill' a 'terrible and evil thing' as I believe it is a God-given discovery, same as all other scientific discoveries, and it can be an incalculable blessing in disease-ridden, famine-afflicted places of the East particularly, but also all around the world. As for the learned gynaecology professor Pip quotes, I always did think him a bit of a 'nut'. You know already that I think he overstates his anti-evolution case more than he can, or should, in all honesty as a scientist. Anyone who wears suits like his must be a trifle odd. (There I go again – depending on personal feelings instead of being objective and impartial). I find it very difficult to apply a rigid standard all the time – it must be one of my bad character weaknesses. For example, signing International Health Certificates (IHCs) is an army MO's most tedious task – keeping vaccinations up to date on all the soldiers. The old major now at the Forward Detachment refuses to sign certificates unless he actually and personally *sees* the injection given, whereas all the rest of us army docs sign on the say-so of our RAP corporals and sergeants. There are so many to be done it's virtually impossible any other way

and old 'Mumbles' inevitably has long waiting lists of people to be given needles and have their certificate book signed – people are being held up going on their R&R because of his rigid interpretation of the laws of international health. I guess he is technically and legally correct, but I couldn't face a soldier and tell him, when it came to signing his book before he could go on R&R, that he'd have to have all his injections done again in my presence because I didn't personally see them given to him before. Do you remember the verse in the Bible from Jude 'And of some have compassion, making a difference'? I think it should be applied in our daily dealings with people and I am sure that the number of people for whom we ought to make 'differences' are many.

4. I had quite a large sick parade today – at least I feel welcomed back. I'm out to the Horseshoe then this afternoon as 108 Battery has gone back there. They all seem pretty well and none the worse for the last op. They are still grieving, of course, but recovering slowly from the loss of one of their members. I believe some of the companies in 7 RAR are very depressed because of the loss of so many men either wounded or down with malaria.

Well that's enough nonsense for one day. I am well and happy.

Much love and thanks for all those letters,

David

PS (for Pip): What is 4th December? Clue: A great day for gunners in the church calendar.[2]

---

[1] Pip did not have a head for heights. He could be unnerved by walking up the stairs to the gallery at the Town Hall in Sydney. I cannot imagine how he was ever persuaded to fly in a two-seater plane. Pip's friend 'Davey' had recently got his pilot's licence and one day the two of them just flew to Canberra. On the return journey they ran into a storm and had to make an emergency landing in Goulburn. It must have been a harrowing ordeal for them both, but for Pip it must have been terrifying. He has never spoken of it to me but I have always regarded his adventure with great respect. I saw my younger brother in a new light after that event.

[2] 4 December is St Barbara's Day. She is patron saint of gunners – also brewers, firefighters, gravediggers and prisoners (amongst many others).

Reflections

Rest and recreation leave and my stay in Saigon were a welcome change from the routine of Nui Dat. The two COs, Reg Gardner and John McDonagh, were admirable people to go on leave with in Taipei, despite the disparity in our ages. They were civilised, sociable, understanding and urbane, as well as being excellent company. The few days spent with them were relaxing and enjoyable, despite my earlier fears.

Santa Fe was a big operation conducted in the north-eastern sector of Phuoc Tuy province by the 1st Brigade of the US 9th Infantry Division supported by the Australian Task Force. My time in Taipei and then in Saigon meant that I saw little of the operation. In some respects, this was unfortunate because it was eventful for our regiment. As he was in regular touch by phone with task force headquarters while on R&R, the CO heard that one of our gunners had been killed and when he told me over dinner in our Taipei hotel we were both very sad about it. Bob Allen gave me all the details when I finally returned to my post – he said he had been very upset that I hadn't been there when Gunner Tregear was killed. He appreciated that my presence wouldn't have changed the outcome for the soldier, but he thought the gunners in both 108 Battery and in the regiment as a whole would have felt more comfortable with their own RMO on the ground at the time and immediately after the tragedy. Officers and men alike told me the latter part of Operation Santa Fe had been extremely difficult for everybody in 4 Field Regiment.

My visits to the army surgical hospital in Saigon and the Australian Surgical Team in Bien Hoa gave me a wider perspective on the war and its human cost. But it was the daily sick parades for Australian troops stationed in Saigon which had the most long-lasting effects on my medical practice. Almost all the soldiers I saw had sexually transmitted infections (STIs), predominantly persistent or recurrent non-specific urethritis, although some had more serious infections. It was in the RAP in the Free World Headquarters in Saigon that I gained my first real appreciation of the psychological repercussions of an essentially simple and minor urethral infection.

Of course I had treated STIs at Nui Dat – considerably more than I disclosed in my letters home. But the gunners had far less opportunity for exposure than the boys in Saigon. One short sharp infection after R&R or R&C and my gunners were easily and quickly cured. Soldiers in Saigon were 'base wallahs'. They were signallers, drivers, admin clerks or personal assistants to important army high-ups and mostly had nothing to do after 5 pm except go to the bars and pick up bar girls. They were often miserable, depressed, lonely and lacked the purpose 'real' soldiers had to sustain them. For many, their twelve months tour of duty was punctuated by one STI after another, most of which were of minor significance, but the cumulative effect of which was to result in serious psychological trauma. Their stress increased proportionally as they neared the end of their tour of duty. Most doctors treated their STIs with scant interest and usually lectured them on the evils of their ways. Surprisingly, given my own total lack of sexual experience, I saw them as kindred spirits and from no knowledge base at that time I did my best to help them. I owe a debt to those non-combatant soldiers in Saigon because they pointed the way to my eventual career path. They may not have faced the same dangers as the infantry, the cavalry and the artillery in Nui Dat, but they had their own demons and they suffered their own unique share of damage from the war. Sexual health physicians are still not very good at managing chronic non-specific urethritis, although it is far less a problem these days than it was in Saigon in 1967. But I look back on those forlorn patients with great sympathy and wish I had the knowledge then which I later acquired. I could have been so much more reassuring.

At the end of November I was more than half way through my tour of duty. I shared in the emotion all members of the regiment felt over the loss of one of our own, killed in action at the hands of the Vietcong. I had lost a great deal of my idealism over the war and was identifying more and more with the men I worked amongst every day. Although my essential Christian faith remained undiminished, I felt less and less sympathy for the trappings of religion. More than anything else I wanted to *belong* to this group of gunners with whom I was serving and to feel I was a part of their lives.

8

DECEMBER 1967

Letters

SEVEN MONTHS IN COUNTRY TODAY!
Dear old Philly-Willy, alias 'Snoopy' the demon flyer,
Did you see 'the Red Baron' in that cloud above Goulburn? Talk about Vietnam being dangerous. It's got nothing on flying with Davey Hampson.

To commence with, on the eve of St Barbara's Day, who you, as an avid student of church history, should know is the patron saint of guns and gunners, we should together sing very lustily that little ditty 'The Screw Guns' composed by Rudyard Kipling. It will be sung in the officers' mess for sure in two days time. 'Screw guns' I need hardly say were the forerunners of our 105 mm howitzers.

Today I have been out to see 106 Battery, who are again on operation. They are all fine, I'm glad to say, compared to 7 Battalion many of whom are 'crook' with malaria at present. I had to see one of the 7 RAR infantry companies who are camped around 106 Battery to protect the fire support base; it's rather tragic to see the number of blokes who really have got 'the twitches'. Poor old 7 RAR have been almost constantly out on ops for the last seven months and have seen a lot of action. Some of the infanteers are really cracking up, which just goes to show that the toll of war is not only in wounded bodies, but in wounded minds too. One of the poor kids I saw today wasn't even game to get out of his weapon pit. He reckoned he was going to stay there until the operation is over, so 'that the b——s can't get me'. It is awfully sad.

So Pip, if you get called up,[1] first of all, apply for the Officer Training Unit at Scheyville and secondly, whatever you do, put infantry last on your preferences. I think artillery is best really, apart from the Medical corps of course.

At the moment I am listening to a record – I bought a really cheap stereo record player in Saigon (a Japanese portable thing) and I'm playing some records bought in Taipei (only US 50c each). There were no classical records available but I bought about half a dozen folk records (the Seekers and Peter, Paul and Mary). They are relaxing and I've developed a liking for them. They have been singing 'The times they are a-changing'. They certainly do seem to be a-changing, but I think it's only an illusion. Things are pretty well basically as they have always been since the Garden of Eden.[2]

The RAP is in turmoil at present. The battery carpenter is in operation putting up partitions and shelves, so things are going to be good soon. I'll have my own proper office with more privacy for the patients and we'll be really well set up. At the moment though it looks like DIY Dad has been at work.

Well, I must away. Behave yourself and stick to solid ground in future, Phil.

Your old affectionate buddy-pal and friend to the last,
Dave

[1]   Pip was nineteen at the time and fortunately was not called up.
[2]   According to the Bible, when Eve gave in to the serpent's temptation to eat fruit from the forbidden tree in the Garden of Eden and then persuaded Adam to do so too, sin entered the world – it has been an imperfect and 'fallen' world ever since. Despite Bob Dylan, and apparent changing times, things are still as bad as they ever were and won't get better until Christ's second coming.

Nui Dat
Saturday night 2/12/67

My dear mother and 'only inspiration',
This is just a short 'hello' letter to send you my love. Life at Nui Dat is fairly quiet at present. 106 Battery is out on operation and all seem pretty fit (I visited them today by helicopter) and 108 Battery is sitting at the Horseshoe and they likewise are all OK. Quite a few 'nashos' have gone home and been replaced by 'reos' i.e. reinforcements from our base in Wacol in Queensland. The regiment has changed quite a bit in the last couple of months with a lot of old faces gone and been replaced by a lot of 'newies'.

I received a rousing welcome back from most of the diggers. The two replacement doctors were described in various terms ranging from grudging respect to various profane utterances which generally classed them (quite unjustly) in the 'village idiot' category. However the 2IC, when he saw me again, fixed me with his usual steely eye and said in an accusing voice that the health of the regiment had never been better, judging from the size of the sick parades, which had dwindled down to about five or six patients a day. I can assure you they have been three times that in the last two days, so I guess I must have brought back a wave of sickness with me. Sergeant Allen tells me that everyone was scared to come and see Captain Grainger, which was why sick parades were so small. Peter Grainger is actually a fine chap, but he does have a rather forbidding external appearance. I guess it just goes to show I am not tough enough on them – too kind-hearted like my father.

I do hope you are used to having a married daughter now, just as you've got used to having a son in Vietnam and that you don't feel too lonely. Never mind, only five months to go and I'll be back home with you all again. The worst is over! The big question is what to do when I get home, but I guess things will sort themselves out.[1]

Tomorrow I'm going to 7 RAR for dinner with Tony Williams, who needs a lot of cheering up at the moment. He is such a conscientious worker and is proud of his unit as I am of mine, so that all the casualties and the big outbreak of malaria are making him feel very flat.

On Monday I am going out with the 2 RAR doctor to help in a sort of Medcap. 2 RAR are to search a village and they want the two doctors on hand to treat any sick locals (to help soften the blow of searching the village). Cordon and searches naturally upset the villagers a lot, having soldiers tramping through their homes.

Well, must close, Mother dear,

All my love,

Davey Boy

[1] I had said so often I intended to study surgery and become a specialist surgeon that I now felt committed to this pathway. My only options were where I did this – Australia, England or the USA.

Nui Dat
Sunday 10/12/67

My dear Mother,

Sunday afternoon again (a very hot Sunday it is too) and I'm listening to some good classical music on the radio from the Armed Forces Station in Saigon while I write to you. I hope you are having a good rest this afternoon, or are you all at Glenbrook?

I am well and happy and things are quiet here. There is a fairly big op going on at present with both our gun batteries out of Nui Dat, but fortunately HQ battery is still here and is not likely to have to move, which gives me a chance to catch up on a bit of work. The RAP renovations are all finished except for the painting, which is going on right now – a nice blue and white colour scheme. It makes a huge difference having proper walls and decent rooms – treatment rooms, store room, waiting room (complete with magazines). The 2IC thinks it's *too* nice and no one will want to do any work and sick parades will get bigger and bigger as people start using our waiting room to relax in. My office is very good too – such comfort.

I have just about finished all my Christmas mail – I've posted cards (corny ones mostly, I'm afraid) to everyone I can think of.

What would I like to do when I come home? I don't care – anywhere you like to go for a holiday, I'll be happy. I'm more interested at present in just having a quiet time somewhere – I'll leave it 'to your own good judgement' (as Dr Piper used to say). I'm still not too sure of any dates, but late April is fairly definite.

All my love to you and Dad,

David

Nui Dat
Wednesday 13/12/67

Dear Mum,

I haven't written for two nights now but things have really been hectic the last few days. Two days ago I had a most unpleasant day. On Sunday night out at 106 Battery FSB, one of the officers (a lieutenant) was killed by a grenade explosion. This, as you can imagine, was a very severe shock to the officers because he was a likeable chap – a real idiot, with great respect to the departed, but an extremely likeable idiot if you know what I mean. He used to particularly delight in shocking me, and his greatest boast was that he would get the doc drunk one night before we left Vietnam, even if he had to pour the beer forcibly down my throat. So it was a real blow to the regiment and we all felt pretty 'crook' about it on Sunday night when the news came through.

On Monday, Sergeant Allen and I had to go to Vung Tau and identify the body, which was a gruesome enough task in itself, but I had strict instructions from the CO and the brigadier to recover some pieces of shrapnel from the body and bring them back for identification, as no one was too sure what sort of explosion had killed him (grenade, mortar, or rocket). Recovering pieces of shrapnel from a body, without going into gory details, is a bit like looking for a needle in a haystack, but after disrupting the whole staff of 36 Evacuation (US) Hospital, getting X-rays done to locate the pieces and doing what amounted to a minor post-mortem, I managed to retrieve two little pieces and brought them back with me to Nui Dat. It was all awful and most unpleasant and took ages and I've always hated autopsy rooms and post-mortems. When it is the body of someone you knew and liked, it is a doubly unpleasant task.

On arrival back at Nui Dat, the CO told me certain things about the explosion, which (without breaking confidences, even to you) makes the whole thing much nastier than an ordinary battle casualty.[1] I can't tell you any more about it, but I'm afraid things are only fair to middling in the regiment at present. I am really sorry for the CO, as it all must be extremely distressing for him. All in all, Monday was one of the worst days I've had for a very long time.

The doctor at the Forward Detachment is a different major now (old 'mumbles' has gone, thank goodness). Major Boyle, the 2IC of 8 Fd Amb at Vung Tau, is now presiding at Nui Dat, but he had to go to Vung Tau for two days (or more) to get a mole removed, so I have to look after both RAPs and it's been extremely busy. I haven't stopped for two days and to make it worse, jolly old Colonel Dunn (the DDMS from Saigon) has been here getting in my way. I suppose it's just as well it's been busy as it has stopped me thinking too much about the other matter.

Then to cap it all today, the hygiene officer of the task force goes and puts in a nasty report (quite unwarranted) on 106 Battery's field hygiene and that has really raised my CO's blood pressure – I've had to try and smooth that out too. Talk about an RMO having to be a master tactician. You've got to look after and give advice to your CO; you're supposed to be loyal to your fellow medical corps officers (including idiot hygiene officers) and to your senior medical officer; so sometimes it's a difficult path. I find that I tend to side with the gunners more than with other medical officers, most of whom, apart from Colonel Dunn, Graham Maynard and Tony Williams, are dill brains, idiots, morons, rude, too fond of the bottle, or just plain odd.

But enough of my problems – apart from our sadness about poor Bob Birse, the lieutenant, I am really quite enjoying myself. I don't mind being busy at all. There is certainly a lot of sickness about at present and I feel useful.

It is a very sobering experience to meet death in a young person you have known quite well. Of course I have seen people die, and the occasional young person, but never until now one I was closely associated with. It is a humbling thought from a Christian point of view – you can't help wondering how much of the Lord that person saw in you. Bob had a few semi-serious talks with me (why I didn't drink, smoke, and so on) but you can't help being concerned. It's too late now, I guess – truly, 'our life is but a vapour', isn't it?

Sorry the old family car is such a wreck. I hope you'll be able to afford a new one next year.

I had a letter from Aunty Audrey[2] today – she's in London with her brother at present. She is amazed at 'how good a letter you write'. I am quite overwhelmed. Perhaps letter writing is my gift. I certainly get enough practice. I will answer Pip's very philosophical letter when I can summon up the required sagacity, which may be never.

Love to you all,

David

[1]   The CO told me it seemed very likely that Bob had been murdered and that one of our gunners was the murderer. A 106 Battery gunner, Len Newman, had been charged. See my Reflections at the end of this chapter for further details.

[2]   Aunty Audrey Bateman was a non-biological aunt who was serving as a missionary, teaching at a boarding school in South India. She was an exceptionally good letter writer herself – always interesting and thoughtful. She never married. Her brother Ralph and sister-in-law Betty became life-long friends of mine, in London.

Nui Dat

Thursday 14/12/67

MEDICAL IN CONFIDENCE – TOP SECRET – DESTROY AFTER PERUSAL – DO *NOT* COMMUNICATE TO THE PRESS!

Dear 'Weevil',

Thanks for your last (of 8th inst). Your news of all your recent activities was very interesting.[1]

I am back at 4 Fd Regt tonight – the major is back at the Forward Detachment so I don't have to 'stand in' for him anymore. I might get a good night's sleep tonight. Last night, what with admissions and things, I didn't get much sleep at all. We had a Kiwi soldier, semi-conscious, with cuts on his face. I was pretty sure it was mainly alcohol but in cases like that you have to keep them under observation in case they've really got proper concussion. Although the medics are pretty good by now, they still can't be completely relied on like trained sisters. Accordingly, I had to get up whenever the medic in charge was worried. The wretched Kiwi, of course, was only drunk and was quite OK this morning. They're a funny mob, those Kiwis – very 'wild spirits'! So I didn't get much sleep last night. I'm safely in my own tent tonight, though.

Now for the philosophy. Your comment on modern man is quite valid – 'completely cynical, with a philosophy of nihilism and a feeling that life is meaningless'. This is why Christians have to show they're different – but not by being negative. It doesn't help people in the world much if we tell them we don't do this, or we don't do that; we frown on this or we frown on that; but it does help if we show a demeanour that completely opposes the cynical, nihilistic outlook at every one of life's queer twists and turns. I like that little poem from the First World War:

> *Give me a healthy mind, Good Lord,*
> *that finds the good that dodges sight;*
> *and, seeing sin, is not appalled;*
> *but seeks a way to put it right.*[2]

I am not getting wiser at all, Phil, and more often than not I am quite wrong. That's another thing we have to guard against – thinking we have all the answers. I remember an agnostic medical student at Nth Shore Hospital when we were doing obstetrics saying to Wilbur and me, 'The thing I hate most about Evangelicals is that they think they know everything. They have a simple, trite explanation for everything'. And he was a right – we aren't humble enough to admit when we don't know. Of course we have The Answer (Jesus Christ), but we don't have all the little answers to all life's questions, or I certainly don't anyway. Last Sunday night I went to bed quite shocked, after hearing about Bob the lieutenant's death at the FSB and pondering, as one does in such circumstances, how suddenly a strong active young life, full of all the joy and vigour of youth, can be just snuffed out like a candle. I felt really devastated and sad. Then I turned to my 'Daily Light', but by mistake read the reading set down for the night before and this verse struck me, 'that ye sorrow not, even as others which have no hope'. The message is that there always IS hope!

Sorry for the sermon, Phil, but the last few days have been rather tough and today for the first time I am feeling a bit happy again.

Behave yourself.

Dave

1   According to family wisdom, Pip, who had always been quiet and shy, was 'coming out of his shell' by 1967. He was doing well at university, had a full life with Evangelical Union activities, Boys' Brigade duties, leading a Christian Endeavour class at church and showing an interest in the opposite sex. In fact, he was soon to meet his future wife and move from Baptist to Anglican, as she and her family were.

2   Thomas Henry Basil Webb, killed at the Battle of the Somme, 1/12/17, aged nineteen.

Nui Dat
Thursday 14/12/67

CHEER UP – ONLY FOUR AND A HALF MONTHS TO GO!

Dear Mum,

You sound quite sad in your letter tonight and the problems of the world seem to have got you down. I got 'carried away' in Pip's letter but then I realised it was *you* needed cheering up, so you had better share that letter with him. I guess it must be your fall[1] that has made you feel like this? I am worried about you. I do hope your foot and all your aches, pains and bruises are better now.

It is good of the church to present me with a Bible in absentia. Please keep it at home. I would like you to look after it for me till I get back. It would get wrecked up here.[2]

All my love,
David

1   My mother had tripped and fallen with considerable bruising on her legs, feet and thighs. Fortunately she hadn't broken any bones. I'm not sure now what the circumstances of her fall had been.

2   It was touching that the church presented me with a Bible and, in fact, I still have it, with the front page inscribed with Pastor Logan's neat handwriting. It always seemed odd it was presented to me seven months after I left for Vietnam!

Nui Dat
Tuesday 19/12/67

Dear Everybody on Christmas leave at Glenbrook,

It's Tuesday night and once again I am on duty at the Forward Detachment, while Major Boyle (who should be here) is down in Vung Tau, 'getting his stitches out' from his little operation. If you ask me, it's an excuse to have a night in the officers' mess at Vung Tau with no possibility of having to do any work. He is, as we say in the army, 'on a swan', which means evading work somehow. 'Swanners' are those people who have that happy knack of managing to get on trips and get out of work as much as humanly possible. There are a lot of them in the army, as there are everywhere else. So I have stepped into the breech again; it's sure to be a busy night. I seem to attract trouble. But things are quiet right now, so I hope they stay that way.

106 Battery are back in base, apparently none the worse for their unhappy last operation. The Kiwi battery is out on operation at present and as their medic has been on R&R and the assistant medic is only trained 'in hygiene' (i.e. how to dig a latrine), I have had to go out every day over the last three days to visit them for an hour or two – that's six chopper rides – I have certainly made up for my previous lack of air travel experience in the last seven months. Anyway, the Kiwis are all amazingly fit. About 60 per cent of the battery are Maoris and they're such huge men. I wouldn't like to get into a fight with any one of them.

By the time you get this I expect Christmas will be over. I do hope you all had a very happy time. It still doesn't seem very Christmassy up here – one day is much the same as the next; but I suppose Christmas Day will be different. Traditionally, officers and sergeants have to serve the diggers with their Christmas dinner on the day. That should be a bit of a laugh. I guess we will have a few sore heads the next day, as the beer will flow freely. There is a concert party coming up too (the ABC Dance Band with such noted swinging personalities as Lucky Starr and Lorrae Desmond) to entertain us all for Christmas – what a thrill. I guess I will go along just to see what they're like.

I have no more news. Sick parades are fairly small, although they are still getting the odd fever at the battalions. Our regiment remains healthy, I'm glad to say. The new battalion (3 RAR) arrives within the next few days so the task force will be a lot bigger; there will be more ops for sure and 4 Fd Regt will have to work all the harder. We have no definite news of our date for going home yet.

Australia is certainly in the news the last few days. It is a bit embarrassing, really. Who ever heard of the prime minister of any other civilised country drowning in the surf?[1] It just doesn't seem very prime ministerial. One would hardly have expected to hear of Churchill or Menzies or JFK losing their lives in such an unexciting manner. But, I guess it is typically Australian; a little bit irresponsible, careless and quite unnecessary.

Well, must finish – my love to you all.

David

[1] Australian prime minister Harold Holt had disappeared while surfing at his favourite beach in Victoria.

Nui Dat
Friday 22/12/67

Dear Mother,

This is just a little note. I heard part of the memorial service for Mr Holt from Melbourne over Radio Australia this morning. The big question I guess is who will be the next PM? With things as they are in Sth East Asia today, our PM becomes an important man and there don't seem to be many statesmen in the offing.

Your surface mail parcel hasn't arrived yet – the latest we have heard is that Christmas surface mail will be lucky to get here by 25th December, so it looks like we will be eating Christmas pudding for New Year.

Yes, I did get the newspaper cutting about Merrie's wedding, but the wedding cake must have gone badly astray as I haven't seen hide nor hair of it. I am keeping the cutting for Merrie, so she can have it back if she likes – it is a literary masterpiece.

The latest tape arrived safely and was really enjoyable. Thanks so much. Did Sergeant Allen ring you when he passed through Sydney on his way south for R&R? I hope so – he will be in Sydney again on Christmas Eve, but I guess then you will all be up the mountains and he'll miss catching you by phone.

I have had tons of Christmas cards – people have been wonderful. I also had a nice long letter from one of the (old) Concord sisters, so I am not forgotten. I know my letters to you haven't been too good or regular lately. Sorry! But thanks for all your letters – you all sound just as busy as ever.

Lots of love for the New Year,

David

PS: Tell Pip I am starting a new organisation called PMAA (Poker Machine Addicts Anonymous).[1] I am the foundation member but am having indifferent success at present. I keep getting this 'itching' feeling in my right hand as if I want to pull a handle all the time. Luckily, there aren't any in Nui Dat – only rubber trees!

---

[1]   Another sign of my gradual 'deterioration'. On a December visit to Vung Tau with some soldiers from the regiment (described in a lost letter), despite my anti-gambling scruples, I had been persuaded to pull the handle of a poker machine in a servicemen's club and this resulted in quite a big win. The gunners were very pleased with me! I felt very guilty about this lapse and compelled to confess it to the family. Despite the experience, I'm glad to say gambling has not become one of my besetting sins.

Nui Dat
Christmas Eve's Eve
Saturday 23/12/67

My dear old Dad,

A letter at last, all yours. After your long newsy letter tonight I felt I really had to churn one out to you.

Congratulations on being the proud owner of a 1700 cc, floor gear shift, Hillman Arrow! But most important, what is it? Second-hand or brand new? You didn't say specifically in your letter, but from the sound of it I guess it is brand new. Is that so?[1] I am really pleased about the new car; it should make things a lot easier for you and will make Mum happy.

All the gun batteries are back in today. 106 were out for a little op for the past forty-eight hours, but are now back for Christmas and 108 returned from the Horseshoe today to have Christmas in Nui Dat. All the battalion companies are in too (except for absolutely necessary security patrols) for three days over Christmas. Tomorrow will be a typical Sunday then Monday, Christmas Day, will be a bit special. At night we are having a big dinner (only a 'family' one) for all the regiment's officers; those who don't usually go to the HQ battery mess, like the other battery officers, and the forward observer officers who work all the time with the infantry battalions.

Today Major Boyle, the present SMO at the little hospital up the road, went on R&R to Australia – some people get all the lurks going – and I 'stood' in for him until five o'clock, then Peter Grainger from Vung Tau came up to take over for the six days he is away. I quite enjoy working up there with the medics at the Forward Detachment – there is always something happening. Today the brigadier had a backache or something and Major Boyle had seen him and promised to send over some analgesic, so this afternoon I asked one of the medics, who rejoices in the most unusual name of 'Smithy', to take the pills over to 'his nibs'. Off he set, found the door to the brigadier's room, knocked and being bidden to enter, walked in. Inside he saw a man with shorts on (no shirt) sitting down taking it easy. Presuming him to be the brigadier's batman, he said: 'Hey, mate, where's the brig?' He was only a little abashed (these medics are no respecters of persons – it must die hard in the medical mind – the respect for authority I mean) to be told by the shorts-clad one: 'I *am* the brig.' Apparently the brigadier was feeling the Christmas spirit or something, so didn't mind at all.

I had a nice Christmas present today too – a brand new sterilizer arrived for the RAP. I only ordered one six months ago, so by army standards, that's not bad.

Well, much love, Dad – don't get booked for speeding in the new car![1]

David

---

[1] This was Dad's third car. It *was* brand new and replaced a very reliable second-hand Hillman Minx which he had been driving for the previous four years or so.

Nui Dat
Sunday
Christmas Eve, 1967

'ARISE, SHINE, FOR THY LIGHT IS COME'

Dear family,
Season's Greetings and the Lord's blessing to every one of you.

Just a short little note on Christmas Eve to say 'hello' and tell you about Christmas doings in Nui Dat. Today started off with a big sick parade (inevitable when all the batteries are back from operations) and I only just made it to church in time; but I got there. The Kiwi padre took the service today and read us one of J. B. Phillips' little ditties,[1] but it wasn't too bad. I had Peter Grainger to lunch in the mess, then this arvo 'Messiah' came over the air, so I had a happy afternoon listening to that. I weakened and opened my presents this arvo too – disgusting, I know, but they reckon the surface mail parcels have arrived and will be distributed tomorrow morning, so I thought I would open all the airmail ones this afternoon. Thank you so much for the cards and all the books ($100 each, Pip)![2] You really shouldn't have bought such dear ones, Phil. The blue (delicate shade) 'undies' are much appreciated too. The books really do look very interesting, so thanks such a lot. The 'little creatures' sent me a beautiful wooden travelling-type chess set which is terrific. I'm sure it will help while away the time on any future operations – there'll always be someone to play chess with, I'm sure.

As well today, a card came from our old 'postie', Jeff Banks – then after tea, a fair-sized parcel arrived all correctly addressed to me (name and all) packed with goodies like toothpaste, shaving cream, boot laces, boot polish, Band-aids, crepe bandages etc. from the 'people of the Redlands (Qld) Shire under Project "We do care" sponsored by the RSSAILA'. Inside was a little card wishing me a Merry Christmas from 'Wolf Cub John Despot' giving his address and all – so what do you know? Anyway, it was a nice surprise and will be useful.[3]

Tonight at midnight the Kiwi padre is holding a communion service for the battery and I am playing the organ. Then again I am playing for his service at 8 am and at the task force service at nine o'clock, so I'll be busy tomorrow at my 'other tasks'.

It's good that your Christmas 'pud' and cake will be here tomorrow, Mum – it wouldn't have seemed Christmas without it.

Well, that's all I guess – I do hope you all had a very happy Christmas Day. Lots and lots of love to you all, Mum, Dad, Pip, old married sister Merrie, and Ian, and of course 'the stranger that is within thy gates' whoever that may be this year.[4]

David

[1]   J. B. Phillips, an Anglican clergyman, was the first to produce translations of New Testament books into modern-day vernacular English. They were held in high regard by Evangelical Christians at that time. They were extraordinarily good, and made the text very vivid and up to date. He also wrote books on religious subjects.

[2] $100 would have been an extraordinarily expensive price for a book in 1967 – I have rechecked the original letter and it clearly is written as $100. It must have been one of my jokes, as Pip wouldn't have had $100!

[3]   This was quite a common practice, especially from local RSL clubs, to soldiers they had come to know about.

[4]   This refers back to the Judaeo-Christian custom of offering hospitality to someone outside the immediate family at festival times. The quote is from the Old Testament. We often did have someone from outside the family for Christmas dinner.

Nui Dat
Thursday 28/12/67

Dear Merrie and Ian,

I have just clambered out of a chopper after being out to visit 108 Battery, who are on a short five-day op. They are in an area that *was* thickly vegetated in the wet season and isn't anymore, and I had to say if I thought there were likely to be nasty scrub typhus mites there. I didn't think there were, so told them they could wear shorts, which caused much rejoicing. Before I have a shower to wash the dust off, I decided to write a letter to my favourite sister and brother-in-law to thank them very much for the exciting Christmas present they sent me.

It arrived right 'on the dot' on Christmas Day. Some miracle occurred – all the mail got here (two three-ton truck loads of it for this regiment).

Your selection was really excellent. I drank those three bottles of apple cider all on Christmas Day – somehow they stayed intact on the journey up; a lot of people's parcels didn't have the same good fortune – there were beer cans and lollies, nuts, raisins and fruit cakes popping out of crushed and crumpled parcels everywhere. I have to say mine all arrived in very good shape. The Pork Publishing Company productions arrived quite safely too – I am really spoiled.[1]

I have told the family all about Christmas here in a tape which I posted today, so I won't repeat all that stuff again – suffice it to say, it was quite a happy time although a bit peculiar being so far away from you all. I was thinking of you a lot enjoying yourselves and struggling to eat Merrie's cooking.

Everything is pretty much back to normal here – operations and things have started again, and the cease fire is long over. We are having a special party on Sunday with a buffet dinner with all manner of big-wigs attending to celebrate New Year's Eve.

Well I really must go and have a shower or I will be late for tea. When am I going to see those wedding photos? By the way, your piece of wedding cake arrived yesterday – parcel posted *airmail* on 21st Nov. Not bad for the post office? It was delicious despite the delay, although I couldn't handle all that icing.

With lots of love and be good,

David

PS See you in May!

---

[1] The Christmas parcel from Merrie and Ian contained three bottles of non-alcoholic cider which they had purchased in Tasmania; and several paperback books. It is a *miracle* the bottles arrived intact.

Nui Dat
Friday night 29/12/67

Dear Mum,

I had your letter and married sister Merrie's letter today written on Christmas Eve. You and Dad sound tired, so I do hope you both had a nice restful time with the 'marriedies' in spite of the 'mangy cat'[1] at nights. How is the posh new car going? Merrie says I won't know you in it when I come home. I doubt that! It's still four and a half months before I come back and in that time Dad should be able to reduce it to the worn out appearance of all Bradford cars. I have been wondering how Pip got on with my old bus going to Gerroa. I hope it didn't give up the struggle on the way down. I sent him a letter to Gerroa, so I hope it gets there.

Merrie's house sounds pretty terrific. I would love to see photos of it PLUS the wedding photos too. Is that character from Richmond a slow worker? What is he doing? Touching up each individual photo?

I am glad to hear the shop was so good the last few days of Christmas. Like I said, it'll become a regular gold mine. Has Jeff Banks been in lately?

You do seem to be looking at your kids through rose-coloured specs lately, mother mine. I don't really think we were the most perfectly behaved kids in church when we were little children. I clearly remember the unwillingness with which Merrie and I were dragged off to the Gospel Hall at Caringbah in the old days and I'm sure some of it must have shown in our later demeanour at those stately meetings. And what about the washing-up on Sunday mornings at Seaforth when Dad was waiting to dash off and pick up his favourites to take to Sunday School, and we were always and inevitably holding him up?

Very much love to the very best mother,
Davey Boy

[1] A stray mangy cat had taken up residence under Merrie and Ian's house. They adopted it, but it wailed at night.

Reflections

The letter of 2 December 1967 mentions a proposed cordon and search of a local village. I truly hated being part of these operations, despite the fact that my work was purely 'medical' and more often than not entailed squatting in a hot tent 'baby-sitting' the frail, the feeble, the elderly and the little kids – plying them with glasses of water all day. The villagers hated the cordon and searches far more than I did, of course. Once the village was surrounded by our soldiers before dawn, no locals could enter or leave, and all the villagers were evicted by force. Soldiers then moved through, searching from house to house. Many of the older women kept up a constant screaming and screeching at the infantrymen who were holding them back from re-entering the village. It was nerve-racking for the men, but I have to say I never saw an Australian soldier lose his temper or act inappropriately or unprofessionally in the face of considerable provocation. As far as I could see, they went about their work with a sort of rough civility. No one enjoyed it one bit, though.

I knew and liked both Bob Birse and Len Newman, the gunner who was charged and subsequently found guilty of manslaughter at a court-martial in Vung Tau in January 1968. Bob was a good-looking second lieutenant. He liked a party, he liked a drink and he was very fond of women. He must have found life in 106 Battery very tedious. He was said not to be very good at managing the gunners under his charge, but I have no way of knowing if that was true. He was very young and very inexperienced. He certainly did not deserve to die by having a hand grenade thrown into his dug-out sleeping quarters at a remote fire support base. We got on well together and I enjoyed his company, as did most of the officers in the regiment. I half envied his casual easy-going approach to life and although he teased me unmercifully, he seemed to respect my more serious and Christian way of life.

Len Newman had been a gunner in headquarter battery and worked in the sergeants' mess before he was transferred to one of the guns on 106 Battery. He was a 'nasho' and had a quiet, slightly withdrawn and serious disposition. He had been a member of the Boys' Brigade in his youth. I knew him because he had accompanied us on Medcaps to both Hoa Long and Ngaio Giao as 'shot gun' on several occasions, including the time we heard small arms fire and had to pack up and leave the little hamlet quickly one afternoon. I found him reliable and dependable. He seemed genuinely to enjoy the Medcap outings with us.

Bob's death caused enormous shock waves throughout the regiment. The regiment was never quite the same after it. I know it inevitably damaged our reputation and our war record for 1967/68. I don't think the CO ever fully recovered and the men of 106 Battery felt it keenly.

I had no previous personal or professional experience of a violent death occurring in suspicious circumstances and I'm glad to say I have had none since that time. I did what I was asked to do, although I found the imposed mini post-mortem, to retrieve some shrapnel pieces from the body, repugnant and highly emotionally disturbing. I have often reflected back on the CO and brigadier's order for me to do that as being irregular and peculiar. There was no proper chain of evidence maintained and I doubt the prosecution or the defence thought the evidence worth much, judging from my memory of the questions I was asked at the court-martial.

I didn't know what to think about the case at the time. I was outraged that apparently Bob had been murdered and I did truly grieve his loss. I went along with the prevailing belief throughout the regiment that Leonard Newman was guilty as charged. The circumstantial evidence was very strong against him. I shared the communal condemnation of his alleged act for its unwarranted violence and cowardice. But I never gave him any benefit of the doubt and I made no move to see him while he was held in the MCE at Vung Tau. I have regretted that ever since. I was a Christian at the time and Christians are supposed to be concerned with justice and forgiveness. I espoused the advocacy and priestly role of the doctor. From my previous contacts with Len, I owed him at least the one visit and chance to talk which I never gave him. I look back and I am sorry for this now.

At a Court of Appeal in Australia later in 1968, the judgement of the Vung Tau court-martial was overturned and Gunner Newman was declared not guilty and released from gaol. Reading the deliberations of the Court of Appeal it seems clear they could reach no other findings – all the evidence was entirely circumstantial. We do not know and now never will know with any certainty who killed Bob Birse. He was another unfortunate casualty of an altogether unfortunate war and is rightly honoured as a young man who gave his life on active service for his country.

Bob's sudden death upset me more than I realised at the time and more than I revealed in my letters home. The circumstances surrounding his death were certainly horrible but, more than anything, my faith in human nature was shaken. Whoever threw the grenade, it seemed clear it was one of our soldiers rather than the enemy. Until that time, I had been seeing members of the regiment, no matter how individually rough or 'godless' some of them might appear, through my own brand of rose-coloured glasses – until then none of them could really do major wrong in my eyes. They all had their own minor peccadilloes, for sure, but they were essentially 'good stuff'. Suddenly now I felt oppressed with a feeling that real evil and wickedness did exist around me.

Harold Holt's death was regarded as totally ridiculous by my fellow officers – I remember Peter Harnwell, the signals officer, literally whooping his way through the officers' lines in headquarter battery singing out the news for us all when it first broke. For thoughtful national servicemen, like Peter, it was symbolic of the whole federal government's tragic mistake in first supporting and then helping the Americans to pursue the war in Vietnam. Having been always brought up to believe the Government was on the side of the angels, I found Holt's death difficult to accept. If a man was reckless enough to risk and lose his life in the surf, was he reckless enough to have risked the future of his country and to have placed young men's lives in jeopardy for precious little gain?

I was getting a little world-weary one way and another and my previous firm articles of faith seemed to be falling around my ears.

9

JANUARY 1968

Letters

Dear old Dad,

I'm glad you liked the Christmas presents – nothing very much, I'm afraid, but I hoped they'd be interesting for you.

I've been really pleased this week that I wasn't sent over with 8 Field Ambulance to Vung Tau – Boy! What a bickering lot the officers down there are. The two doctors who've done virtually all the work for the past seven months have just got their 'confidential reports' from the CO of the Field Ambulance and he's really given them both a shocking report. Both are getting out of the army, but that's beside the point – their work deserved more praise than they got. How different it is here at 4 Field Regiment – even the 2IC is bearable – at least you know where you are with him. The officers in our regiment are really one big happy family. Brian Mitchell is one of the steadiest, most honest and loyal people I've ever met – he's no Christian (in fact a bit anti-established church or organised religion) but a fine character for all that and a pleasure to know; Peter Snowden, the LAD (engineer) captain – a very youthful-looking thirty year old is reminiscent of a male version of Aunty Marge, with the same type of outlook on things;[1] old John Martin,

231

the quartermaster, a 'brown-boot army man' – thirty years in 'this man's army' is sensible and soft-hearted for all his bluster; and the two young, slightly wild second lieutenants whom the 2IC keeps a firm steadying hand on, are very good-hearted and friendly. They are my regular breakfast, dinner and tea fellow diners and we get on well despite our different characters and outlooks – no unpleasant undercurrents despite the grumpiness of the 2IC, who doesn't really worry us.

Today I got a great heap of information from the Postgraduate Committee in Medicine after my recent request, so I really will have to settle down and work out what's to be done in the future.

There are three alternatives as I see it:

1. Sydney Uni course for the Fellowship of the Royal Australasian College of Surgeons (FRACS) – the easiest way to get this is to apply again for an anatomy demonstratorship.

2. Fellowship of the Royal College of Surgeons England (FRCS) – this takes four months study to get the primary exam, in residency in London. Then if you want the English second part (final exam) it means three years residency in an English hospital followed by the clinical exam.

3. Mayo Fellowship in the USA to work for four years at the Mayo Foundation in Minnesota.

So that's it – goodness knows what's the best thing to do but I feel a kind of urge to apply for the American one – I don't know why, when I've always hated American ways. I'm not rushing into it and I won't write any letters off till I hear from you. I know what Mum will say, 'Do the exams in Australia'. And of course I can't blame her for that.

I know it is hard for you to advise me, Dad, but do pray about it for me won't you? One thing I am sure of at present – I am determined to have a go at being a surgeon while I'm still young and unattached.[2]

Well, lots of love, proud car owner,

David

---

[1]   Aunty Marge was my mother's only sister. Unlike my mother she was fun-loving, cheeky and a heavy smoker. Her younger boy Greg was a pilot and, unluckier in the draw than my brother Pip, was called up for national service. Greg did well in the army and subsequently had a distinguished career as a Qantas pilot flying 747s.

2   My announced plan to become a surgeon had been received with great
    encouragement by my family and their enthusiastic reinforcement of
    the idea made it difficult for me to contemplate anything else. To be fair,
    though, I was *very* slow to allow myself to accept what I was really inter-
    ested in and best suited for.

8 Field Ambulance (!)

Vung Tau

Friday 5/1/68

Dear family,

Well, here is an epistle penned from a bed of sickness. Yes, the
RMO himself has fallen foul of the dreaded virus or whatever it
is that causes a high fever for a few days. At any rate I haven't
got malaria, which is something to be grateful for. I got sick three
days ago – just felt off-colour for a day or so, until I took my temperature and found it to be 103 degrees F. When, after aspirin etc.,
nothing relieved it I thought I had better get some professional
advice – Peter Grainger happened to be the doctor at the Forward
Detachment and he said I ought to go to hospital for a few days,
so here I am.

I am feeling much better now and my temp is down to 99, so apart
from feeling weak, I'm having a good rest. No one really knows what
this particular disease is, but lots of people have had it. It isn't malaria
and it isn't scrub typhus, so I can't be accused of setting the troops a
bad example by not taking my paludrine (antimalarial) or not anti-
miting my clothes.

I have now been in hospital twenty-four hours. It is an awful
business being in hospital and today I've felt an awful fraud, but I
guess the break will do me good.

Well, I'll leave it there for now. Don't worry though – I am quite OK.

Much love,

David

PS My official diagnosis is 'PUO' (pyrexia i.e. fever of unknown
origin). I have an enlarged spleen too, if Merrie is interested.

Nui Dat
Monday 8/1/68

My dear Mother,

I'm very sorry my letter writing has been rather poor over the last few days, but really I didn't feel much like writing letters while I was in hospital. I got out today and am back in my little tent – my temperature has been normal for the past forty-eight hours, so they decided I was cured and packed me back to Nui Dat this morning. I really do feel much better, although pretty weak. Goodness knows what I had – just one of those viruses, I guess.

I had a surprise on Sunday – Trevor Weekley from Penno[1] dropped in to see me in hospital. I had completely forgotten that he'd rung me from Saigon last Thursday to say he would be coming to visit Nui Dat on Saturday and that he would look in on me. He arrived at the RAP and they told him I was in hospital, so Trevor, ever innovative, stays at Nui Dat overnight and hitches a ride down to Vung Tau on Sunday. He looks very well and seems to be enjoying himself in Saigon; he is the same old Trevor, full of self-assurance. He breezed in and out and then ducked off for a swim in the sea at Vung Tau before catching a plane back to Saigon. It was very good to see him.

I'm glad you at last bought a TV from Uncle Bill for the princely sum of $15, even if the real reason Dad bought it has now come out in a recent letter from Ian Lloyd. I got the full 'low down'. Dad really bought the set, so as cousin Billy Lloyd should not 'rip it to pieces with his unmerciful hands'.[2] A real dog in the manger attitude, Dad. I hope you've managed to rig up a proper antenna for it by now, so that it actually works.

The wedding photos arrived today and I am extremely pleased with them – they really are very good, aren't they? You certainly look a ball of style, Mum!

I couldn't send Pip a telegram about his excellent results,[3] as I only heard about them when I was in the wretched hospital. He is a real old conundrum, isn't he? You never know what he will do next.

I had a very cheery letter from Gran and Grandad Lloyd today.

Well, lots of love from the ex-hospital patient,
David

1   Trevor was a 'nasho' and was serving in the service corps, assigned to an army unit in Saigon. He was one of the younger members of Pennant Hills Baptist Church.

2   'Billy' Lloyd was the only son of Uncle Stace, my mother's elder brother. Bill had a passion for old steam cars and all things electrical and electronic – hence cousin Ian's amusing reference to Billy getting his 'unmerciful hands' on the old TV set. Bill is now a retired Sydney patent attorney.

3   Pip had done exceptionally well in his exams (Bachelor of Arts) at the University of New South Wales, so well that he was able to stay on for an honours year.

Fire Support Base Berryman
Op Duntroon
Saturday 13/1/68

Dearest Mother,

Just a little note from out on Operation Duntroon to let you know that I am OK. I've just about recovered from whatever 'wog' it was I had last week and am now back to my normal healthy appetite and am feeling my usual self again. One good thing about having been sick – everyone is very solicitous of my health and the 2IC told me I wasn't to do any digging or filling of sandbags or anything strenuous but just to take it easy – so I have been doing just that. It isn't a bad spot we're camped in except a bit open and very hot during the day and it gets quite 'icy' at night now – the temperature drops to about 65 degrees F. Although that sounds good to normal Sydney dwellers in winter, it is very cold up here once you are acclimatised to tropical conditions. We have a new officer just arrived from Sydney and he can't understand us all shivering in the cold early morning conditions – he thinks it's the best time of day and spends all the rest of the day sweating profusely.

This op is just the same as all the others – helicopters hovering around, landing important people and picking them up again; big crane helicopters dropping in supplies of high explosive ammunition, the guns firing periodically and so on – just normal routine, which we are all getting a little bit sick of after eight months. Still, there can't be many more ops to go in the next few months, I hope.

I will be interested to hear how Merrie is getting on with her new job at Penrith Hospital. At least it's a bit different from when she was a student nurse at North Shore or Hornsby – she can leave if she doesn't like it or if the hours aren't suitable[1] . . .

(Remaining page of letter is lost)

[1] Student nurses (as Merrie had been at Royal North Shore Hospital) and student midwives (as she had been at Hornsby) were paid very poorly, worked extremely hard and long hours, and could only leave when the course was completed – unless they were willing to forfeit whatever time they had already managed to get through.

Fire Support Base Berryman
Op Duntroon
Monday 15/1/68

Dear Mum,

It is Monday evening and I am sitting on my little camp folding chair, in the Vietnamese sunset, writing this note to you. It is the fifth day of the operation and we have all the work finished now – I have a most glorious RAP – I wish you could see it! A bulldozer dug out a huge scrape of earth about six feet deep into the ground. We sand-bagged both open ends and then across the top laid a dozen very big logs which some engineers cut down with chainsaws from the surrounding bush and laid sandbags on top of those. So you see, I am pretty safe – it would take a major direct hit from a big bomb or explosive device to do any damage to this RAP – bigger than the VC possess anyway. At this stage everything is very quiet and I think we shall finish off this op on Thursday without anything very eventful happening. I hope so anyway.

I really haven't anything else to tell you. Sergeant Allen is out here in the bush with me, being as incorrigible and irrepressible as ever; Corporal Williams (medic) from 108 Battery went on R&R to Singapore today and Chuck (106 Battery medic) is in Vung Tau as one of the 'star' witnesses in the court-martial which commenced today and which I am sure you will read about in the papers.

I have spent my time out here reading – the underground RAP is nice and cool during the day (when the temperature must get up well into the nineties). The nights are very cold still, but my army blanket keeps me warm. Who ever heard of needing a blanket in Vietnam? But at this time of year you really do.

How is the TV going? Has cousin Max managed to fix it for you, or has Uncle Bill really diddled you out of $15? Maybe little Billy Lloyd may yet get his 'unmerciful hands' on that set.

Well it is getting almost too dark to write – it is a lovely sunset though. Even Vietnam can look beautiful at times. It is 'stand-to' – the diggers all sit in their dug-out pits with their weapons – this happens every morning and evening faithfully – It is a delightful little carry-over from the Rudyard Kipling days of the British Army when the wild 'navvy' hordes of Afghans on the Indian border would attack either at sunset or daybreak. Why, I can't imagine and I am sure the VC have never heard of the idea and attack whenever they feel like it. But without fail, out on operation, at morning and evening we still 'stand-to' for forty-five minutes. The Yanks think we are quite mad.

It is really too dark now so I'll finish off with much love to all the family,

David

Fire Support Base Berryman
Op Duntroon
Wednesday 17/1/68

Dear old Mum,

Goodness knows when this letter will reach you as latest news we have heard is that there is a nation-wide postal strike back home. I haven't had a letter for three days now, so something must have fouled up somewhere. What on earth is wrong with the PMG[1]? They seem to have been 'on strike' more than they've been working in the last twelve months.

We are still out on operation and likely to be that way until 20th January at least. I had an exciting day yesterday – a 'chopper' just arrived and they told me it was for me – apparently I was required for the court-martial at Vung Tau, so they flew me to Nui Dat where another 4 Field Regt Officer was waiting to join me on the chopper. You can imagine how I looked after being in the bush without a shower for five days. I flatly refused to go on to Vung Tau until I had showered and got some clean greens on, so they had to cancel that idea and call another chopper for me fifteen minutes later. You can hardly walk into a court-martial smelling strongly of BO and with scungy old greens on.

I at last got to Vung Tau suitably dressed and washed. When the other officer and I got there the poor old CO was very distressed – 106 Battery now has only one young, recently arrived officer left at Nui Dat to run the battery and all its firing – all the rest are being held at Vung Tau for the court-martial. The CO has to be there too, for some legal reason. Anyhow the CO stirred the 'legal eagles' up a bit and told them I had to get back out on operation by last night, or else 'the whole FSB would be without adequate medical coverage' – he made me sound very important to the war effort. So they heard my evidence about identifying Bob's body and extracting the bits of shrapnel from him, straight after lunch, then the president of the court told me that, in view of 'operational necessities', I would be excused by the court and could return to the bush. I am a pretty seasoned witness now, after twice in the witness box at courts-martial. This one is a very big affair and the army legal officers are enjoying themselves immensely, I'm sad to say. I hate legal people! Two CMF barristers have come up from Australia as counsels for the prosecution and the defence. As far as I can see the prosecuting counsel is an old 'ditherer' and the defence counsel is smooth and suave – I just hope it doesn't mean the accused will just 'get off' if he's really guilty. It would be a travesty of justice if the gunner is released, but I can just imagine how the defence and the newspapers are going to play it – you know – poor national serviceman who didn't want to come to Vietnam in the first place and couldn't stand the strain; unpopular young bumptious officer (which he wasn't really), bad discipline in the battery (certainly not true). The poor old CO is really worried about it all and I feel very sorry for him.

Anyhow, the defence didn't seem to think I was worth wasting questions on, so I got off easily. No one is sure how long it will drag on.

Well, I had better finish off if I want this letter to 'catch the mail' – that's if there is any post left in Australia, of course,

Much love,

David

[1]   The PMG was the Postmaster General's department, the forerunner of Australia Post.

Fire Support Base Berryman
Op Duntroon
Friday 19/1/68

Dear family,

It will probably be March before you get this letter, despite assurances which we hear on the news that 'forces mail will get through' even though there is a postal strike at home. It certainly doesn't seem to be working this end, as it is a week today since I had any mail at all and everyone else is much the same. It's a real nuisance, as mail is one of the most eagerly awaited events of the day. I suppose they'll sort it out within several months at least. You don't notice the lack of letters so much back at Nui Dat because there's always something else to occupy your mind, but on operation where there's nothing much to do but sit and read books, mail becomes very important.

I have nothing of any interest to tell you, I'm afraid – this has been a very quiet operation – no one has given us any trouble and the gunners have had very little firing to do. Everyone has been very bored.

One good thing – they have transported out a mobile shower unit this time and everyone has been able to have a shower in the afternoons. A shower unit consists of a pipe leading down into a creek, a filter, a high pressure pump and a sort of arrangement of multiple shower heads which squirt out water from all directions under high pressure – a trifle primitive, but a welcome relief on a hot afternoon. It allows about eight–ten people to shower together at one time. We are fortunate in this position, as there is a decent stream nearby where we can get water for showering and washing. It is much better having a good shower than just a wash out of a dish of water. Unfortunately the shower unit broke down yesterday and is being shipped back to Nui Dat for repair, so we will all be dirty again today and tomorrow – the last two days of the op.

The court-martial is still dragging on but they don't seem to want me anymore as I haven't been recalled.

I hope you are all well and that the shop is going well and the new car is behaving itself.

It's awful getting no letters! I'm not sure what scrapes you are all getting into back home.

That's all for now – will be back in Nui Dat on Sunday, all being well.

Lots of love,
David

Fire Support Base Berryman
Op Duntroon
Friday 19/1/68

Dear Gran and Granddad,[1]
Just a short note from out on an operation, which has been going now for about a week and which ends on Sunday. It will be good to get back to the base camp at Nui Dat, although this op has been quite enjoyable – no rain, nice sunny days and quite pleasantly cool nights. The operation has been very quiet too and I have had virtually nothing to do – there has been very little even normal 'sticking plaster and aspro' stuff this time, I'm glad to say, and I have spent most of the time sitting in the sun reading. I thought to bring a medical textbook out with me which I have been wading through and thus 'brushing up' a bit on things I was getting very 'rusty' on. That has certainly helped fill in the time quite well and profitably.

I do hope you are both keeping well and strong. I was glad to hear in your last letter that Gran has been pretty good in the last few weeks. I hope the weather is OK in Caringbah and not proving too hot and trying for you.

Lots of love to you both,
David

[1]   My Lloyd grandparents – Mother's parents. Grandmother Lloyd was chairbound with chronic rheumatoid arthritis. Unknown to me, my Granddad Lloyd was already dead when I wrote this letter.

FSB Berryman
Op Duntroon (last day)
Saturday 20/1/68

Dear Mum,

Just a very little note to tell you we finish off this op tomorrow and go back to Nui Dat. I think ten days in the bush, sitting in the sun with practically nothing to do except read my medical textbooks, has done me good. I feel much better than when I first came out here, and I think I have regained some of the weight I lost in hospital.

Someone found an amazing waterfall not very far from where we are, so we have been having our showers in that since the discovery. It has been terrific! The force of the water on your back nearly knocks you over. Waterfalls are not the sort of thing you expect to see in Vietnam. It has certainly made things much more bearable on our last few days. Mind you – operations in the dry season are infinitely better than those in the wet, as you can imagine – no glutinous mud, no continually being wet and sticky – it's far better to have the (dry) heat to put up with during the day and the cold at night, as far as I'm concerned. As the wet season doesn't start again until April, I doubt I'll see much of it again, thank goodness.

I wrote to Dr Wheeler the other day (you remember, the urologist from Concord) to see if he could give me any advice on future study in surgery and particularly to see if he knew anything about the Mayo fellowship in the USA; so at the moment I am just waiting for answers to my letters.

I had a funny letter recently from Gunner Scroope, my ex-batman, who went home in October.

Much love,

David

PS No letters from you all for eight days now – wretched PMG workers!

Nui Dat
Monday 22/1/68

My dear mother and all at home,

Well, I am beginning to wonder if I will ever hear from you all again, but I guess the mail *must* eventually get through – the news this morning said that it would probably be settled today – the strike, that is. So I certainly hope so. It is quite upsetting to the morale of the troops – I guess it is all a 'commy' plot.

At any rate, today has been 'flat out' one way and another (first day back from an op always is) and there seemed to be many people to see and fix up, and all sorts of paperwork to get through; but at last it's finished. Things are quiet for a few days now, but you never know when the next op may be just around the corner; 'war is hell' as the diggers are always saying.

'Digger' (Major) James has been here at Nui Dat about ten days now and has taken over at the Forward Detachment – already welcome changes are being made and it is beaut to have a *genuine* army doctor at last – at times I almost despair of the Australian army Medical Corps until I meet someone like Major James – he is really refreshing.

While I write I am munching little bits of your Christmas cake, Mum, which is still nice and fresh – I seem to be taking a long time to get through it, but I find you can't eat too much fruit cake at a time in this climate.

Not having had any news, there is nothing I can comment on from your end, but I just hope you are all well and keeping out of trouble (especially Pip and Merrie).

Give my love to Gran and Grandad too – I had some lovely short-bread from them the other day – goodness knows how it got here, but it arrived out of the blue.

Well, lots and lots of love to you all,

David

Fire Support Base Harrison
Operation Coburg
Saturday 27/1/68

My dear family,
Well, it sure is a long time since I heard from you all, but the mail started to come through again today with a postcard from an old friend on the Blue Mountains with a picture of the 'Three Sisters' on the front – it made me quite homesick when I saw Jamieson Valley.[1]

Here's hoping I get a letter from you tomorrow night – I'm beginning to wonder if I'll remember your writing when I see it. It's a curious feeling not getting any mail at all for a couple of weeks – you feel all cut off, isolated and unnatural.

I haven't written myself for the last few days as they have been very busy – we left Nui Dat on Wednesday morning by road convoy – about 30 to 40 miles [48 to 65 kilometres] all told and it was a rough, dusty old ride – we were all very glad to get to FSB Anderson. We then had to turn to and 'dig in' (that is create a little trench about 2 feet deep, 6 feet long and 2 feet wide [60 × 180 × 60 centimetres] to sleep in overnight) and the ground was very hard. We had an uneventful night, got up early, had to pack everything up again and then went by chopper another 10 miles [16 kilometres] or so to this new site (FSB Harrison). The last three days we have been busily 'digging in' (our own 'hutchies' – sleeping holes, the RAP, the HQ battery command post) and sandbagging everything, as things are a little bit more lively here than back in Phuoc Tuy Province, where our operational zone normally lies. The infantry have already had several battles and our gunners have been firing their guns flat out in support of the infantry. And the temperature has become really hot.

I guess by now you will have heard all about the court-martial result and sentence? Five years for being found guilty of killing a man! A bit laughable, isn't it? I believe, although naturally none of us here have seen any newspaper reports from home, the regiment has had a lot of bad publicity over this, as signals are coming thick and fast to the CO and battery captain of 106 from Army HQ with 'please explains', e.g. why wasn't there an RMO on the gun position at the fire support base? why only one medic? why weren't the hand grenades locked up? – 'locked up', I ask you, with a war going on! Apparently Army HQ is basing all their questions on newspaper reports. I would be very interested to see the news reports if you still have them – newspapermen are not too popular with the regiment at present, as you can imagine.

Well, it is too dark to write anymore, so I'll finish off with my love to you all,

David

[1]   I was born in Katoomba and lived the first seven years of my life there, hence this reference to a card from the Blue Mountains making me feel homesick.

Fire Support Base Harrison
Operation Coburg
Sunday 28/1/68

My dear Mother,

It was only lunch time today that your letter about Granddad Lloyd arrived – I did get a shock and it seemed especially awful that I had to wait twelve days to hear about it.[1] I'm really just as glad that you didn't send a telegram, but the wretched mail strike does make you mad, doesn't it? I can imagine what a sad time it must have been for you, old thing, and the worry about Gran and her future must have been a big problem. I will be anxiously awaiting later news from you about what you are going to do for Gran. I expect by now the initial shock will be over and you will all (Gran included) be missing Granddad very much and realising the full import of the loss. As you say, it was the best way it could have happened and it seems somehow just like dear old Granddad – to be found in the back yard just outside his canary cage. You are quite right – he will be missed by many people for many a long day. I just can't imagine life without Gran and Granddad at Dolan's Bay and our fortnightly visit out there; I know it often seemed a terribly long way and a tie and all that, but somehow to me it always seemed a vital part of our family life – you know – things would change – exams would come and go, holidays and speech days and anniversaries and things would come and go, but our fortnightly trips to Dolan's Bay would go on just the same and always Gran and Granddad would be there, to tell things to and to show things to – somehow it was one of the most stable parts of our daily life as children and teenagers. And now, Granddad won't be there anymore to make us cups of tea and stuff us full of food and fill our baskets and bags with crumpets and jars of honey and things won't ever be quite the same again, will they? But for all that, Merrie and Pip and I will always be able to remember our grandfather as an outstandingly kind and good man – perhaps he didn't have the most outstanding knowledge of Christian truth, but

I sincerely believe that he knew the Lord for all that – no man is naturally as kind and loving as Granddad became without the grace of God touching his life. And I am sure Granddad will have received a 'well done, good and faithful servant'.

Of course the big problem for you will be what to do with Gran and I'm afraid there is just nothing I can do to help or advise. I do just pray that God will provide for her and you, Mother dear. I will be thinking of you especially in the next few weeks.

With all my love,
David

[1] Grandad Lloyd was 83 and had kept himself amazingly fit. He died suddenly and unexpectedly in his back garden and was found outside the cage of his canaries. Grandma was totally helpless and needed full nursing care after his death.

Fire Support Base Harrison
Op Coburg
Wednesday 31/1/68

Dear old Mum,

I had your letter yesterday telling me about the details of your one week spell as nursing sister for Gran. It really must have been an awful time for you, and you must have been tired out at the end of it. I'm glad you were able to find a good nursing home for Gran, so close to home too.

What is going to happen to the home at Dolan's Bay? I suppose you will sell it will you?

I'm glad Gran has settled in OK – she will probably be all right as long as she has someone to talk to and a view of people and cars to watch and plenty of visitors. But it is sad, isn't it?

Today, the war seems to have livened up a bit – in spite of all the Yanks' efforts, most important US installations were attacked last night, including the President's Palace, the US Embassy, Bien Hoa Air Base (which we are supposed to be defending in part) and so on. If you ask me, the Americans haven't a clue how to fight this sort of war – for example the area where we are at present is only 5–10 miles

[8–16 kilometres] from Bien Hoa and Long Binh, two of their biggest bases, and yet the area is teeming with VC. They (the Americans) just don't seem to worry about patrolling near their vital bases. It seems doubtful to me if they will get anywhere in this war. It is so futile and frustrating. No ground is ever gained and the capital Saigon is still very vulnerable to VC attacks. Oh well – only three months to go and I won't be directly concerned. I hope old Pip manages to escape the call-up – at least he will get a deferment till he finishes uni, won't he?

Well, I had better finish off for today – I am still praying hard about the future – I guess it will sort itself out in time.

Much love,

David

PS When is someone going to tell me definitely about Merrie and Ian's 'news'? You forget I won't 'be able to see for myself', as Ian's mother hinted, in a month or two.[1]

---

[1]   The big news was that Merrie was pregnant. I was very happy for them both.

Reflections

I t was a dark month. This was an unhappy time for the Americans and their allies in Vietnam because of the major communist offensive throughout the country beginning with Tet (the Chinese New Year). It was a sad time for me and for my family back home. I had been unwell, the mail strike in Australia totally disrupted mail supplies for two weeks and then the Tet Offensive further disrupted mail for the troops because of attacks on Tan Son Nhut airport. I and the regiment were away on operation for most of the month. At home, my grandfather Lloyd died suddenly and unexpectedly, leaving my mother with the problem of my totally disabled grandmother.

My feverish illness settled fairly rapidly (although I continued to get a bout of fever lasting a day or two, intermittently, over the next twenty years – my own little physical legacy of Vietnam). I lost about seven kilos and looked even more skeletal than usual when I arrived back at Nui Dat. I very slowly regained weight over the next three months. I was really grateful to the 2IC for his ban on my doing any heavy physical work on the fire support bases because then I really did feel too weak.

The disruption to mail caused enormous anger and upset amongst the troops particularly as Australian forces, especially the infantry, were now involved in quite nasty conflicts with an increasingly active and aggressive enemy. Any complacency about the progress of the war had now died completely. My comments on the way the Americans were fighting the war and their ultimately doomed strategies merely reflected the sentiments expressed at this time by many of the Australian army officers I associated with daily. It was becoming apparent that we might lose the war.

On a personal level I was especially upset that I didn't hear about my grandfather's death until almost a fortnight after the event, because of the mail strike. The only letter to my grandparents included in this collection is written four days after my grandfather died when I was in ignorance of his passing – my mother must have found it at their home and added it to the shoe box. There is also reference in one of my letters to shortcake from my grandfather inexplicably reaching me during the mail strike well after he had died. My granddad looked after my grandmother, with no outside nursing assistance, for the twenty years over which she had been crippled with arthritis. I felt his loss quite keenly. It must have been much worse for my mother, who was devastated by his death.

At home, my mother managed to cope with my grandmother for about a week until a nursing home placement became available. It was a very difficult time for both my parents. The mail strike and the daily bad news from Vietnam must have only added to their woes.

Life on the FSBs throughout the two operations Duntroon and Coburg was pleasant enough for me, as the weather was quite beautiful. The gunners worked very hard on their guns, firing multiple fire missions in support of the infantry. I was kept busier with illness than with injuries, mostly heat exhaustion, stress reactions, high fevers, snake bites and the occasional sick infantryman brought in from the surrounding countryside.

Meanwhile, back at Nui Dat, things had improved medically with the arrival of Digger James as SMO of the task force. After Jack Blomley had completed his stay in Nui Dat, medical services at the Forward Detachment of 8 Field Ambulance deteriorated. I was away a good deal of the time so could not pass personal judgment on the regime of 'old Mumbles', but the medics there, never ones to curb their tongues, were outspoken in their dissatisfaction with the situation. My comments about Digger James throughout the remainder of the letters would be shared by many. He was a pleasure to work for, and with, and continued to have a very distinguished army career after Vietnam. After retirement he became President of the RSL for some years.

At the end of January 1968 I felt as if things were getting a little out of control. I had several causes for anxiety – worry over my mother grieving the unexpected loss of her father; my own sadness over Granddad; the uncertainty of the war with the onset of the Tet Offensive; a heavier work load due to more illness and particularly stress-related conditions in the gunners out on Operation Coburg; and the breakdown in good communications with home due to the mail strike, when mail supplies were still not entirely regular at the end of the month.

However, I wasn't doing too badly in myself. When you're happy in your job, the actual physical environment doesn't matter all that much. Being gunners' doctor suited me so well, I was not to feel quite as happy and satisfied in my work again until I became Director of the STI Clinic in Melbourne in the early eighties.

10

FEBRUARY 1968

Letters

FSB Harrison
Op Coburg
Thursday 1/2/68

Dear Pip,

You have probably given up hope of ever hearing from me again, but lately I have only had time to churn out family letters. Now that we've been out here in the bush for a week or more, all the holes are dug, the RAP is well below ground level, sandbags have been filled and laid, my sick parade is over for the morning (one case of sunburn and one sore ankle) and I have time to write you one of my literary masterpieces. Mail from home is still all haywire (no letters again last night). I suppose none of you had much time for letter writing during that week when Gran was with you[1] – please try to fit in time to tell me, in a nice long letter, just what is going on at home at the moment – after twelve days without letters I feel all in the dark.

As you will no doubt have seen in the papers, this crazy war has only been going 'so-so' for the Allies in the last few days. This operation (Coburg – what a name – remember Pentridge Gaol?[2]) was switched on all of a sudden because of a sudden call from the Yanks – their Intelligence had apparently found out about ten or eleven days ago that the VC were planning all these Chinese New Year terrorist

249

attacks on Bien Hoa air base; Long Binh, a huge Yankee logistical support centre; Tan Son Nhut airfield and Saigon – so they called us in to clear a jungle area near Long Binh where the VC were likely to set up sites to rocket and mortar important areas. Ever since we moved in, the infantry have been having contacts with quite big VC forces and there have been a number of Aussie casualties – but we've killed a lot of VC too. Our guns have been firing constantly and have got through terrific amounts of ammunition and the general view is that we have succeeded in keeping this area free of VC; but Bien Hoa and Long Binh still got attacked – I just can't understand it – the Americans seem to have no idea how to fight this war sensibly – imagine having unpatrolled and uncleared areas of jungle around huge and vital bases like LB and BH – it seems they never bother doing routine patrolling around their base areas – just depend on their big guns and big air strikes and rocket-equipped choppers. I can't see them winning ever, if they don't change their tactics. But then, I wouldn't know – I'm only a simple physician. Anyway, we haven't been mortared, rocketed or attacked, thank goodness – probably not important enough to worry about, and on Sunday we go back to Nui Dat.

You still haven't told me what subjects you're doing at uni for your honours year. I expect a big long newsy letter soon.

Lots of love to everyone,

Davey-Baby (as one rude second lieutenant insists on calling me)

PS Hope you 'beat the draft' but you can always resort to burning your draft card on the steps of UNSW or something.[3]

---

[1]   I was seriously worried about my mother. My grandmother was a 'dead weight', being able to offer no help in her lifting, transfer to a chair from bed, or in toileting. My mother was reasonably robust but not physically strong and had no nursing training.

[2]   Pip, the little creatures and I had once camped in a tent at a caravan park in Coburg, almost under the walls of Pentridge gaol.

[3]   Increasing numbers of young Australian men were conscientiously objecting to being called up for national service. My suggestion to my brother, after my nine months in Vietnam, was at least half serious.

Operation Coburg
Friday 2/2/68

NINE MONTHS IN SVN TODAY!

Dear old Mother mine,

This is just a short note which will take several weeks to reach you, I guess, but at least I have done my bit. On top of the recent Australian mail strike comes the VC disruption of our mail for a few days (at least until Monday). It really is frustrating – you've no idea how awful a feeling it is when the resupply helicopter comes in and again there are no letters – it's something one never gets used to. Mail arrival time is certainly the high point of the day. But I'm not Robinson Crusoe – everyone else here is in the same boat.

The news this morning is that Nui Dat got a few rounds of mortar bombs last night while we were all away in the next province. Some of our 'tankies' were wounded when they went out in their APCs to help restore law and order in Baria (the provincial capital) after the terrorists had a bit of a go there. So even quiet little Phuoc Tuy province seems to have come in for its share of VC disturbances over 'Tet'.[1]

I hope things are getting back to normal at home by now and you've all (you especially, Mum) recovered from the shock and emotional strain of Granddad's death. I hope you are feeling strong and well in spite of it.

Lots of love to you all and especially to you, Mum,

David

PS: We are all safe and sound here at this FSB, except that the poor old gunners are tired out from so much firing.

[1] The North Vietnamese and Vietcong Tet Offensive is now recognised as the turning point in the Vietnam War: the psychological blow that undermined America's confidence in their ability to win this conflict.

Operation Coburg
Saturday 3/2/68

Dear Mum,

It was a real brain wave of yours to give a letter to the two army boys[1] you knew were coming up here last week. The result was that I got a letter yesterday (which you had written last Sunday) despite the mail muck-up caused by the terrorist activities in Saigon. One of the boys must have dropped the letter in at 4 Fd Regt in the task force area and they forwarded it out to me here. I was about the only one to get a letter and the first to know that the tanks had arrived at task force. I notice from the name of his unit that one of the boys works on tanks.

It was so sad to hear about poor old Gran. I do hope she is feeling better again now – has the doctor seen her? It may all just be nervous reaction. She should be well taken care of at the nursing home and Dr Gill is a good doctor. I'm really more worried about you, Mum, knowing how anxious you must be, especially with the strain of having to go to work every day too. It sounds as though you could do with a good holiday.

It's not official yet but 'they' reckon our going home date will be either 7th or 8th May (that could be changed hundreds of times yet, of course, knowing the army). It's quite likely we'll land in Brisbane (as this is a Queensland unit) but of course that's not at all certain. If we do, how about meeting me in Brisbane and we could go on holiday straightaway in Queensland? Don't worry about money – I've got stacks saved up by now – we can stay in motels all the time if you like. That's just an idea but it might help my acclimatisation – straight from Vietnam to cold old Sydney in May might be a bit of a shock to the system.

Well, must finish – I am thinking of you all a lot at the moment.
David

---

[1] I do not now know the names of these two army boys. I presume they must have been Baptists whom Mum had come across somehow – they were not from Pennant Hills church. My mother believes one of the boys was the son of the sister of my Aunty Olive (Mum's sister-in-law).

Operation Coburg
Tuesday 6/2/68

Dear Mum,
Yes, we are still out on operation. Sunday was to have been the going home day but now they've extended it until Thursday or Friday, so we still sit here in the bush. As you will have seen in the papers, we have

had quite a few casualties – none here at the FSB (the enemy have left us alone fortunately), but the infantry have been running into big forces of VC and although they have done well – I believe they have killed over 100 VC on this op – they have had casualties themselves (understandably enough). They tell us the worst of the VC uprising is over now; but it will be a couple of days before we go back to the comparative peace and safety of Nui Dat.

Yesterday and this morning a lot of letters arrived, for which I was very thankful, although very upset to hear about poor old Gran.[1] Gran and Granddad really lived only for each other in the last few years and I can just imagine how terribly lonely it must be for her now Granddad has gone. Do give her my love especially, won't you? I probably won't be able to write to her again before the end of this op, as I have been very busy the last day or so.

Well, I had better close, Mother dear – all my love and thanks for all the letters and for the parcel of 'goodies' for Medcap which arrived in one piece. Please thank all the people who contributed some money towards it for me. I will write to them as soon as I am able.

Lots and lots of love,

David

PS: What is all this about Mr 'Personality' Pip and 'this Fay girl'[2] as Dad so cryptically says?

[1]   Although Gran had settled into a nursing home at Eastwood, she was depressed and non-specifically unwell. She seemed to have lost her previous interest in life and those around her.

[2]   Fay was a fellow University of New South Wales student doing maths, from the Evangelical Union. There was never any truth to a serious romantic involvement with Pip.

FSB Harrison
Op Coburg
Thursday 8/2/68

Dear Mother-mine,

Another letter from Op Coburg! We have now been here exactly two weeks and look like being here another week as the operation is being so profitable. One company of 7 RAR got into quite a bit of trouble when they came across a large enemy camp yesterday (only about three miles from where our FSB is situated) – they couldn't get 'dust-off' helicopters into the area to get casualties out for quite a long time. Officers in the command post here were debating whether or not to send *me* in with a patrol from here (walking the three miles) to help out, until the 'dust-off' helicopters could land. I was all ready to go (kitted up with medical supplies) but they decided against it and at last the helicopters were able to pick up the seriously wounded. I can't say I was too disappointed. I'm no hero, I can tell you. Sergeant Allen now tells me I have missed out on my one big chance to get an MID ('mentioned in dispatches'). I can't say that worries me too much.[1]

Things are still pretty quiet here at the FSB, although the gunners have worked harder than they ever have before in support of the infantry. Both batteries have fired about 6000 rounds of ammunition in the last two weeks since the op started, so they're both very proud of that.

Today our fourth intake of 'nashos' left to go home to Australia next Monday, fifteen in all from the regiment out here in the field, so fifteen reinforcements arrived in this morning – a pretty rude shock for them as they've only been in SVN for one and a half days. Gunner Thomas went back today – he says he will drop in to the shop and say hello to you and Dad sometime.

I managed to write a letter to Gran yesterday – your letters about her sound so sad. It must be a great strain for you. I wish I were home to help you a bit. But it's not too long now before I will be well on the way back. 106 battery and Chuck go back in exactly one month's time, then HQ Battery (and me) are replaced in early May and 108 Battery in late May/early June.

Well, lots of love,

David

---

[1]   Walking in with a patrol was a scary prospect, but I was quite prepared to give it a good go.

FSB Harrison
OP Coburg
Friday 9/2/68

Dear family,

This is just another hurried letter from the bush. We have just received the rather sad news that we have to stay another ten days or so here in the field because the Yanks are 'still worried about Saigon' and they need the valiant Australians to help defend it. Of course, now we are all set up and well established it does not really matter, but it is just a nuisance – you can't help missing some of the home comforts of Nui Dat now and again. 106 Battery, however, are going back to Nui Dat tomorrow or the next day to get ready to go home to Australia. The Kiwis are coming out to replace them and the rest of us carry on as usual. Things have quietened down a lot and the guns have hardly fired at all today. The worst part is the mail – I just hope some letters come in on the resupply.

It's a very small world; yesterday I was over at the 108 Battery position talking to people in the command post when I saw one of the new surveyors who arrived yesterday morning to replace the 'nashos' who went home. I thought he looked vaguely familiar but couldn't think who he was. Then he came up to me and said I looked vaguely familiar to him. It turned out he was one of the old Seaforth Boys' Brigade boys. Pip would remember him – Dennis Gorrick.[1] He seemed very amazed to find me here when he found out who I was, which is hardly surprising given my generally unmilitary appearance and the seven or eight years that must have elapsed since I saw him last. He *volunteered* for national service – apparently he was doing commerce at UNSW part-time, but failed one subject so decided to go into the army and 'get it over with' before he completed his course full-time. He likes the artillery and has a pretty good job. The surveyors are the most intelligent of the artillery, who work in the command post calculating distances and things – it's all trigonometry and therefore a closed book to me. You never know who's going to turn up over here next.

Please excuse me writing on the back of these medical documents, but I am running short of paper.

Lots of love,
David

[1]   I had always liked Dennis. He was a very pleasant teenager and had grown into an extremely engaging, intelligent young man.

FSB Harrison
OP Coburg
Saturday 10/2/68

EXACTLY ONE YEAR SINCE I JOINED THE ARMY

Dear Mum and Dad,

Yesterday afternoon I received a notification from the Royal College of Surgeons (RCS) in London in answer to my letter.

The situation is that they hold courses, lasting eighteen weeks, twice yearly. These courses are to help people study for and get through the primary exam for the fellowship (FRCS). The primary exam is on basic medical sciences – anatomy, physiology, pathology and is held three times per year. Applications are still open for the course beginning 9th Sept 1968, which goes through to 17th January 1969.

There is a residential college next to the RCS which provides a centrally heated room, dinner and breakfast for 8 pounds 10 shillings per week (about A$20 per week = $360 for the whole course).

The problem then is where to do the second part of the course.

There are two possibilities:

1. Stay on in England and get a job at an approved hospital and do the required training and then the part two exam. I think at least one of my Concord years would count, so I should only have to complete two years in England.

2. Come home from England and do the second part of the exam in Australia. Apparently, this is quite legitimate (even though you end up with the English primary and the Australian second part). This would involve working at least two years in an Australian approved surgical hospital (of which Concord is one) before sitting for the exam. I'm fairly sure Concord would always employ me again. The great advantage of this is that I would only be away from home for six months to get the primary exam and would then be home again to work for my second part. The primary exam is the hardest one to pass and they say this London course is very good.

It all seems to have worked out well as far as timings are concerned – home from here in May; have a month's holiday; get a locum somewhere to make ends meet June to August; go to England and do the course September to January; sit the exam; be home again (penniless) in February with the primary fellowship. Of course there must be countless hidden snags (it couldn't be quite that straightforward), but it's a start. I was quite excited when I got the information yesterday. At any rate I will consider it carefully for the next few days before coming to a decision – I have rather 'gone off' the American idea in the last few weeks as four years in America would be a little too much . . .

[Last page missing.]

Op Coburg
Monday 12/2/68

[Last bit of a letter to my brother – the rest is lost.]
Some church youth leaders only set themselves up as such to satisfy some of their own psychological problems. Do you agree, Mr clinical psychologist? And that is a dangerous thing. Young people (as well as 'oldies') will accept and respect a person when that person has shown themselves worthy of respect. And what is it that makes a person worthy of respect? Just plain 'genuineness' (if there is such a word); in other words by showing they've got a set of standards and that they stick to them. Or better, to quote Chuck (on officers) 'those who show they will do the "rightey" by the blokes'.

Well that's quite enough homespun philosophy! I am probably, as usual, way off the track.

See you soon,

Davey-baby

PS: I had a long talk to Dennis Gorrick today – he was telling me about some of our old 'colleagues' from Seaforth. He plans to go back to uni when he finishes the army. He has grown up a very nice fellow.

Nui Dat
Wednesday 14/2/68

Dear family,

Well, at last we're back in Nui Dat after three weeks out on operation in Bien Hoa province – not that it's anything like the papers have been saying. The way they carry on you would think we had been to the DMZ – after all, Bien Hoa is only the next province to ours, about 50 miles [80 kilometres] north of us. We flew back this morning by Chinook helicopter and got here about ten o'clock. The rest of the day has been spent in clearing up, putting all the stores back in the RAP and so on. We are in the throes of inoculation parades again too (six months since our last one – time is really flying by). 106 is the first battery of 4 Fd Regt to be replaced and they go home in eighteen days, so it really isn't much longer before we all leave. People are starting to talk about going home now, so the worst of the tour is well over.

Today I sent my application form to London to apply for the course for the primary FRCS which starts on 9th Sept 1968. Yesterday I had a reply to my letter to Dr Wheeler, the urologist – a very good and helpful letter. He said quite decisively that the American course at the Mayo Clinic was no good for me for two reasons:

1. the American diploma isn't recognised in Australia – you must have a fellowship

2. the pay is too poor for the four years even to eat properly on.

He suggested I enrol in the English FRCS course and do the English primary exam. In the same mail yesterday came my passport photo (which I had written back to Nui Dat requesting, as I knew the English FRCS required one) and the two just seemed to tie together and I felt I should go ahead and apply for the English course. I feel sure, if I really set my mind to it and study hard both before I go and also when I'm actually on the course, I'll be able to make it. I have never had any trouble with anatomy as a subject anyway, and that's the bulk of it.

I thought I would try and get a half day job for the three months (June to August) and study the rest of the time . . .

[Rest of the letter lost.]

Nui Dat
Thursday 15/2/68

My dear Mum,

I do hope some of my letters are getting through to you people. The mail has been absolutely shocking since the New Year. The poor old adjutant went on R&R in Singapore in early January and met his wife there, but although she writes every day he hasn't had a single letter from her since return from his R&R. (He has had a few telegrams, fortunately, so he knows she's all right.) That's just one example of the mail situation. The big parcel of things for Medcap came through today though, so parcel mail is getting through OK. Thank you all so much on behalf of the people of Hoa Long!

I have done a dreadful thing and lost the letter Dad sent me outlining the names of people who gave money and soap for the parcel – I'm ashamed to say I have forgotten who they all were. Would you be so good as to thank them all personally on my behalf and please let me know the names and addresses again, Dad, and I'll write them letters of thanks.

Tomorrow I am going with the Civil Affairs doctor to Hoa Long to do a Medcap all day, as the battalions are doing a surprise cordon and search of Hoa Long itself. After the recent Tet Offensive, Hoa Long is supposed to have turned largely VC again, or I should say, the VC have managed to reassert their influence there. So they are going to search the place and get rid of any obvious undesirables and we docs are being sent there to soften the blow to the local villagers. I should be able to get rid of a bit of soap in the process.

About the MAL: I am quite happy to pay the $200 for a new engine, as I must have contributed considerably with my interstate trips to the poor condition of bearings and crankshaft. And after all it is theoretically my car, so go ahead, Dad, and pay for it out of my 'money bins'. There's no need to pay that back.

The news is out tonight about going home dates – 'semi'-official this time. I will be almost certainly coming home on 7th May flight with the remainder of HQ battery. 'Vital' people like the CO and adjutant go home on 23rd April but the poor old doc is left till last – probably because they won't have a replacement doctor until the last minute.

Anyway that will only be twelve months and one week, so I can't complain. It's only 81 days from today, I've worked out – a bit better than 365 days, isn't it? The best part is that it's a Qantas charter flight 707 jet all the way home.

Well, lots of love to you all and especially to Gran at Eastwood.[1]

David

[1]   By now Gran had become more comfortable in her new situation and her health had improved. She never regained her old spark, though.

Nui Dat

Saturday 17/2/68

Dear family,

At last! The mail is coming through and I feel quite up to date on all the family news. Some letters, like Merrie's one telling me her glad tidings, must be irretrievably lost. Sorry to hear you haven't been well, Mother dear, what with 'headaches and dizzy spells'. Do take care. Only seventy-nine days 'and a wake-up' to go now and I'll be home again, so please don't go getting sick or doing anything stupid like that.

Enclosed is a black and white film which I would like you to get developed for me, Dad. I am sorry I am such a terrible nuisance. I have promised Col Dunn photos of the boys firing the guns and the mortars wearing their ear muffs for hearing protection. He wants them for army medical records. So would you mind getting enlargements done (the size above PC size[1]) of any photos depicting ear muffs? Thanks a lot, Dad – I feel embarrassed asking you but I did promise the colonel and he is my most senior MO.

I had a letter from Mr Simpson from Penno today telling me his son Ian is off to Canungra in a week. I expect I'll see Ian in Vietnam; he is sure to be coming up as a gunner with one of the 12 Fd Regt batteries replacing ours. He may even be 'one of my flock' (if that's what you call prospective patients) for a few weeks. Please thank him for the letter, Dad.

Please tell Merrie and Ian I'm sorry they've been a bit neglected in letters lately – I've been up all hours answering the jolly things. I just haven't time during the day, and tonight already, before this one, I've written four. It's a never-ending battle to keep up. I like doing it, but finding time is the big problem.

I am thrilled to bits about the coming baby – of course it will be a boy! Another David coming along? And I will be just in time to see it before I depart for London. Tell Merrie if it's twins or triplets other good names are Alistair, Jeremy and Michael.[2]

Yesterday, as I told you, I went on an all-day Medcap to Hoa Long which was singularly boring. All the poor usual old people trotted up whom we could do nothing much for, except to let them lie down in a tent and give them lots of water while the village was searched. The operation wasn't boring, though. Fifteen VC were found sheltering in Hoa Long and shot and one Aussie soldier was killed in the process, so it's all still as hostile as ever. Nine months of Medcaps and soap don't seem to have caused much change of heart.

Well, that's all except lots of love – I am well and happy and counting the days.

David

[1]   Postcard size.
[2]   Merrie had a boy called David, born in August 1968. He is now a Baptist minister in Bega, NSW. She named her second boy Jeremy; and my partner is Michael. 'Alistair' didn't eventuate – Merrie's third son is Tim.

Nui Dat
Tuesday 20/2/68

Dear Dad,

Well – the hide of that Trevor Weekley[1]! Telling everyone I sounded 'lonely' in my letter. What a lot of bosh. As a matter of fact I wrote giving him the names and addresses of lots of missionaries and similar people in Saigon that someone gave me before I left Australia. I never had a chance to look them up when I was there, but I thought Trevor might have had some time.

I'm not surprised Mr Logan's leaving Pennant Hills Baptist. One thing I am going to find a bit hard when I get home is settling back into 'Baptist' fervour. Pip's summary of the Centenary Day sermon from Mr Logan made me chuckle – 'people of the Book'; 'makers of religious freedom'. In fact, the old Anabaptist record (apart from people like John Bunyan) is rather the opposite of the promotion of 'religious freedom', I would have thought. But the Penno Baptists, whatever their funny ways, are good and kind people and that makes up for a lot.

It's now Wednesday night (21/2) – I have been out all day on another Medcap (there are no Band-aids, soap or combs left at all), this time at Long Dien, one of the villages near Baria over towards the Long Hai Hills, while another cordon and search went on. It was exceedingly boring. On a cordon and search they set up a 'Medcap' tent and the lame, the halt, the blind and the aged, who are tipped out of their homes for the day while the soldiers search the village, congregate in this tent. Of course, there is little you can do for them (or need to do for them) – they just sit or lie there and I sit and look at them, or give them glasses of water and try and make them comfortable. It's not very exciting. Just lots of poor old things and millions of little kids – it's so sad. Life doesn't hold much for them here; no security, no peace, little money and rickety old homes.

Well, I had better go to bed as I am really tired tonight.
David

[1]   A young man from Pennant Hills Baptist Church who served as a national serviceman in Saigon.

Nui Dat
Friday 23/2/68

Dear Mum,
Well, after another little mail hold-up because Tan Son Nhut airport has been bombed again in the last few days with mortars and rockets, a good little stack of mail arrived today. Tell Pip his answers to my questions have not quite set my mind at ease about this 'Fay girl'. I feel she may very likely hold a special place in his affections.

Mother, you are the limit. What hope have I of cutting all my associations with the army and getting back into normal civvy life with you raving on about the 'Charge of the Light Brigade'? Colonel Dunn doesn't help either by telling me he thinks that at heart I am 'a good Aussie digger'. I thought you would have given up all your funny old Empire Day notions by now, but I see they die hard in you. One thing is certain, there is no gay flag flying or trumpet sounding gallantly about this Vietnam War. I sometimes (like on Wednesday down at Long Dien during the cordon and search), but not often, feel that the critics might be right – maybe it is an immoral war we're fighting; maybe the Yanks are the aggressors – there is so much good young life lost, so much suffering amongst civilians, so many tears, so much blood shed and so little progress seen. Maybe we should withdraw and let the Vietnamese sort it out themselves? Who would be President Johnson today? In the good old days there were only 'goodies and baddies' in wars, but everything is so complicated these days. But I guess if Communism is to be stopped, we must carry on here and see if some sort of non-communist stable government can be salvaged out of the wreckage.

Last Sunday night we lost five Australians at Fire Support Base Anderson (the one we stopped at briefly overnight on Op Coburg). One of our gunners was killed – it was probably his own fault, but that doesn't make it any better – he was sleeping out in the open because it was too hot sleeping in his underground bunker, which is very understandable – they do get oppressively hot. When the mortars started falling, he was killed almost instantly.

Thank Pip for all the photos. The new car looks a beauty and even the MAL doesn't look too bad. I was quite shocked to see the great change in Gran's appearance. I guess it's only to be expected, from your letters about her, but it still gave me a shock. The lounge room looks as ever but the music books on top of the piano are not quite as untidy as when I'm home.

Lots of love to you all,
Davey Baby

Nui Dat
Saturday 24/2/68

Mother, I am SO sorry!
I completely forgot yours and dad's wedding anniversary on 19th. How could I forget it? I was really upset when I got your 'nostalgic'

letter. Happy twenty-seventh anniversary, very belatedly. I do hope you both had a happy day. The last few weeks must have been very hard for you, dear old thing, so I do hope the next two months before I get home are very happy and stable ones for you. It is good that Gran is so much better and more settled. If she is eating well and 'giving cheek' she can't be too bad and even worrying 'about her bowels' is a healthy sign. Do give her my special love.

Mum, what is all this about me lecturing the local Girl Guides, when I get back, on 'Vietnam' and 'the hills and woodlands of the SW tablelands'? Pip has to be joking. Not even to promote your trade in Castle Hill could I go that far. After all I am one of Her Majesty's Commissioned Officers and I can't go lecturing all over the place. What will you 'dob me in for' next?

Lots and lots of love,
Davo

Nui Dat
Thursday 29/2/68

Dear Mum,
It is Thursday morning after sick parade, which was surprisingly small this morning, and for once there is nothing to do, so seeing I missed writing a letter last night I thought I would drop you a line now.

Yesterday we had a visit from two 'big wigs' in the medical corps, one a doddery old full colonel with a broad Irish accent who would be sixty-five if he's a day, and another nondescript-looking half colonel. Colonel Dunn accompanied them and showed me and the RAP off like we were his prized possessions and then proceeded to tell them how I'm planning to go to England in September to study surgery. The old colonel then said that the only sensible thing to do was to stay on in CMF full-time duty until then. I replied I would consider that only if I could get a Sydney posting and didn't have to go anywhere outside Sydney for that three months. They are sure they can get me a job at 2 Camp Hospital at Ingleburn for the interval, so that would be quite good and wouldn't mean I had to be away from home at all and it would save me having to hunt around for a suitable locum job. But apart from everything else I still haven't heard back from England. I just hope I get on that course.

The story about coming home is that the plane will land in Brisbane (as most of the regiment comes from there) but will then fly on to Sydney for the remainder of us. The final arrangements still aren't out officially, but I will let you know as soon as I possibly can. It somehow still seems an awful long way off (sixty-eight whole days or whatever it is), but I guess it will go pretty quickly.

I think that's all the news for the moment,

Lots of love to you all,

David

Nui Dat
Thursday 29/2/68

[Two-page fragment of a letter to Pip.]

. . . discussion with Colonel Dunn and the two 'big wigs' from medical corps headquarters today. I said I wanted to live at home before I went off to England in September, but that I would be happy to do sick parades somewhere, or work at the Camp Hospital for that few months. (I suggested Scheyville might need a good army doctor for RAP work – that would be nice and close to home.) If there is nothing satisfactory in the army, I will just resign. Colonel Dunn definitely doesn't want me to resign though as he says, if I ever plan to do any army work later on, it is much better to stay on in the CMF and not lose seniority.

I must admit I do like army work (well – perhaps not army work itself, but I enjoy being a doctor who looks after sick diggers). I would hate to just get stuck in an army 'rut', though, when there is so much medical work of a more necessary nature in civvy life. It would be a tragedy if a doctor spent the rest of his life looking after sprained ankles in great hulking soldiers when there are really sick people in the world who need him more. On the other hand, soldiers are human beings too and have peculiar problems of their own and are entitled to good doctors (rather than just army career doctors, who are often not good doctors or good soldiers). I really don't know what it is, but there is something appealing about soldiers and the army in general (or there is to me, and lots of other doctors feel it too). I guess it is our mother and her liking for that wretched fellow Kipling!

Colonel Dunn even suggested I get a transfer to the Territorials when I go to England and spend my spare weekends with English gun batteries looking after 'tommies' instead of 'diggers'. Apparently he did that when he was in England doing his FRCS.

How did I get onto all this? Sorry, Phil. Please tell Mum when she scrutinises this letter (as I am sure she will) not to fear. I am not planning to consign myself away to the army forever. The thing I miss most over here (apart from all of you, of course) is some good hospital medicine and surgery and once I get back I am sure I'll be happy to be an ordinary civilian again.

[Remainder of the letter is missing.]

Reflections

The letters for February are briefer and fewer and some are only fragments. With the war heating up as a result of the Tet Offensive, it was much less easy for me to find time to write than it had been in my first six months in Vietnam. The gun batteries of 4 Field Regiment were intimately involved in dealing with the Tet attacks by supplying artillery support around the clock for our infantry battalions. The battalions were assisting the Americans in support of Bien Hoa air base, the massive US military compound at Long Binh and Saigon itself. The gunners fired incessantly – I know because I was there on the ground during Operation Coburg to hear it. I saw first-hand the reaction of the gunners in my everyday dealings with them as I did my rounds from gun to gun. They were all very tired. We all heard Armed Forces Radio from Saigon and despite the attempt the announcers made to sound cheerful, as if Tet were only a minor setback, anyone could tell the Americans were more than a little rattled. Australian and ARVN infantrymen passed frequently through Fire Support Base Harrison, often bringing with them Vietcong prisoners, clad in traditional black pyjamas, for interrogation by Army Intelligence units. I was struck by how young, slight, worn-out and vulnerable these prisoners seemed. It was difficult to believe that it was men such as these who had managed to attack the American Embassy in Saigon only a few weeks before.

Out on Operation Coburg I appear to have run out of writing paper on occasions, as some letters are written on the blank back page of a document which said:

This is to certify that –

Name:

Rank:

Number:

Unit:

is fit for RTA – return to Australia, within 7 days from this date . . .

Capt DL Bradford, RMO 4 Fd Regt – Fire Support Base Harrison.

For the first time, return to Australia was starting to sound like an approaching certainty rather than a distant dream.

Baptists have come in for more than their fair share of criticism and some good-natured ribaldry (originally intended only for my family's benefit) throughout the letters, so it's important to redress the balance where church people are particularly mentioned, as in these February letters. The people of the Pennant Hills Baptist Church were incredibly supportive throughout my time in Vietnam, with their prayers, their letter writing and their sending of articles generously and consistently for Medcap work for distribution to the people of Hoa Long and Ngaio Giao. Some of them wrote to me very regularly, first and most particularly Mr Frank Atkinson (whom I dubbed my 'war correspondent'). The church may have been furnished austerely and the venetian blinds at the front may have been lacking in grace, but there was nothing austere or ungracious about the spirit of the good people of that church. They gave generously for good causes and supported their own unstintingly. The church gave at least three more of its sons to the army as national servicemen – Trevor Weekley who served in Saigon, Len Miller who served as a medic in the Field Ambulance at Nui Dat and Ian Simpson who became an artilleryman in Malaysia.

Many Allied soldiers began to question the rightness of the cause and the morality of the war during and after the Tet Offensive. I was no exception. I particularly remember my horrified reaction (private rather than public) to the Australian cordon and search operations at Hoa Long and Long Dien which are described in the February letters. Although my task was tending the children, the old and the infirm in a separate tent, I was very aware of the inhumanity of forcefully driving people out of their homes, then systematically searching homes, land and possessions, and the inevitable sullen resentment which could be plainly read in the faces of the locals. It was painful too to see the rounding up of Vietnamese men suspected of being VC and to hear the occasional short bursts of small arms fire throughout the day which we knew meant the shooting of the odd young man who offered Australian soldiers any resistance to capture. To see and hear all this in Hoa Long was especially painful for me. I couldn't resist voicing some of my growing concerns in one letter home.

Youth is a wonderful time. How resilient and uncaring people are in their twenties. If it were not so, it would be much more difficult for politicians to wage wars. Things were now quite grave in Vietnam – our FSB could have been attacked, with substantial loss of life, at any time. I knew that and had to plan for the eventuality – yet I seemed to live, as we all did, in a sort of fool's paradise. My last letter in February mentions my plans for future training in England and this occupied a good deal of my thoughts. While part of me would have liked to stay on in the army, I knew that option was not really viable. I thought that getting away to London offered me the best chance to work out how I was going to live the rest of my life. My career choice of surgery was quite secondary to that fundamental aim of sorting myself out free from the restraints of family, church and now the army.

11

MARCH 1968

Letters

My dear Mum and all the family,
Well, in reference to Leap Year, I don't know about 'designing females'.
I recently had a letter from 'Googly-Eyes'[1] – she calls me 'boy' and
'a busy little RMO' in one or two places which doesn't exactly impress
me much, but I guess she is good-hearted. I have also had a letter
from Miss BM (listen Phil) and she finishes up her letter 'with Christian LOVE'!! (my exclamation marks and capitals) and in the course
of the letter she has some nice things to say about Pip cutting a
dashing figure in 'an old pair of your army greens doing *callisthenics*
for the little chaps at the Boys' Brigade camp'. I have also had several
letters (plus numerous 'Peanuts' cartoons, little bookmarks, pictures
of 'friendly mice', an 'un-birthday' card) and two 'Peanuts' books
sent special delivery via an 8 Fd Amb nurse who went on R&R to
Singapore, from Vicki – the army sister from Terendak Hospital in
Malaysia. It only leaves me to get a letter from 'the front-end loader'
and then all my female fans will have had a go at Leap Year. Seriously
though, of all of them, I like Vicki the best – I think she would get on
well with you, Mum. Of course, she is what good Baptists would call
'worldly' and her surname sounds a bit Catholic, so I had better be

careful. I am not getting carried away, so don't get upset, but she does write nice letters, she doesn't call me 'a busy little RMO', and from what I remember of her at 2 Camp Hospital she is a very nice girl. But, as Phil would say, our correspondence is 'purely platonic', 'purely platonic', 'follow? follow?' to quote Dr Piper, and that's that.[2]

It was very good of Mr Logan to visit Gran. I can imagine what you mean about Gran being better and yet frail and sad – how could she be anything else? She must be like a person without an arm or a leg now Granddad is gone and no matter how good they are at the nursing home, it can't bring Granddad back to her. Do give her my love every day you visit. I can only write to her about once a week. And give my love to Aunty Frieda[3] too. She was always rather a favourite of mine – red lipstick and all. How is her grandson Robin getting on? He should be out of the army by now, I guess.

Do congratulate Pip on being a warrant officer in the Boys' Brigade – I had forgotten about that until tonight. I saw Dennis Gorrick again today – he seems to enjoy the army. I haven't yet met the two boys[4] who brought the letter back for me during the mail strike. I really should drive over to the tank unit and find them but I haven't had a chance.

There was great excitement today. I was just finishing sick parade when I got a call to say a fellow out at the Horseshoe had been burnt and they wanted a doctor to go out with the 'dust-off', so Sergeant Allen drove me straight around to the helipad and off we shot in a chopper. When I got there, of course, it wasn't nearly as bad as they had made out (fortunately), but he did have rather a badly burnt face. All I did was superintend his evacuation in the dust-off chopper and I then stayed on at the Horseshoe all morning as two gun batteries are out there at present, so there was plenty of routine stuff to do. So you never know what is going to happen next up here.

I haven't been to my Medcap at Hoa Long much lately (owing to the increased danger of ambushes), so I haven't seen a great deal of the people themselves. I saw the film *The Ugly American* last night. It was rather frightening in a way, being so true. It is all very difficult in SE Asia. I don't honestly know if the West is really winning or losing in any of these countries. I guess the whole fact of the matter is that unless the West can give the main thing it's got that's worth giving (i.e.

the Christian message) and back the message up with the genuineness of the lives of its representatives, the communists will win hands down in the long run.

Well, much love, Mother mine,

David

[1]   My father, despite his serious nature and firm Christian faith, had a gift for creating apt and outlandish nicknames for people. Almost all the church people we ever met had a nickname, known only to the family. Any young ladies from the church who showed any interest in either Pip or me were quickly labelled. If I recall, poor 'googly eyes' had a pair of thick glasses and the 'front-end loader' was a well built, rather strapping young woman.

[2]   The 'girlfriend issue' always caused me great discomfort, and like most gay boys from families who have strong expectations of their son making 'a good marriage', I sent up the usual smokescreens.

[3]   Aunty Frieda was my Grandmother Lloyd's younger sister. She was quite a character and notable for an enormous fear of thunderstorms. At the first rumble of an approaching storm she would take up residence under her bed until the danger passed.

[4]   I can't remember their names. One was a nephew of an aunt of mine.

Nui Dat

Tuesday 12/3/68

My dear family,

Well, here it is eight weeks to go until I see you all again ('D.V.',[1] as one of the church people is always putting in his letters to me). I still don't know when we land on the Tuesday night.

About our holiday – I don't really mind if we spend it in a little cottage at Leura, or in Merrie's backyard at Glenbrook, or on the beach at Manly, or camped in Lane Cove Caravan Park, or under Echo Point, or even on top of Ayers Rock, as long as:

1. we are all together preferably without anyone else
2. there are plenty of cups of tea going
3. there is plenty of good old Aussie scenery to feast the eyes on
4. there aren't any guns or helicopters or flares at night.

I don't mind at all – 75 Castle Hill Road will do me, although it would be nice to get away on our own, from curious neighbours, church people, customers, Girls' Friendly Societies, Girl Guides, and the Children's Free Library. One of those car tours stopping overnight at motels appeals too just so long as it's leisurely; we can stop when we like and we don't have to rush to get 'there' quickly. If Dad's worried about the cost, remember my money bins. I think the Halvorsen cruiser idea is 'out', though, as Mum wouldn't enjoy it and it would probably make Merrie's morning sickness worse. I'll just leave it to Mum (who will decide in the end anyway).

Oh I forgot:

5. No 'goffers' (which being interpreted is cans of soft drink). I am beginning to hate the sight of dry ginger ale, lemonade and Coca-Cola. If I stayed over here any longer I would start drinking alcohol just for a break from the everlasting soft drink. The problem is that there is simply nothing else, except super-chlorinated water or instant tea or coffee and they only appear at meal times. Before dinner, when I come into the mess hot and thirsty, I sometimes just long for something to drink which doesn't make you 'burp', but flat fruit drinks are unknown here. Anyway I am firmly convinced (quietly, in my own mind you must understand) that the value of being a strict teetotaller is all rubbish. People like the CO can have an old style gin and tonic, or something like that, before tea with quite obvious refreshment and enjoyment and I am quite sure there can be no harm at all in such practices. Mind you, I've never tried and I may not even like it. I've tried the glass of wine which everyone always has with the evening meal here at Nui Dat a couple of times, but I don't like that much. I am dying for many cups of tea when I get home, so stock up, Mum. And I agree with English Evangelicals who believe in drinking alcohol, provided it is in strict moderation. St Paul indubitably wrote, 'Take a little wine for thy stomach's sake', to Timothy who was probably ruining his digestion with fizzy drink, or the ancient equivalent. And I'm certain that when he wrote 'wine' he didn't mean unfermented grape juice.[2]

Yesterday I went to Hoa Long for a Medcap and it was a good well organised one, as we had an excellent interpreter – it makes all the difference. I got rid of the last lot of Band-aids, combs and soap. I don't think you should send anymore now – it would take the usual four to six weeks to get here and I shan't be doing Medcaps at that stage. Of course I would hand it on to the Civil Aid Unit if you have people eager to send stuff, but don't worry otherwise.

I have been out to the Horseshoe again today and tonight I had a long discussion in the officers' mess with the barman bombardier and his friend the HQ battery laundryman on a vast number of topics ranging from sex (the number one topic always here), 'the pill', death, heart transplants and finally some more serious matters like 'where would you go if you died tonight?' and is there life after death. All the other officers had gone to the movies, fortunately. The boys are convinced I am a number one wowser.

Well, must close. Sorry for the long dissertation on alcohol but I feel fairly strongly about it, so Pip had better rake up some good arguments if he disagrees with me.[3]

Lots of love,
David

1   'Deo volente' (Latin) – God willing.
2   Used in place of communion wine by Protestants.
3   Pip was a strong Evangelical Christian at this time, and he is still; I am not sure whether he would have agreed with my new views on alcohol, sex, etc., at this stage. I expect he might then have had a few reservations supporting me uncritically, although I suspect he would agree with me now.

Nui Dat
Monday 18/3/68

Dear family,
It has been a busy day, with three helicopter rides around the place, visiting 108 Battery at the Horseshoe and the Kiwi battery at a new FSB located in a ghastly hot sandy area. Nothing else exciting has happened, though – all the troops seem well and I just spent my time 'gas-bagging' as usual. Still, it wears you out all this air travel.

I'm glad to hear the scripts are so good at the shop, but a bit sorry to hear that Dad is so worn out. Couldn't you get another chemist to help now and again if it's that busy? Perhaps on your busiest morning (say Saturdays)? There is no sense in Dad killing himself with overwork. At least our holiday isn't far off now – only fifty days before I leave Nui Dat forever.

I enclose the answer I had to my Concord request. At least they still remember me, so I may get a job there for the last six months of 1968[1] even yet. I'll now just leave it up in the air until I get home – go and see the DDMS Eastern Command and find out what he can offer me in the army. If it's not suitable, I'll resign and try Concord Hospital. If they can't help, I'll just do locums or something.

Tell Merrie and Pip, the copy of *Witch Wood* is quite safe wrapped up in plastic, so I will definitely bring it home with me – 'No sweat', as the Yanks say.

Everyone sounds busy with preparations for the 'stirring days' of the Billy Graham[2] campaign – prayer meetings, counselling classes. It must be getting close.

Tomorrow will be Merrie's last day at work, so then she can retire to being simply an expectant mum (much to your relief, I'm sure, Mum).

If the mail is still playing up at home – in case this is the only letter that arrives before April 7th – have a very happy birthday and I send all my best love, Mum, and to Grandma for the 4th April.

Lots of love,
David

[1]   I had received a reply from London saying I did not get a place in the September FRCS course. The letter telling my family this must have gone missing.
[2]   Billy Graham was a hugely successful American evangelist who made two crusading trips to Australia in 1959 and 1968. Following these two visits, more junior members of his evangelistic organisation conducted further Australian campaigns over ensuing years.

Nui Dat
Wednesday 20/3/68

My very best Mother,
Your homemade biscuits were really delightful and we all ate them for morning tea today. They made the doughy so-called buns the cook

had made for morning tea pale into insignificance. All the officers (except the 2IC, who wouldn't have one) said to tell you they tasted 'beaut'. And, by the way, the Gamophen arrived safely too. I wonder if some letters are still going astray?

I was meant to do a Medcap at Hoa Long today, but the local Hoa Long VC have been 'playing up' again and the village is deemed unsafe (despite the Civil Aid Unit's protests to the contrary). However, I see no point in sticking my neck and my medics' necks out needlessly. Not with only forty-eight days to go! If the CA Unit want us to do Medcaps they can jolly well provide the necessary protection as far as I'm concerned before we'll go again.

Tomorrow I've another day of chopper rides visiting 108 and the Kiwi batteries – I am getting to be as much of a 'flying doctor' as Tony Williams used to be. 102 Battery has arrived to replace 106 Battery, and the new medic with 102 Battery isn't bad. I still miss Chuck a lot, though. The new medic is a large, fat (well, 'well built' would be a better term, I suppose) lad and seems very competent. He is very easy to get along with and does what I ask without question.

No more news tonight,

All my love,

David

PS Don't worry about more Gamophen – I think I have enough left to last seven weeks.

D.

Nui Dat
Friday 22/3/68

Dear Phil,

Thank you for your letter. I am sorry to hear Merrie and Ian's mental condition remains unchanged[1] – never mind! Aunty Marge, in a recent letter, states that they will make 'wonderful parents'.

Don't whisper a word of this to anyone but I am not really 'cut up' about missing the 'stirring days'.[2] I always was a bit of a heathen, I know, but I find it's all a bit much for me. I am glad the counselling classes are well attended and that there is a lot of enthusiasm behind all the preparations. We ought to be very thankful for the keenness of

Christian Sydney, even though they are so funny. It is not so in other capital cities of Australia.

I have been to Vung Tau today – there is a new CO at the Field Ambulance now – Colonel Watson, who used to be CO of 2 Camp Hospital. He is a 'big, bad bachelor' of about mid-forties and can consume enormous quantities of alcohol 'they' tell me, but for all that is a good CO and is expected to change 8 Field Ambulance from the worst unit in Vung Tau to the best virtually overnight. I hope so! Things are a lot better down there now – they have a specialist physician and a pathologist, as well as the surgeon, and much more equipment, so things are improving all the time. And so they should. Our casualties continue in a steady stream. While I was there today four were brought in with bad wounds from a minefield explosion on the current Operation Pinaroo.

Yesterday I visited the batteries out on the op and nearly got stranded because the RAAF fouled up my chopper flights somehow. I thought I would have to spend the night at the Horseshoe. The regimental radio net was crowded with messages most of the afternoon about 'starlight' and his travelling arrangements. No one was too sure where I was or where I was trying to get to half the time and I climbed in and out of the wrong chopper on numerous occasions. Just as well it happened in my eleventh month in country rather than my first. Such is life – in the army.

Well, all the best, Phil, and love to all the family,
Davo

<hr />

1   This was a joke – Pip and I frequently suggested unkindly that Merrie and Ian were mentally unhinged. We still do!
2   A reference to the extraordinary excitement that in certain Christian circles surrounded Billy Graham's visits to Australia.

Nui Dat, SVN
Monday 25/3/68

My dear Mum,
Thank you for your letter which arrived today and in which you so justly observe that it is now only six weeks to go. Hurrah! The new 2IC arrived today and the old one departs in two weeks, so things are

changing – the new regime is here. I am to be the last bastion of the old regime, apparently. Even Peter Snowden (LAD), who was to have gone home with me on 7th May, has discovered that his replacement will be here earlier than expected, so he has decided he will go home two weeks earlier himself. I am to be the last HQ battery officer left of 4 Field Regiment. 12 Fd Regt still haven't a doctor, the new 2IC told me tonight. The medical corps certainly doesn't hurry itself. Never mind – I don't have to stay past the 7th May. Digger James said he would arrange a 'stand-in' doctor from the Field Ambulance, if no replacement has arrived by that time for 12 Field Regiment. I can't be expected to stay on here forever even if the medical corps probably thinks fondly 'that nice kind Captain Bradford' would extend his services to help out. Like fun, I would! The American Army makes anyone who wishes to extend over here for another six to twelve months have a compulsory psychiatric interview, and a good thing too.

I don't dare think too much about the holiday – it sounds too good to be true and 'any old where' will do. I just hope it's not going to be too cold. Please look out a few jumpers for me, Mum. Mine have probably all been eaten by moths or else worn out by those two raiders Pip and Dad.

I'm so glad to hear Pip has had a permanent deferment from the army. It is a good experience, I'm sure, for most boys, but it can be a terrible waste of two good years of one's life. I'm sure Pip would have handled it without any trouble if he had been 'called up', but it's good he wasn't. There are a lot of things in army life which one can well do without (including being shot at and killed), but then again there are a lot of 'fine, brave and real things' too (to quote your newspaper article[1] which you sent and which I did enjoy and mostly endorse). When one compares the lazy, self-satisfied, 'priggish and parasitic' youth depicted in the article with the healthy, beer-drinking, admittedly often foul-mouthed, happy-go-lucky Australian digger, the latter wins hands down. At least they are alive and real and don't live in a shadow world of their own manufacture. Soldiers have their besetting sins, but if I may be so bold as to say, they are at least 'honest' sins and not of the Pauline variety listed in Timothy II, 'covetous, boasters, proud, blasphemers, disobedient to parents, unthankful, unholy, with-out natural affection, truce breakers . . . despisers of those who are good'. Not too much of that list can be imputed to the average soldier. Why is it we don't condemn sins like that with the same relish with which we enter into battle against the four old monsters alcohol, sex, gambling and tobacco? We Christians are funny people. Maybe Pip had better write and set me straight on that one, as well as on the 'drink' question.

There are many imponderable questions in life. I often wonder what good my twelve months up here have done. There is no little group of Christians in the regiment now, the church services are no better attended, Sergeant Allen's colourful vocabulary is in no way depleted or curbed, the officers still 'grog on' as before, when they can safely do so, and the Hoa Long locals still smuggle 'goodies' to the VC. Not much positive to show for my time here.

But I must stop 'gibbering on', as Chuck would say. Much love to all and happy birthday, Mum.

David

[1] Possibly an editorial in *The Sydney Morning Herald*, as it was the only newspaper my family read.

Nui Dat
Wednesday 27/3/68

Dear family,

Only time for a short one tonight, I'm afraid. Every now and again the doctors in the task force have a 'meeting' in the evening with 'Digger' James at the Forward Detachment. It doesn't end up happening too often because of all our various commitments but it's nice when it does. They drink beer and I drink lemonade (or something). It's his idea and it's a good one. It merely involves sitting around outside his tent chatting – we can share stories about our patients and the war and really discuss anything within reason; including difficulties we might be having with our units. It's a welcome break from just talking with the few officers in our artillery mess because there is little chance for doctors to get support from their colleagues up here. Now 'Digger' is here he's providing some leadership for us all and I know we appreciate it.

The sessions do tend to go on a bit, though, and not being a beer drinker I feel just a bit on the outer.

Anyway, must close as I am falling asleep here – the guns are quieter tonight.

My love to everyone,

Davo

Nui Dat

Thursday 28/3/68

Mother-mine,

I had a letter tonight which you only wrote last Sunday, so the mail seems to be behaving itself again – but perhaps I shouldn't speak too soon. It doesn't really matter much now with less than six weeks to go (into the thirties tomorrow – thirty-nine days to go).

Today is exactly one year since I arrived at 4 Fd Regt – that morning when I drove through the gates at Wacol in my brand new uniform, full of trepidation, not quite knowing what to expect. I wouldn't like to do that again, but looking back I'm glad I did it. It was quite a coincidence too in that it was lunchtime today when Colonel Dunn rang through from Saigon telling me he had just received a signal from AHQ containing a fresh posting order for me after I complete my forty-five days leave. They have posted me as an MO at 2 General Hospital at Ingleburn (which is presently a non-existent unit until the proposed general hospital is actually built at Holsworthy). In practice what happens is that all the members of 2GH are detached to the existing 2 Military Hospital (the old 2 Camp Hospital) where I worked before. This was quite a surprise and I'm not quite sure what to do about it. Apparently as a CMF full-time duty officer I have the right to resign a post with the maximum of a month's notice. So if the army tried to pull its old tricks of sending me off here there and everywhere, there would be no problem – I could just resign. Working there would mean I had a definite job for the next eight to nine months and it would be work I'd enjoy. On the other hand, it is further away from home than Concord and I would have to do night and weekend duties, of course. Being an army officer and not just a civilian working for the army there would always be the chance, if there was a big exercise for example, they could always tell me I had to go to it and they might detach me to a field ambulance or something for a week or two. This is the only major flaw in the idea. Colonel Dunn read me a letter from the general saying that I had obviously proved myself a satisfactory army MO up here and that the corps would therefore do everything in its power to assist me 'further my studies'. I guess the work at Ingleburn wouldn't be nearly as exacting as at Concord and I should have plenty of time for study.

What I would like to do is wait until I get home and go and see Dr Ada at Concord; if he can give me a job, I would then resign this posting before I start it. But that seems a bit mean, and if I don't intend to take the job with the army I would really like to say no in the next few days and let them know I was finishing full-time duty when I return to Australia. Do you see my dilemma? What do you and Dad think? I will ask Digger James what he thinks tomorrow, but it has really thrown me into confusion. Could you put up with having your son in uniform for a further eight months?

So old Greg has been called up! I can imagine Aunty Marge's concern but really for a pilot he has nothing to lose. There is flying aplenty in the army at the moment and I would think that being a 'chopper' pilot over here [is] much less dangerous than being an infantry man. And army pilots lead lovely lives – no living in mud or slush, no digging holes in the ground and filling sandbags.

How are Dad's sinuses and antrums? He must be having a bad time at present with those and his bad back. I hope he isn't overworking – never mind; only six or seven weeks to that holiday. I hope my present arrives in time for your birthday and that you have a very happy day. I am sorry to burden you both with my problems re the future. Please don't worry too much, as I am sure it will all work out. It's just hard to know what's best sometimes.

Much love and all my prayers for you all back home,
David
PS I hope Ian's exams[1] go OK. Give him my best wishes.

---

[1] Ian was slogging his way through chartered accountancy exams one subject at a time.

Nui Dat
Saturday night 30/3/68

Dear Dad,

A tiny note tonight.

I'm so sorry to hear that your back has been playing up lately – it must be that you're overworking and need a good rest. I guess you are looking forward to that holiday almost as much as I am. I hope you have managed to find a suitable reliever by now.

Thank you for getting the enlargements done for me – they haven't arrived yet, but I am looking forward to seeing them.

Well, take care of yourself, Dad, and lots of love from me,

David

Nui Dat
Sunday night 31/3/68

Dear Mum (and everyone else),

It has been a funny Sunday – high Church of England this morning, a lecture to the 'tankies' at 3 Cav Regt at lunchtime on VD, followed by lunch with the 'tankie' officers in their mess, a party this evening at HQ battery gunners' mess (the snake pit) marking the end of HQ battery 4 Fd Regt (it becomes 12 Fd Regt officially with the arrival of their advance party in a week's time) and that's my Sunday. Not really inspiring, I guess. At least my lecture went over well – I am becoming quite adept at VD lectures but I won't try it out on the family when I get home so have no fears.

I like the 'tankies' – they are much rougher and tougher than gunners and are mostly a good lot underneath. I don't envy them their job – two or three of them driving around for weeks on end in those hot little tin box APCs of theirs. They often live in them and sleep in them at night. Not really much fun. And they're always at the mercy of attacks with rockets, which the VC love to use against APCs. I suppose you can't blame them for letting their hair down a bit when they go to Vung Tau for a day – hence the need for the VD lecture.

Today I had a letter from 'a member of Dr Meredith Foxton's lady helpers and the people of the Redlands Shire' enclosing a postal note for $3 for me to buy 'goodies' at the nearest canteen. The people of the

Redlands Shire have been extremely good to me since Christmas – I have had about three different lots of parcels with tinned food from them. I'm completely perplexed as to how they got my name. The only thing I can think of is that Aunty Nell's son-in-law[1] may have given my name to them as a worthy cause. I think he is in an RSL group near there, so that may be it. Anyway this letter writer cheers me up by assuring me 'there's always a silver lining', so that's good to know. It is a kind thought of theirs, whoever they may be.

Enclosed is a copy of the signal describing my new posting order which I told you about in Thursday's letter. Don't worry about the 'tenure of not less than one year' – this is standard on all army postings and is a safeguard for the soldier rather than the army. It means the army is duty bound not to move you again for at least a year (barring accidents). It does not stop me getting out at a few weeks' notice if I want to. I still haven't completely decided what to do about it. Digger James thinks I may have to work too hard at 2 Camp Hospital (long hours, with not much time for study), but he thinks it unlikely they'd try to send me off on exercises and things. He advises I see Colonel Finley, the DDMS of Eastern Command, when I get back, as he is a CMF officer and a Macquarie Street specialist and pretty sympathetic to civilian army doctors like me. I will try to do that before I go on holidays.

Well, lots of love, Mother dear; I packed up a big parcel of medical textbooks which I bought in Taipei and am posting them on. Do keep well and strong and don't overwork.

All my love and prayers,

David

---

[1]   Aunty Nell was Granddad Lloyd's sister, who lived in Brisbane. She and her husband, Athol, were very kind to me when I was at Wacol for the weeks prior to leaving for Vietnam. Her grandson was a national service-man and had served in Vietnam prior to my leaving for overseas.

Reflections

Unusually, and in response to a letter from my father, the March letters start with a discussion of 'girlfriends'.

Unfortunately my memory of these potential girlfriends is extremely hazy now, but I do remember Vicki, the army nurse 'with the Catholic surname', a truly sweet and funny girl, who faithfully wrote and sent me all sorts of cheery messages throughout my year in Vietnam. We lost contact after my return to Australia – I am sure this was my fault. It's a shame she picked a gay boy to waste her energies on for a year or so, but wherever she is now I remember her with considerable fondness.

It's obvious by the reduced number of letters home, I was still busy in March even though based back in Nui Dat. Operation Pinaroo, in the Long Hai Hills near the coast north of Vung Tau, took up a lot of the month and was a difficult one for the infantry. The gun batteries fired many rounds in support from the Horseshoe and from another fire support base. I visited very regularly by helicopter.

There is a story I can now tell. During March I did many medical examinations for RTA – an endless succession of chests to be sounded, ears to be peered down, toes to scrutinise for fungus infections and genitals to check for STIs. Out of many good-lookers, one young man stood out for his extreme attractiveness – dark hair, olive skin, stunning build, naughty smile. Two nights later I was awakened by a phone call – they were bringing 'a very sick gunner' to see me from the far side of the task force. I sighed and rolled out of bed and walked up to the RAP. A Land Rover arrived with a soldier huddled on a stretcher. The story came from his mates – suddenly very ill, high fever, severe headache, aches and pains, must see the gunners' doctor. Once he was alone with me in my office, his head emerged from under the blanket with the same wicked grin. There was instant recognition. He didn't look ill. I examined him carefully – under the blanket, he was dressed only in a pair of army green underpants. Normal temperature, normal pulse rate, normal blood pressure, pupils normally reactive, no neck stiffness, chest clear, no lymphadenopathy, no palpable liver or spleen. He knew and I knew what this was all about. 'You're not sick, gunner,' I said brusquely. 'You're wasting everyone's time and I ought to charge you.' He smirked. 'Back to bed with you,' I added more gently, 'and behave yourself in future.' They took him back to his lines and I went back to bed. I didn't sleep easy, visions of his saucy smile flitting across my mind. One gunner seemed to have sussed me out despite all my caution.

My future plans were gradually crystallising. I had received word from London in March that I hadn't obtained a place on the course for the primary

FRCS for the second half of 1968, but they had reserved me a place in the first course for 1969. The letter telling this to my folks is lost. This meant I needed to find work for the months July to December 1968. The army had provided me with a posting to the Military Hospital at Ingleburn where I had worked before, but I was also considering trying to get work back at Concord Hospital.

My further 'deterioration' was no doubt in evidence in my waning adherence to total abstinence from alcohol. I doubt members of my family were convinced by my new-found defence of 'taking a little wine for thy stomach's sake'. I seem to remember my good friends at 3 Cav Regiment had even managed to persuade me to try one or two glasses of beer on a couple of occasions in my last months in Nui Dat, although I never stooped so low back in the mess at 4 Field Regiment. The Cavalry Regiment have much to answer for. It's a relief to know the barman and the laundryman, after our long evening discussion on life's ultimate questions in the officers' mess, still considered me a 'number one wowser'. I can't have deteriorated totally.

Like everyone else I was counting off the days until I returned to Australia. By the end of March people were talking about little else. I wanted to get back as much as anyone, but I did experience some concerns about how I was going to pick up the threads again on the home front. I might appear the same to my family and friends – and indeed for the seven months or so after I got home and before I left for England, I resumed exactly the same sort of life I had before I ever went to Vietnam and acted superficially as I always had done – but deep inside I knew I was different. I remember Digger James saying to some of us Nui Dat doctors that we would never be quite the same again and that our year in Vietnam would always remain a vital part of our future lives – we would never quite get it out of our system. He was right.

I recognised I was going to have some regrets. I would miss the unique position and privilege I had held as the gunners' doctor; I would miss the officers I had lived with, worked with, showered with, messed with; most of all I would miss my gunner and trooper patients – their easy talk, their confidences, their hurts and often their friendship. Parting from some of them was going to leave me with an ache I can feel even to this day.

12

APRIL 1968

Letters

Nui Dat
Monday 1/4/68

Dear Dad,

Well, April Fools Day and March is done with at last. Would you believe I am coming home *next* month. Hurrah!

I have just been listening to Mr Johnson's speech describing how he plans not to run again for president this year. It was kind of a sad speech, really, as though he was a tired old man who had done his best and somehow not done well enough. One can only feel sorry for him, as his position is probably the most unenviable one in the world today and no one can blame him for wanting to be well rid of the burden. Whatever anyone says, it is a failure for him (even if he has no other choice but to step down); because the very fact that he has no other choice indicates that he has failed to convince his people and the world in general that his policies were right. There is no doubt that the VC and Hanoi scored a notable psychological victory over the Tet Offensive period. Even though I am usually quite an optimist I can't help thinking that America's star has begun to wane. Perhaps if they had another Churchill at the helm over the past few years, things would have been a little different now.

I do hope you are feeling better now, Dad. I am very worried about you and Mum. I realise how upset Gran must get if you don't go to see her every night, but it is absolutely foolish to kill yourselves in the process. Be sensible about it – it'll be no fun if I have to visit you both in hospital when I get home, and it won't help Gran either, so stop gobbling your food down and rushing around like a crazy idiot, Dad. You will have a coronary if you aren't careful – you are getting mighty close to fifty you know and dashing your food down is about the worst thing you can do. If you can't manage any other way, you will just have to visit Gran every second or third night. That is not being cruel, it's being sensible. At the moment it just sounds as if you and Mum are working yourselves to death in the shop during the day, missing meals or eating them on the run and then dashing off to Ryde to see Gran every spare minute. It is just CRAZY, STUPID and the sort of idiotic martyrish thing you two would do. I am sorry to sound so angry, but I am worried about you both and so are Merrie, Pip and Aunty Jean, judging by their letters. You two sound as though you are as senseless as some of the soldiers I have to deal with every day. It seems as if my health is a good deal safer than both of yours, even though I am in a war zone! I jolly well hope I sound SEVERE and that you and Mum get shocked into some sense. Hectic lives are all right for twenty-year-olds but not for near fifty-year-olds and I would like to have my mum and dad around for a few more years yet, thank you very much.

Lots of love and prayers for you both,

David

Nui Dat

Tuesday 2/4/68

ELEVEN MONTHS IN SVN TODAY AND EXACTLY FIVE WEEKS TO GO!

My dear Mum, Dad and family,

I have felt *awful* all day today for posting you that cranky letter last night. It was just that I was so worried when I had your recent letters saying how busy you have been and what a rush it is for you to see Gran every night. But I was a bit sharp in last night's letter, I must admit, and I have been conscience-stricken today so I must say a big 'sorry'. Of course I realise you want to visit Gran every night and that she would be upset if you couldn't come, so I really have no right to make it more difficult for you by 'blowing you up'. Please forgive me, but all the same, do take good care of yourselves.

Today I was very extravagant and bought myself a nice little tape recorder at the PX for only $50. I decided against one of the great big stereo ones that cost about $300. It takes a 5-inch tape and you can plug it into a radio or radiogram and record music straight off. The reproduction is very good even though it isn't stereo. I will sell my tiny letter tape recorder as this one can be used to play even the little 2 inch tapes. The only things of any great price I have bought up here are my radio, this tape recorder and my camera. The amount of electronic equipment some soldiers buy is just astonishing.

I'm afraid my news is pretty unexciting at present. 108 Battery is still at the Horseshoe and the Kiwis are at a dusty sandy FSB below the Long Hai Hills where the present Op Pinaroo is still going on. I am visiting the latter again tomorrow. I do so much flying now I think I must nearly qualify for wings. Please congratulate Greg for me – I completely forgot to say that to you the other night when your letter about his excellent flying results arrived.

The weather is shockingly sticky at present and I feel very tired tonight – there is plenty to keep me busy even though I'm based at Nui Dat.

Well, all my best love and sorry for last letter's outburst.
David

Nui Dat
Friday 5/4/68

THIRTY-ONE AND A WAKEY!
My dear Mother,
Well, I must be coming home soon. Some friend of Dad's has written asking me to address the Westminster Rally in Scots Church on 18th May. Apparently he has a testimony in mind (or is it 'testimonial' now)? Anyhow I wrote and told him I was sorry I couldn't do it as I will be away on holidays with the family then (which is true, isn't it)? Even if it isn't, I'm afraid I don't want to do any speaking when I first

get home. I would like time to collect my thoughts a bit and readjust
to normal life. After all it would be rather awful to forget where I was
and start launching into a lecture in front of the august Evangelical
Presbyterians. Dad will probably be shocked at my turning down such
a request, but I really couldn't have faced it so soon. I hope you see
my point.

Talking about holidays – yes – Bowral sounds great – probably a bit
cold, but if we have a log fire that won't matter, will it? Anything will
be good after smelly old Vietnam with its red dust, rubber trees, sand
and mud.

I should have sent you all another tape but I just haven't had time.
Never mind, in four weeks we won't need tapes or letters. The photos
came today, thank you so much, Dad. They are pretty good, aren't
they? The mortars aren't so clear, but I think they should satisfy the
colonel.

Pip has got me wrong. He takes me to task for an alleged attack
on uni students, which I am not guilty of. Long ago I was a uni
student – not a very willing one, I admit, poor long-suffering parents,
but a uni student none the less. I am always defending them hotly in
the mess (where they come in for quite a bit of attack). The real uni
student is not lazy or parasitic. He/she is a hard-working, much
downtrodden, exam-ridden, normal likeable kid and of course
he/she is every bit as good as the average soldier. I am talking about
the pseudo-intellectual type who has never passed a uni exam in his
life, who squanders pots of his 'old man's' money, who leads all the
protest marches, talks all the bilge and washes infrequently. They
are the sort I'm comparing unfavourably with soldiers. As Pip very
well knows, the real uni student hasn't time to sit about talking
about 'the ultimate reality', unless Arts is very different to Medicine.

Lots of love, Mum,

David

PS Don't get too worried if you have some of my 'beery' visitors.
Peter Snowden, the LAD officer, vows he will 'pop' in when he comes
to Sydney in May to tell 'your godly parents all about your evil
doings in Vietnam, doc'! He is really harmless and very likeable,
though.

Nui Dat
Sunday 7/4/68

MUM'S BIRTHDAY AND FAREWELL TO 7 RAR

Dear family,

Well, another Nui Dat Sunday is almost over and it's been a quiet day – sick parade (a couple of suture jobs on cut hands, etc.), then a special dinner at 7 RAR for their battalion farewell (the current 7 RAR doctor had invited me to come – not Tony Williams as he went home several weeks ago). It turned out to be quite a good party – they had the best steak I have tasted in SVN for barbecuing, so maybe I'll put on more weight and will look less like a skeleton when I arrive home. The day finished with just some quiet talking in the mess. Oh! I forgot, I went to church this morning too. The Kiwi padre officiated with one of his vague sermons (about 'courage' this morning). The brigadier was there and he gravely congratulated me on my organ playing when he saw me at the 7 RAR party at lunch time so there is no doubt I am quite famous – such an old task force identity now.

I told Merrie in her letter that Trevor Weekley dropped in to see me yesterday – a little more subdued and thinner than when last I saw him but still the same old Trevor. Tell the Weekleys I saw him and that he looks well and fit.

I'm glad Bombardier Dickinson's paintings arrived OK.[1] You must be on the same wave length as all artists, Mum. 'Dicko' tells me the little girl is by far the better painting of the two but I agree with Pip – I like the little boy painting the best. They are real children 'out of Dicko's head' – I can tell you no more than that.

The night of 7th May for arrival seems very definite. Please don't have any great deputations at the airport, though – just the family. Often army flights are late or get cancelled until the next day – you can never be quite sure. But I really only feel like coping with the family when I arrive; not other people (especially 'Googly-eyes' or the 'Front-end loader').

About the future – I will just wait until I get home to finally decide. I have plenty of leave, so that gives time to make enquiries and to resign the new posting if I want to do so. Mum, there is absolutely no fear of my being sent off to Vietnam again, not while I remain CMF –

the Australian Regular Army is a different matter, of course, but I have absolutely no intention of becoming ARA.

I guess the 'stirring days' are just about to begin. Now don't go rushing out to the Showground every second night and to Gran's every other night. Stay home and watch Billy[2] on TV. And don't go working desperately on the house for my return. I don't care if it looks like a bomb has hit it – it will look like that five minutes after I hit the place, anyway, so please don't waste time on extra housework.

Lots of love,
David

[1] Dicko had given me two quite large paintings on plywood. One was the face of a boy, the other of a girl. I posted them both home. Sadly I have lost them both in multiple moves since that time.

[2] Billy Graham, the American evangelist.

Nui Dat
Monday 8/4/68

My dear family,

This is just a short note to wish you all a very happy and blessed Easter this year and to send you two lovely photos of your son/brother/brother-in-law at the 4 Fd Regt HQ battery party a couple of weeks ago. As you can see my looks haven't improved after a year away – my hair remains as unmanageable as ever; my teeth continue crooked and my smile is as lopsided as before. And of course my ears need not be described. You will see that in each picture I have managed very successfully to conceal my can of beer. In actual fact, on this auspicious occasion, it was Coca-Cola (ugh). That is all the snake pit runs to in catering for non-drinkers. And cola more than any other fizzy is most conducive to indigestion. It was a happy party anyway.

Tomorrow, the first lot of HQ battery people leave – the 2IC and four others – so the exodus has started. Only four weeks before we leave.

Well, that's all for the moment. I hope you like the photos.

Lots of love,
Davey Boy

Nui Dat
Thursday 11/4/68

Dear Mum,

I am so glad the roses arrived in time and that you enjoyed them. I was worried they mightn't turn up as I had ordered them so long before, but they did, so all is OK.

Yesterday we held a full regimental parade on the newly finished oval and dedication of a plaque to the memory of the four officers and gunners who have been killed over here in 4 Field Regiment's twelve months. It was a simple little ceremony with a few words from the CO and the brigadier and a couple of prayers from the Kiwi padre and the RC padre – quite moving, really.

The CO of 12 Fd Regt is here and on Sunday our CO hands over to him officially, so soon I will be 12 Fd Regt's doctor (for a couple of weeks anyway). That is a bit of a blow, as they are still fussing around trying to find a replacement doctor for me – whether they do or don't doesn't really matter as I am definitely leaving on 7th May come what may. Every other HQ battery officer will be gone by then except muggins. As Sergeant Allen says, 'You can't win 'em all, doc'. Sergeant Allen is sticking it out until 7th May as are the great majority of HQ battery gunners, so I guess one officer has to stay behind with them.

Tomorrow is Good Friday – there will be services tomorrow especially, but otherwise it's just an ordinary day. It will be a funny sort of Easter; not the most ideal circumstances for thinking about the Easter story, but its message is still as applicable to men everywhere (including Nui Dat at the tail end of a twelve-months tour of duty). I do hope and pray that you will all have a very happy and blessed Easter-time.

As you see, I am a bit 'down in the dumps' today, mainly because I have a cold in the head and am not operating at my normal high level of biological efficiency. So don't worry about my whingeing.

Very much love to you all,
David

Nui Dat
Friday 12/4/68

My dear long-suffering family,

I have just written a letter to Judy 'Bex' Nicholas[1] thanking her for the big box of Medcap stuff which arrived today (plus a yellow and red flannel which they suggest is 'to keep my neck warm').

Today has been fairly busy – sick parade; visiting Colonel Dunn at the task force RAP (old Forward Detachment), as he is having a day in Nui Dat from Saigon, to talk over the posting a bit further; and hygiene inspections for the rest of the day (ugh! grease traps, kitchens and latrines – how gruesome they are, and especially on Good Friday). Nothing very exciting but enough to keep me busy. Then tonight I watched a film at HQ battery – like a drive-in without the cars. I enjoy being with the gunners and hearing their irreverent comments.

I haven't yet fully decided what to do when I get home. I expressed all my doubts to Colonel Dunn this morning. He was emphatic I was not bound in any way. If I do not like the job (because I don't get enough time to study), or if they try sending me off on exercise or something, he says they can do nothing about it if I just hand in my resignation. He maintains it is a good posting and that the army is bending over backwards to help me (as they are at least being definite and I have an actual posting in my hand, rather than vague promises).

I will need a car if I work at Ingleburn. I wonder if you could speak to Mr Hughes about keeping his eye out for one for me, Dad? I don't think I could drag the 'MAL' back from Pip – not now. He would be lost without it, with his vast social life to maintain. I will only need one for eight months and almost anything economical but reliable would suit me. A nice red second-hand Mini-Minor would be terrific.

Well, I guess I have exhausted my supply of news – my love to every-body. I hope you are all well and counting the days off faithfully until my return. I certainly am this end.

Lots of love,
David

¹ There is a note about Judy Nicholas (née Renn) for the letter of Wednesday 27/9/67. Dad (who else?) had added the 'Bex' because of Judy's fondness for Bex Powders (an over-the-counter analgesic agent popular in the fifties and sixties) for her headaches.

Nui Dat
Saturday 13/4/68

My dear Mother,

The mail is playing up a bit again as I haven't had a letter for two nights now. I do hope you are all OK and not too tired out. You should be able to have a good rest over the Easter period, and then it's only about four weeks and we'll be on holiday.

The world is in a sad state this Easter – wars, rumours of wars, financial problems, racial problems, violence even in the capital of the greatest 'Christian' nation in the world. Poor old America! But it ill becomes us carefree Australians to point the finger at the Americans – one day we are going to have to grow up awfully suddenly and I doubt we have any more real solid foundation than America has.

But not long now and I will no longer be a 'cog' in the Vietnam war machine – I won't be sorry about that. With new talk of peace prospects and the possibility of a new government in Washington before very long, I just hope and pray that a satisfactory peace may be won and that the awful cost so far in young American and Australian lives (not to mention the vaster numbers of Vietnamese) won't all go for nothing. It is so easy for sacrifices made to be forgotten by all except the sorrowing families.

Well, after being so mournful I must conclude. Tomorrow is Easter Sunday and there is no place for mourning and hopelessness on Easter Day.

Lots and lots of love and see you in three weeks time,

David

PS: Rev 21.4. 'and there shall be no more death, neither sorrow, nor crying, neither shall there be any more pain: for the former things are passed away'.

Nui Dat
Easter Sunday 14/4/68

Dear Mum,

Just a little note tonight to tell you about Easter Sunday in Nui Dat. I went to church this morning (decided to be a heathen and go to the C of E service as Sergeant Allen said he would go with me at 8.30 am). The 3 RAR (Anglican) padre is terribly, terribly 'high' and sort of 'intense', if you know what I mean, but his sermons are surprisingly good. It was a nice service.

After sick parade there was a big ceremony at the 108 Battery position when 4 Fd Regt fired their last round and 12 Fd Regt fired their first round, (the brigadier pulling the cord on the gun on each occasion). We and all the assembled guests then withdrew to the officers' mess for a farewell party to 4 Fd Regt (given by the incoming CO and his officers). Then tonight the Kiwi battery had a formal dinner for officers to farewell Colonel Gardner and 4 Fd Regt, which I was invited to. The menu is enclosed – it is in reality just normal fare with a few trimmings, but it sounds wonderful, doesn't it?[1]

So it has been quite a day – not the usual way I spend Easter Sunday, that's for sure.

Tomorrow morning the CO leaves, so I will go and see him off on the plane at 7.45 am. Then the next day most of the other HQ battery officers leave (the adjutant, the assistant adjutant, the QM). It will be sad seeing them go. Never mind; only three weeks left.

Until then, lots of love,
David

[1] The menu included a seafood cocktail with shellfish from Baria and (deep-frozen) roast turkey from the Americans.

Nui Dat
Monday 15/4/68

Dear everyone,

This morning we saw off the CO (with an illegal bottle of champagne at Luscombe Airfield – i.e. the Nui Dat airstrip). Most of the officers were quite unsuited to eating breakfast, let alone drinking more alcohol, but they struggled manfully – I took photos to prove it. The CO said I was not to use them in evidence against him. As he climbed aboard the plane the two gun batteries in Nui Dat fired a special 'fire plan' of coloured smoke in his honour so the plane taxied down the runway to the sound of the guns booming all over the task force – it was quite impressive. We gunners do things in style. And now, for three weeks I am the RMO of 12 Fd Regt, which is a bit of a 'come down', but I guess I will survive.

There are more farewells tomorrow morning (the adjutant and his party), so I will be getting good at seeing planes off.

Best love to you all,
David

Nui Dat
Wednesday 17/4/68

My dear family,
I have just received your Good Friday letter and I am so glad to hear that you all had a nice restful day, although I was sorry that Granny has been so sick.[1] It must be pitiful to see her like that.

I am sorry to hear that Mr Begbie[2] has had a heart attack and is in Concord Hospital. I didn't think he looked terribly well when I saw him that time up here.

All being well I leave here on Tuesday 7th May at about six or seven o'clock in the morning. We fly in C123 planes (small Hercules) to Saigon and then have about a three hour wait in the hot sun at Tan Son Nhut airfield until about 12.30 when the plane takes off for Darwin (a 707 Boeing jet charter aircraft). It refuels in Darwin, then flies on to Brisbane and then Sydney. We should arrive about 1.30 am on Wednesday morning 8th May, although it is said never to be on time and can arrive as late as 3 or 4.30 am. As you can see, it's a long tiring trip but at least better than the way we came up in that horrible Hercules for eight hours from Darwin. Anyway, who cares? I would paddle a canoe home if there was nothing else available. The charter flights are supposed to be very good – they even have beer on board; can anything be better than that? A good genuine cup of tea would do me, but will they be able to supply that?

Robbie said in his letter he was hoping to stay a few days at our place so he could come to the airport to welcome me. I hope you can fit *him* in, but I don't want hordes or multitudes there to welcome me – it would be too embarrassing.

I am a *teenager* now! Nineteen and a wake-up!

Lots of love to you all,

David

[1] My grandmother had suffered lung complications of her rheumatoid arthritis and was subject to frequent chest infections in the last few years of her life. She died in 1970.

[2] Reverend Alan Begbie, Chaplain-General of Australian Forces.

Nui Dat, SVN

Sunday 21/4/68

My dear Mother (and everyone else at Lantern Woods),

It is Sunday afternoon and I have just tuned in to the BBC for the afternoon news – it is easily the best and most unbiased of all the available radio stations.

I guess by now you will have had my letters telling you of the letter from Concord Hospital offering me a position on the surgical side which falls vacant in May and of my subsequent decision to turn it down. I do hope you are not disappointed that I didn't take the job, but I prayed about it and thought about it a great deal for forty-eight hours and finally decided it would be best if I let it go. Now I feel quite happy about my decision. It seems to me that my main job over the next eight months is to get a lot of reading and studying done before I go to England, as I do not want to have to sit this exam about a hundred times like a lot of people. If I worked at Concord, although I would get the same time off as I used to, I don't think I would study all that well. I get too involved in the work and I wouldn't take my due afternoons off and just leave the junior resident to get on with it. I am not like that and I would end up working really hard and not getting enough study done. If I go to Ingleburn, the volume of work won't be nearly so much. Of course I won't get a lot of surgical experience at Ingleburn but that isn't the important thing at this stage – I've got to pass the primary exam before I can even think of further experience. Also, the army owes me eighteen days leave for this year which is due on 1 July, so I should stay in until that, to get the benefit of them. And the army has been really quite good to me giving me the job at Ingleburn, which is definitely the best army MO job in NSW, so I guess I shouldn't grumble. I will meet plenty of specialists there who visit regularly. So that's the story. I will be in uniform until the end of the year.

Sorry to worry you with all my problems. See you in two weeks.
Much love,
Davo

Nui Dat
Monday 22/4/68

Dear Mum,
You and Dad really are cruel to the Baptist minister at Castle Hill – shocking him by not displaying enough crusade fervour. Fancy putting money-making first! I am ashamed of you. Did you tell him that you are just doing what St Paul said Christians ought to do 'studying to be quiet and to do your own business and to work with your own hands . . .'? Pip is representing you all at the crusade very well in any case, what with being a children's counsellor and all.[1]

I'm sorry to hear Aunty Jean is unwell. Do give her my love and apologise that my correspondence hasn't been too good lately. I'm afraid I've lost my letter writing zest, with only two weeks to go. I will be seeing you all again soon, Aunty Jean included.

Lots of love,
David

[1] These comments reflect the extreme enthusiasm with which the Billy Graham crusade was greeted by many Christians. My brother, Pip, spent a great many hours at crusade meetings, counselling children and teenagers who came forward to commit their lives to Christ. My mum and dad found it hard to get to the campaign meetings in at the Showground (Moore Park) during the week due to the demands of the shop, thus earning the disapproval of the Castle Hill Baptist minister.

Nui Dat
Saturday 27/4/68

Dear Mum and Dad,

Here it is my second last Saturday in Nui Dat and only nine days to
go before I leave here forever, so time is really running out. It can't go
too fast for me now – the old regiment has gone and most of the
officers of 4 Fd Regt have left except for the one from 108 Battery who
is coming home on the same flight with me. Besides, most of 12 Fd
Regt are out on operation right up in Bien Hoa province near where
we were on Op Coburg, far away from here, so we are a select little
group back at base.

As I told you before, I have been helping Digger James at 8 Field
Ambulance and it's been really busy up there – you never stop all day
and it is most exhausting. I'm feeling like I need a holiday at present.
Major James has given me the day off tomorrow, so I'll be able to have
a bit of a breather.

Len Miller from Penno has arrived at Nui Dat and is posted to
8 field ambulance (it's no longer the Forward Detachment – it's the full
field ambulance and the unit at Vung Tau is now the 1st Australian
Field Hospital). I think he is wondering what he's struck since he
arrived the other day, it's been that busy – a little different for him
than raking leaves at the CCS at Wacol. He looks very well and has put
on weight since last I saw him. He tells me Ian Simpson is not coming
here but got a posting to the gun battery in Malaysia – a very coveted
post for artillerymen.

No more news except I'll see you in ten days time and that's not
long at all.

Love from your son, brother, brother-in-law,

David

PS I am now feeling well again – the cold is better and I'm getting
used to the antimalarial 'going home' pills.

Nui Dat
Sunday 28/4/68

EIGHT DAYS AND A WAKE-UP TO GO!

Dear Mum and Dad,

This will be my third-last letter from Sth Vietnam. I will try and write tomorrow night and Tuesday night, but it will be pointless writing after that.

There's another change to the plans. We fly direct from Tan Son Nhut to Darwin (that's in Uc-Dai-Loi) to refuel but then it's straight on to Sydney. We are not even stopping in Brisbane. That means we should be in earlier (about 11.30 pm). Check with Mascot on the day, though – specify it's the charter flight from SVN, NOT the R&R flight, but the RTA flight. The whole fifty-five of us HQ battery personnel under command of those two capable officers, Captains Dennis Moore and David Bradford should walk, or more likely 'roll' in most cases, as it's a 'wet' flight, off the plane. The Brisbanites, like poor old Sergeant Allen, whom I will be able to introduce you to now, have to then get another charter flight to Brisbane and have to pay their own airfare. The army will only pay train fare prices, which has to be mean in the extreme.

It's a funny feeling, the thought of coming back to civilisation after a year away – I am sure it will take some adjusting. That's why I'd prefer only family there; besides I will be too scungy-looking (to quote Pip) to see anyone else.

I went to church this morning – being loyal, I thought I should support the Kiwi padre at the OPD service, but I was the only congregation there, which was a bit embarrassing. He took the opportunity of telling me his theological outlook, which he describes as 'very liberal liberal'. He is not a bad bloke and I think his heart is in the right place but his theology is corny to say the least. I had my little say and he thinks I am a very bigoted Baptist. Me? A bigoted *Baptist*?

Then, for lunch, I went to the 'tankie' officers' mess (3 Cav Regt), who are a wicked but nice friendly lot of chaps. They have always been very good to me and seem to think I am a suitable person to look after the medical needs of the senior corps (the cavalry). They are very snobbish! The gunners aren't half as bad as the 'tankies' for superiority complexes. It is a little unsettling having lunch there, as one is confronted by an entire wall of *Playboy* pin-ups for the month dating back to January 1966. I had a chuckle to myself thinking about the zealous young man in Mr Logan's story and how busy he would have to be pulling down all the 'rude nudes' on the 3 Cav Regt mess wall. Still, it is only anatomy after all and fairly harmless. Our RAP is the only place in the entire task force which isn't decorated with nudes, but for how much longer, I wonder? Sergeant Allen, it's true, has a little corner with his favourite pin-up stuck there, but she has a bikini and is really quite decent. Someone witty has written in biro on the top. 'To Bob, with all my love, Veronica XXXX' and to the uniniti-ated it is a big puzzle how Bob came to meet Veronica, as the writing looks very authentic.

I must stop shocking you.

Lots of love until next Tuesday 7th May,

David

PS Len Miller seems to be settling in very well, tell his folks.

Nui Dat, SVN
Monday 29/4/68

LAST LETTER FROM VIETNAM TO HIS GODLY SISTER AND BROTHER-IN-LAW

Dear Porky-girl and Chicken-Chest,

Please reserve one room at Gilchrists' Glenbrook Guest House from 10th to 18th May incl. for bed and breakfast (in bed) of course and all other meals (not in bed), for one war-weary soldier-doctor lately returned from the wars to the bosom of his family. He is looking forward to having a complete rest without interruption, particularly by members of the nursing profession, so it would be appreciated if the proprietors of said guest house could put off all their other frequent clients for this period; suitable compensation will be made for this. In particular if the Misses AMcP, BM, Front-end Loader, HL or Googly-eyes request accommodation at the same time this client reserves his right to withdraw his application STATIM (if not sooner). The shock to his already jangling nervous system would be too much and I fear complete nervous collapse, shell shock or combat fatigue would occur in their most refractory forms. The mere thought of Miss Googly-eyes and 'the little RMO' sends this prospective guest into 'flat spins'. Requirements (other than this) are simple:

- Plenty of tea
- No coffee
- No soft drinks
- Plenty of warmth
- No lectures to neighbours
- Plenty of hot showers and baths
- No mosquito nets
- No helicopters
- No guns
- No night calls
- No 'etherised' eggs[1]

Anyway, seriously, I am much looking forward to staying with you both at Glenbrook if you're sure it's all right. I am just dying for a good holiday – not having to get up to do a sick parade at eight o'clock every single morning with the usual, 'I think I've got a drip, doc', sequence to be heard at least twice every day (often far more frequently than that).

Tonight I am on duty at task force RAP again – we have already had one bad 'dust-off' in – a soldier from one of the battalions who got shot through the leg and the upper arm this afternoon out on operation. We put a drip up but seeing how badly smashed up his femur must have been, he was in amazingly good shape – no obvious clinical shock. After a bit more morphine we sent him off to Vung Tau. I hope it is quiet otherwise tonight, as tomorrow will be another busy day, I suppose. At least time is passing for me quickly now. Only eight days and a shave to go!

See you about 11.30 pm on Tuesday 7th May at Mascot, but remember – no 'fans' there other than family.

Much love,
David

---

[1]   For troops in Vietnam, eggs were preserved by the injection of some chemical – popularly believed to be ether. They did taste terrible!

Nui Dat
Tuesday 30/4/68

Dear Mum,

This will be my last letter from Vietnam, as by the time it reaches you by the weekend I will be almost home.

Today was a good day because my replacement doctor[1] arrived. Actually in the flesh! The poor chap thought he was going to the Field Hospital at Vung Tau till he landed at Saigon to be met by Colonel Dunn telling him he was now the gunners' doctor. Anyway here he is and here he stays. And I am free to leave next Tuesday morning 7th May. I should be home anytime between half past ten and half past twelve on Tuesday night May 7th. But you'll have to check with the airport to be sure of the time. If anything changes, I will let you know at once by telegram.

You have no idea what a relief it was, seeing the new doctor – he is only very young – 'looks even younger than you, doc', said one of the gunners today. My next few days will be spent showing him the ropes now.

Thanks for the cuttings about Nobby Clark – isn't that beaut?[1] He really deserved it and it is a great thing for 4 Field Regt.

Lots of love,
David

[1] Captain John Stephens.
[2] Lieutenant Neville Clark won an MC for his outstanding bravery at the battle of Suoi Chau Pha, as described in my Reflections on the August 1967 letters. The award was officially announced in April 1968.

Reflections

My last month in SVN was a busy one. There was plenty to do medically and I spent a good deal of time working with Digger James at 8 Field Ambulance (the old Forward Detachment). I found the work very satisfying; dealing with the casualties who came our way was now well within my capabilities, as described in the letter of Monday 29/4/68.

It was a month of farewells. As the month progressed, I said goodbye to all my fellow officers of HQ battery as they departed in dribs and drabs. The farewell to the CO, Reg Gardner, was the most emotional and I felt a real lump in my throat as his plane took off and the guns of the new regiment sounded a final salute to him and to 4 Field Regiment itself. That was when I knew my personal adventure had ended, even though I had another two weeks or so to serve in Vietnam.

In April I made the decision to stay in the army and to accept their posting to 2 Military Hospital in Ingleburn for the remainder of 1968. Accordingly I turned down the offer of a surgical job at RGH, Concord. When faced with a clear-cut choice, I found I couldn't yet give up the army and decided to postpone the final cutting of ties until the end of the year. For a would-be surgeon this move was probably not very sensible. I might have remained a surgeon even until today if I had made the opposite choice, but I am glad I decided as I did. I have had a much more satisfying career as a sexual health physician than I would ever have had as a surgeon. I am sure too I have made a better doctor in the field of sexual health than I would ever have been in the field of surgery.

As the Caribou, loaded with HQ battery gunners and me, took off from Luscombe airstrip on that final May morning, I looked down at the familiar terrain of Phuoc Tuy province and realised this would be the last time I would see it for many years – perhaps forever. The gunners were cheering as we left the ground. I could only feel overwhelmingly sad – sad at our losses; sad at the remembrance of those wounded and sick because of their time here; sad for the Vietnamese and their still war-torn country; and sad for myself. I didn't try then to analyse my own deepest feelings. Looking back, I think I was sad because a chapter in my life was ending – as it turned out, one of the most significant chapters in my life. In a lifetime, you only get a few chances to live life really vividly and intensely for a little period. My twelve months in Vietnam had been one such time and I regretted its passing.

POSTSCRIPT

The men of HQ battery, 4 Field Regt landed at Mascot in Sydney in the early hours of Wednesday morning 8 May 1968. I introduced Bob Allen to the family and said my goodbyes. With the exception of Bob and Jeff Banks, I have seen no one from headquarters battery since that morning.

Soon after my return, my family and I had a holiday in Bundanoon on the southern highlands of NSW. It was bitterly cold and the rented cottage we stayed in was draughty and had rats in the walls. In the last few days I had a recurrence of my feverish illness with bad gastroenteritis. It wasn't a very successful holiday.

I stayed in uniform and worked happily at 2 Military Hospital Ingleburn while living at home in West Pennant Hills. As I had hoped, I had plenty of time in which to study. As Dad had failed to organise a car for me to buy, I soon found a very reliable second-hand VW 'Beetle'. I continued to attend Pennant Hills Baptist Church on Sundays when I was not on duty at Ingleburn. I did not find this too arduous a duty, as I had to work every second or third weekend at Ingleburn. Mostly, when not on duty, I resumed my old job of playing the organ on Sunday mornings. While at Ingleburn, several times I came across the nocturnal gunner with the wicked smile. He would nod briefly and knowingly. He seemed to have found a friend – a driver who used to accompany us on Medcaps.

The army kept its promise and did not send me on field exercises, but it would have been uncharacteristic for them not to spring a surprise. One Monday morning I was posted suddenly and unexpectedly for three weeks to the small hospital at Kapooka Army Base, Wagga Wagga, where I did medicals on what seemed like millions of new national service recruits (including my young cousin Greg). I was discharged from full-time duty in the army in December 1968, and although I remained on the books as a CMF officer I have never worn the uniform again.

I arrived in London in March 1969 to begin my surgical studies and finally obtained the FRCS in 1972. I had been correct in my original letter on the subject – there *were* 'countless hidden snags' in my quest for the surgical qualification. The most formidable was passing the primary examination – I failed the first time. I should add that I was not unique in this achievement – most people failed the first time; but I felt it keenly. The first three months in London were the most difficult in my life. I was lonely, I missed the companionship and structure of the army, the weather was foul, the food at the residential college was terrible, the room was tiny and looked out onto a grey brick wall, the church I had been recommended was extremely conservative and unfriendly and I couldn't study or concentrate. I could think about nothing but sex!

I was fortunate to meet by chance an Australian psychiatric registrar whom I had known at Concord Hospital – Dr Frank Lappin. I realised I needed to talk to someone and with great difficulty told him my problem. I had never tried to talk about my homosexuality with anyone before and it was an amazing relief to get it off my chest. He was unfazed and over the next year or so provided enormous support and sensible advice. Without him, I might not have survived intact. In the Christian circles in which I had my upbringing, consulting a psychiatrist except for severe psychotic mental illness was thought to show a lack of faith, so despite my medical training, I felt quite guilty even informally talking to Frank.

I felt the need to consult a Christian leader as well, so over the next few months I had a couple of appointments with a leading Evangelical, the Reverend John Stott, rector of All Souls, Langham Place. Mr Stott received me kindly but his message was uncompromising, as I had expected – indeed it was entirely what I would have heard from my own father: being homosexual was not intrinsically evil in itself but homosexual acts were sinful; Christ called Christians to deny themselves and follow Him. It came down to a clear choice for me. Choose Christ and His way, or indulge myself by following my own nature. He pointed out that I was at a crossroads and whatever decision I took would determine my future destiny.

Black and white, clear-cut messages were what I was used to and what I had been brought up to consider right and appropriate. But Vietnam taught me, if nothing else, that life's choices, though inescapable, are rarely clear-cut or black and white. Sexuality seemed to me then, as it seems to me now, an intrinsic part of a person's life and character. How could I live as a whole person when 'denying myself' meant not just refraining from homosexual acts, but having to deny the real me? It would be living a sham. Over some months of substantial turmoil I did make my choice. I was homosexual and I would live with it and if an appropriate time, place and person happened along I would not be restrained from acting on what was natural for me.

After the FRCS primary exam I decided to stay on in England. Having more or less 'come out' in England, it seemed easier to give myself time to adjust to my new life well away from home and family, so staying on seemed appropriate. When I was home in Sydney on holiday for six weeks over Christmas/New Year 1972/73 I met Michael, my lifelong partner. He joined me in England in August 1973 and we have lived together ever since. As well, I 'came out' to my family in 1973. Although my coming out was not funny then, it is funny in hindsight. After I met Michael, there was a week of regular phone calls before I returned to London. I told white lies as to whom they were from, but my mother soon cottoned on and told me, over the ironing board, that I was homosexual. Thus challenged, I had no option but to agree. Fortunately, there was a pile of handkerchiefs handy for the tears that followed. I wonder how many boys have been told by their mothers they are gay? Probably quite a lot. My mother exhorted me not to tell my dad. I agreed for the moment, but soon after my return to London, I devoted a free afternoon to writing him a long letter – cowardly perhaps, not to have taken time to speak to him before I left for London, but it was all I could cope with at the time.

My parents did not take it well, which was understandable given their firm Evangelical faith and their loyalty to the Bible as they understood it. For years I had not taken it well either, for exactly the same reasons. The next years were extremely painful ones for them and for me. My homosexuality and my relationship with Michael were difficult for them to accept, although my brother Philip and his wife Rosie were always supportive towards us. It is a measure of the close bonds which tie us all together as a family that, after many years of pain and hurt on both sides, we have managed to reach a stage where my mother, my sister and my brother and their families all joined in wishing Michael and me well as we celebrated our marriage in

Canada in August 2006. It is sad we are unable to marry in our own country, where our families could attend, simply because the government, which I once served as a soldier, refuses to allow same sex couples to marry in Australia.

We returned home to Australia in early 1980 and settled in Melbourne, Michael's home city. I was then a venereologist (a specialist in sexually transmitted infections), having completed appropriate training in England. I become Chief Venereologist for Victoria and eventually had a practice looking after substantial numbers of people living with AIDS. I buried about 150 patients and friends in those dark days before effective treatments for HIV infection were developed. In 1993, we moved to Cairns, where I became director of the Cairns Sexual Health Clinic until I retired in 2004.

The time in Vietnam changed me profoundly. Who knows what might have happened had I not enlisted. Without the Vietnam experience, I might have taken the black and white path John Stott set before me.

I should now fill the reader in on what happened to other people mentioned in the book, where I possess that knowledge. First, my family – my father, Camden, worked on as a pharmacist in Castle Hill for several more years and after retirement on the Blue Mountains died in 2003. My mother, Noelle, is a sprightly octogenarian and now lives in a nursing hostel in Leura. My sister, Merrie, whose wedding I missed, had three children and intermittently worked as a nurse at Nepean Hospital until qualifying as a hospital chaplain. She worked on in that role at Nepean Hospital until her retirement. She and her husband Ian now continue to live on the Blue Mountains. My brother, Philip, completed a master's degree in psychology, and then worked as a clinical psychologist in the Commonwealth Acoustic Laboratories until he felt the call to train as an Anglican minister. He is now rector at Hunters Hill in Sydney and together with his wife Rosemary has four children.

The little creatures have prospered – Ian, the youngest, eventually became a Queen's Counsel; Robbie developed a passion for Indigenous rights and the rights of people with mental health problems; while Peter became an internationally recognised nurse educator and health systems manager.

Reg Gardner, the CO, was awarded the OBE in 1968 and wrote me the following at that time, in response to my congratulations: 'I would be delighted to hear from you from time to time, so that at the appropriate time

308 The Gunners' Doctor

I will be able to say, with due modesty, "Yes, I have known Dr David Bradford for years – in fact he was once my personal physician."' Sadly, he has now passed away.

Bob Allen, my irrepressible sergeant, had the sort of career in the army he richly deserved and rose to the rank of lieutenant colonel in the RAAMC. He retired from the army some ten years ago and since then has done work in many troubled places of the world for Care Australia. He lives with his wife in Tasmania.

Alex 'Chuck' Berry, one-time 106 Battery medic, did another tour of duty in South Vietnam in the early seventies, this time at the 1st Australian Field Hospital at Vung Tau. He qualified as a radiographer and wrote a textbook on the subject for rural and remote nurses. We have stayed in touch over the years. He has a large family and now lives in Toowoomba.

I have lost touch with Peter Williams, 108 Battery medic, but it is believed he became an Anglican priest in Queensland.

It is difficult to believe, when many of them meant so much to me during that unforgettable year, that I know nothing directly about the fate of any of the other soldiers I served with in Vietnam.

I don't think any Australian soldier who served in Vietnam for more than a moment was at all surprised to see the television pictures in 1975 of the first victorious North Vietnamese tank breaking through the gates of the Presidential Palace in Saigon. It was bound to happen and somehow we all knew it *would* happen some day. Every day we were there in Vietnam, we saw the seeds of defeat sown in the way the war was waged. More than that, we recognised the war was lost, because our enemies had a cause they believed in fervently. While I wasn't surprised to see the pictures, I was surprised that seven years later, in far away London, I was so affected by the fall of Saigon. I felt choked up. What was it all for? All the heartache, all the bloodshed, all the young lives damaged or destroyed, the hatred, the bitterness, the maiming, the mistakes, the muddles, the murders? It seemed so pointless and futile.

Vietnam in 2004, when we visited, was readily recognisable. The heat and humidity, the hustle and bustle, the semi-tropical landscape, the rice paddies, the South China Sea at Vung Tau – all unchanged from my memories of 1967. But there were marked differences: an air of affluence prevailed in many places – most notably in Hoa Long, once the scene of abject poverty; military vehicles were no longer in evidence, helicopters no longer filled the skies, and the ambience of menace we all knew so well in 1967 seemed to have been entirely dispelled by the coming of peace; finally and most notably, the people had cast off their despondency, apathy and lethargy and now would give the Thais a run for their money for friendly, winning, heart-warming smiles. Why should they smile at us I wondered, middle-aged, well-to-do American look-alikes that we had become? Just one of the imponderable questions cast up by that enigma of a country: Vietnam.

I felt the need for answers when we parked in the street outside the People's Assembly Building in the town of Long Tan. The town looked prosperous and busy. People were going peacefully about their business. Two flags waved lazily over the building: the flag of the People's Republic of Vietnam – yellow star on red background; and the flag of the Communist Party of Vietnam – yellow hammer and sickle on red background. Was it really to stop this happening, to prevent those flags ever flying over the town, that eighteen Australians were killed and twenty-four wounded during the fierce battle of Long Tan just down the road, in the rubber plantation, in August 1966?

The fact is that those flags do fly proudly today in Long Tan as they do all over the People's Republic of Vietnam, despite the efforts of our valiant soldiers, the sacrifices of Americans and their allies and the strategies of LBJ, Robert Menzies, Harold Holt, Richard Nixon, General Westmoreland and all the rest. Did our Aussie diggers die in vain, victims of the misguided policies of unscrupulous or naïve politicians?

There is no ready answer to these questions but one thing is clear – Australians must not forget Vietnam and its lessons. I hope these letters will play a small part in keeping memories fresh in the consciousness of our nation.

GLOSSARY

adjutant (adj) – assistant to the CO

AHQ – army headquarters

APC – armoured personnel carrier – small armoured vehicle on tracks

army – military forces of a country excluding the navy and air force

artillery – the army corps concerned with guns and their science

arty tac – central artillery command post

ARVN – Army of the Republic of Vietnam – South Vietnamese army

Australian Logistic Support Group – grouping of army supportive units (e.g. 1 ALSG)

batman – army officers of the rank of captain and above often had a private soldier assigned to them as a sort of personal valet and driver

battalion – an infantry unit composed of three or more companies

battery – a unit in an artillery regiment; usually composed of six guns

battery captain (BK) – captain in command of gun battery

battery commander (BC) – major in overall command of a battery and its forward observers; usually located with an infantry battalion

BEQ – bachelor enlisted quarters – quarters for enlisted men (ORs)

bombardier – a corporal in the artillery

BOQ – bachelor officer quarters – quarters for officers

brigadier – most junior rank of general

captain – commissioned officer above the rank of lieutenant

cavalry – corps in the army mounted on armoured vehicles

CCS – casualty clearing station – emergency medical unit for army

CMF-FTD – Citizen Military Forces full-time duty

CO – commanding officer – top-ranking officer in charge of an army unit

colonel – commissioned officer just below brigadier general

command post – nerve centre of operations for a military unit

company – a subdivision of a battalion

corps – a major military unit – artillery corps, infantry corps, medical corps etc.

craftsman – a private soldier in the engineering corps

DDMS – Deputy Director of Medical Services – medical officer in charge of medical services over a large military area

DGMS – Director General of Medical Services – general in charge of RAAMC

field ambulance (Fd Amb) – army medical unit designed to provide emergency care for army in the field

field hospital (FH) – an army hospital providing tertiary medical care for army in the field

field marshal – officer of highest rank in Australian army

fire for effect (FFE) – the order for a gun battery to fire

forward detachment (FD) – a small unit of a field ambulance sited close to active fighting forces designed to provide emergency medical support

forward observer (FO) – member of the artillery attached to a company of infantry in radio contact with the command post of a gun battery

FSB – fire support base – a site consisting of one or more batteries of guns deployed in the field

gunner – private soldier in the artillery

harassment and interdiction (H&Is) – an artillery fire plan directed at random into curfew areas to cause stress and fear to the enemy

headquarter battery – battery of an artillery regiment which contains support services for the whole regiment

howitzer – a type of large gun

infantry – the foot soldiers

JRMO – junior resident medical officer

LAD – light aid detachment (of the engineering corps RAEME)

lance-bombardier – in the artillery, equivalent of lance-corporal

lance-corporal – lowest NCO rank – i.e. just above private

lieutenant – commissioned officer ranking below captain

lieutenant colonel – commissioned officer above rank of major – a 'half-colonel'. COs of regiments and battalions are usually lieutenant colonels

major – commissioned officer above rank of captain

major general – commissioned officer above the rank of brigadier

maximum security night (MSN) – a night in the task force area when there was deemed to be high risk of a VC attack. Unnecessary movement between units, movies, mess parties, and the showing of any lights were all banned on such nights.

Medcap – Medical Civil Aid Program

medic – short for medical orderly – a private soldier or NCO in RAAMC

mess – place used for eating, drinking and other recreational activities

MO – medical officer

NCOs – non-commissioned officers – i.e. above the rank of private

Nui Dat – 'small hill' in Vietnamese – one such small hill was the site of the first Australian Task Force (1 ATF) base

officer – one who holds a commission in the army

operation – a specific military campaign or action carried out over a set time period

ORs – other ranks – non-commissioned members of the army

platoon – small sub-unit of an infantry company

private (soldier) – lowest military rank

quartermaster (QM) – officer in charge of quarters, clothing, rations

R&C – rest and convalescent leave

R&R – rest and recreation leave

RAAMC – Royal Australian Army Medical Corps – corps that provides medical support for the Australian army

RAEME – Royal Australian Electrical and Mechanical Engineers

RAP – regimental aid post – the medical centre for an army unit

regiment – large military unit consisting of a number of batteries in the artillery, a number of squadrons in the cavalry and a number of battalions in the infantry

RGH – Repatriation General Hospital

RMO – regimental medical officer – army doctor attached to an army unit

Royal Australian Army Nursing Corps (RAANC) – corps that provides nursing support for the Australian Army

Royal Australian Artillery (RAA) – the Australian artillery corps

Royal Australian Cavalry (RAC) – the Australian cavalry corps

Royal Australian Regiment (RAR) – an Australian infantry corps composed of a number of infantry battalions e.g. 2 RAR (2nd Battalion), 3 RAR (3rd Battalion) etc.

SVN – South Vietnam

second in command (2IC) – the deputy commander of a military unit

second lieutenant – most junior commissioned officer

sergeant – non-commissioned officer above the rank of corporal

sergeant major (SM) – non-commissioned officer of highest rank, as in battery sergeant major (BSM), regimental sergeant major (RSM)

shell – projectile containing high explosives fired from a big gun or cannon

sick parade – appointed time when soldiers report to see a doctor or medic

SMO – senior medical officer – army doctor holding the most senior position in an area – e.g. the CO of 8 Fd Amb in Vung Tau

squadron – a subdivision of a cavalry regiment consisting of several troops

starlight – radio call sign for regimental medical officer

sunray – radio call sign for CO

task force (TF) – a large military unit under the command of a brigadier general

task force area command (TAC) – the command post for a task force

troop – a small unit of a cavalry squadron

trooper – private soldier in the cavalry

warrant officer (WO) – member of army holding a warrant, i.e. of intermediate rank between NCOs and officers

Also published by Random House Australia

You're Leaving Tomorrow: Conscripts and correspondents caught up in the Vietnam War
Malcolm Brown, Stuart MacGladrie and Candace Sutton

The Vietnam conflict was an event that bitterly divided Australian society. While many people supported the government's military response to the perceived threat posed by expansionist communism, many others violently opposed our participation and took their opposition to the streets. The servicemen and conscripts who had to undertake active service and the members of the press corps who reported on the action found themselves caught up in the mess and mayhem.

You're Leaving Tomorrow provides a fascinating insight into these turbulent times. It is full of striking images that evoke the full emotional spectrum of a nation as much at war with itself as another country. Malcolm Brown shares his experiences of National Service as a young man who was deeply ambivalent about both the war and the peace movement. Stuart MacGladrie was a photographer who spent a nervous three-month tour of duty stationed at Bien Hoa with 1RAR, and his photographs record the daily realities for the troops, from showering to going out on patrol. Candace Sutton describes the course of the war from the perspective of the correspondents of the AAP in the combat zones. She considers how the papers of the day presented these accounts and reported also on the turmoil at home.

Together, these three highly respected Fairfax journalists take a multi-faceted look at these dramatic times in this fascinating and richly visual book.

Write Home for Me: A Red Cross Woman in Vietnam
Jean Debelle Lamensdorf

Working as a journalist at the Adelaide *Advertiser* in 1966, Jean Debelle yearned to be involved in the biggest story of the decade – the Vietnam War. But only male journalists in Australia were being sent to cover the escalating conflict. Instead, she volunteered to work in Vietnam for the Red Cross to tend to the non-medical welfare of the sick and wounded ANZAC forces. Jean had planned to report on the war in spare moments, but there were none. For one year she lived in the spotlight: a young Australian woman among 5000 men.

This intimate personal account is told from the rare and compassionate perspective of a young woman living close to the battlefront. Jean tells of the resilience of the soldiers in the face of daily atrocities and of the international medical personnel fighting to save lives and to rebuild shattered bodies and minds. It is also the story of the Vietnamese, struggling to maintain not just their traditions but their very lives in the face of brutal hardship.

With infectious humour, Jean tells of striving to be like a sister to the men when sex was in the very air they breathed. She experienced stark terror when she faced a crazed gunman, had a close call in a minefield and was caught in the midst of a Vietnamese skirmish. Jean also offers an unvarnished look at the Australians' worst battle in Vietnam, Long Tan, and their worst landmine disaster. With unblinking candour, she writes of the harsh realisation that after nine months in Vietnam she had grown cold to the unrelenting horror of war.

From diaries, letters and Red Cross reports, Jean Debelle Lamensdorf has researched and written a story not only of tragedy but also of hope and humour. It is a compelling adventure story – and one of love.

'Her style seems a perfect vehicle for recounting a personal experience that is also a tribute to the courage and determination of the people she served with.'

The Sydney Morning Herald

'This gripping account of her experiences is written with humour and profound insight. It's a marvellous book, written with great sensitivity.'

Good Reading

Modern Military Heroes: Untold stories of courage and gallantry
Narelle Biedermann

Meet the real heroes of Australia — today's soldiers, sailors and airmen who have been honoured with awards for their outstanding acts of bravery and courage.

Australians have always admired the heroic actions of our countrymen in the heat of battle. From our nation's proud history we all know of heart-stopping stories of courage from Gallipoli, Kokoda and Vietnam, and they have shaped the way we see ourselves as a nation at war. But who are our modern military heroes, the real men and women of our modern elite defence forces, decorated for their unswerving duty and courage in the line of fire?

Narelle Biedermann interviewed 13 members of the Australian Defence Force who have been awarded medals in the service of their country in the last 25 years, and here they tell their own stories. In these extraordinary testimonials, each person tells of the drama and danger, the emotional challenge, and how their training — and personal daring and fortitude — helped them to perform these remarkable feats of courage and bravery. Perhaps most revealing is that each of these proud people was humble and self-effacing in receipt of their award — though none could deny they were strongly affected by what they saw and did.

From actions carried out in Rwanda, during the Black Hawk disaster, during the ill-fated 1998 Sydney to Hobart yacht race, in East Timor and the Gulf War — and more — the medals achieved by these courageous individuals include the Medal for Gallantry, the Star of Courage, the Bravery Medal and the Distinguished Flying Cross, which are all awarded for outstanding acts of gallantry, courage, bravery or valour in dangerous circumstances.

Narelle Biedermann served four years as an officer in the Royal Australian Army Nursing Corps. She now lives at Puckapunyal, Victoria, with her husband, Tom, and their two daughters.

Tears on My Pillow: Australian nurses in the Vietnam War
Narelle Biedermann

'Don't forget your cotton underwear, girls!'

With little more than this sage advice, a total of 43 Australian Army nursing sisters were sent to Vietnam between April 1967 and November 1971, undertaking tours of up to 12 months. The nurses were assigned to a military hospital in a war zone with no advance preparation for what they'd encounter: caring for horrifically injured soldiers straight off the battlefield, understaffed, using basic equipment and often in difficult circumstances.

Books about the involvement of Australians in the Vietnam War rarely refer to the role of nurses. But war and nursing are closely linked, and the contribution of these women undoubtedly affected many soldiers in profound ways. In *Tears on My Pillow*, author Narelle Biedermann explores the experiences of nursing in the Vietnam War through the words, voices and photographs of these servicewomen.

The veterans share their tales of living and working in a war zone with emotion and humour. Their stories reveal trauma, tears and grief that went on for many years, but also the moments of fun and laughter when they were able to forget the harsh realities of their lives for a short time.